MAN WALKS INTO A BAR 2

5 7 9 10 8 6

Published in 2007 by Ebury Press, an imprint of Ebury Publishing

A Random House Group Company

Collection Copyright © Jonathan Swan 2007

Jonathan Swan has asserted his right to be identified as the author of this Work in accordance
with the Copyright, Designs and Patents Act 1988

The Random House Group Limited Reg. No. 954009

Addresses for companies within the Random House Group can be found at
www.randomhouse.co.uk

A CIP catalogue record for this book is available from the British Library

The Random House Group Limited makes every effort to ensure that the papers used in our
books are made from trees that have been legally sourced from well-managed and credibly
certified forests. Our paper procurement policy can be found on www.randomhouse.co.uk

Printed and bound in the UK by CPI Mackays, Chatham, ME5 8TD

ISBN 9780091913694

To buy books by your favourite authors and register for offers visit
www.rbooks.co.uk

Man Walks Into A Bar 2

THE ULTIMATE COLLECTION OF JOKES AND ONE-LINERS

JONATHAN SWAN

EBURY PRESS

 CONTENTS

A

B

F

G

H

i

J

K

L

M

N

O

P

U

V

W

Z

'When I first said I wanted to be a comedian, everybody laughed. They're not laughing now.'

Bob Monkhouse

ACCiDENTS

* A heavily bandaged man was sitting up in bed in hospital when his friend came to visit. 'What happened to you?' his friend asked. 'Well, we went to Alton Towers and decided to ride the roller coaster. As we came up to the top of the highest loop, I noticed a little sign by the side of the track. I tried to read it, but it was very small and I couldn't make it out. I was so curious that I decided to go round again, but we went by so quickly that I still couldn't see what the sign said. By now, I was determined to read that sign so I went round a third time. As we reached the top, I stood up in the car to get a better view.'

   'And did you manage to see what the sign said this time?' asked his friend.

   'Yes. Remain seated at all times!'

* I had a terrible accident. I had the right of way but the other guy had the truck.

* 'Dodo died, Dodi died, Di died, Dando died… Surely Dido's looking a bit worried.' *Colin & Fergus*

1

✳ Every time my wife has an accident in the kitchen I get it for dinner.

✳ He's so unlucky that he gets into accidents that started out happening to someone else.

✳ I never had an accident until 1997. Then I got a car.

✳ He was killed in a terrible accident. He flew his plane into a tunnel without checking the train timetable.

✳ 'How did the accident happen?'
   'My wife fell asleep in the back seat of the car.'

✳ 'Have you ever had a car accident?'
   'Well, I met my wife at a petrol station.'

✳ To avoid scalding your hands in hot water, feel the water first before putting your hands in.

✳ Safety tip: When you drop cigarette ash on the carpet, spill a little of your beer to prevent a fire.

🐕 ACCOUNTANTS

✳ What happens when you cross a transatlantic aircraft with an accountant?
   A Boring 747.

✳ An accountant is having a hard time sleeping and goes to see his doctor. 'Doctor, I just can't get to sleep at night.' 'Have you tried counting sheep?' 'That's the problem – I make a mistake and then spend three hours trying to find it.'

aliens

How does an alien count to 35?
On its fingers.

What did the alien say to the garden?
Take me to your weeder.

🐶 AMERICAN PRESIDENTS

✳ Besides Lincoln and Washington, what other presidents happen to have been born on public holidays?

✳ What do you get if you cross a US president with a shark?
Jaws Washington!

✳ When I was young I was told that anyone could be president. Now I'm beginning to believe it.

AMISH

You know your Amish child is going off the rails when...

* He sometimes stays in bed until after 5 a.m.

* In his sock drawer, you find pictures of women without bonnets.

* He shows up at barn raisings in full 'KISS' make-up.

* When you criticize him, he yells, 'Thou sucketh.'

* His name is Jebediah, but he goes by 'Jeb Daddy'.

* He defiantly says, 'If I had a radio, I'd listen to rap.'

* You come upon his secret stash of coloured socks.

* He uses slang expressions: 'Talk to the hand cos the beard ain't listening.'

* He was recently pulled over for driving under the influence of cottage cheese.

* He's wearing his big black hat backwards.

🦁 ANTS

✳ Where do ants go for their holidays?
Frants!

✳ What do you call an ant who skips school?
A truant!

✳ Why did the ant elope?
Nobody gnu.

✳ What do you call a greedy ant?
An anteater!

✳ What is smaller than an ant's dinner?
An ant's mouth!

✳ What do you call an ant who lives with your great uncle?
Your great-ant!

✳ What do you call a 100-year-old ant?
An antique!

✳ Who is the most famous French ant?
Napoleant!

✳ Why don't anteaters get sick?
Because they are full of antibodies!

✳ What do you call an ant who likes to be alone?
  Independant!

✳ What do you call an ant with five pairs of eyes?
  Antteneye

✳ What do you call an ant with frogs legs?
  An antphibian!

✳ How many ants are needed to fill an apartment?
  Ten ants!

appliances

What runs but doesn't get anywhere?
A refrigerator.

🗣 ART

✳ Why did the picture go to jail?
  Because it was framed.

✳ A picture is worth a thousand words, but it uses up a thousand times
  the memory.

✳ Modern artist: Someone who paints on a canvas, wipes it off with a cloth, and sells the cloth.

✳ What is red and smells like blue paint?
Red paint.

✳ Recently a man in Paris nearly got away with stealing several paintings from the Louvre. However, after planning the crime, and getting in and out past security, he was captured only two blocks away when his Renault van ran out of fuel. When asked how he could mastermind such a crime and then make such an obvious error, he replied: 'I had no Monet to buy Degas to make the Van Gogh.'

✳ I painted her in oils because she had a face like a sardine.

✳ The best way to tell if a modern painting is finished is to touch it. If the paint is dry, it is.

✳ It's easy to understand modern art. If it hangs on a wall, it's a painting. If you can walk around it, it's a sculpture.

✳ She was so ugly that her mirror was out in a museum of modern art.

✳ What do you call an American drawing?
Yankee doodle!

✳ They say a picture is worth a thousand words, yet the guy at the gallery wouldn't trade me that painting for my newspaper.

✳ After his wife divorced him, Joe asked his best friend, Bill, to fix him up with a blind date. Bill obliged. The next day Joe called up Bill and shouted at him angrily: 'Bill, what kind of a guy do you think I am? That girl you fixed me up with was cross-eyed; she was almost bald; her nose was long, thin and crooked; she had hair growing on her face; she was flat-chested; and her ankles were as thick as her thighs.' Bill answered: 'Either you like Picasso, or you don't like Picasso.'

✳ Artist Pablo Picasso surprised a burglar at work in his new chateau. The intruder got away, but Picasso told the police he could do a rough sketch of what he looked like. On the basis of his drawing, the police arrested a mother superior, the minister of finance, a washing machine, and the Eiffel Tower.

🐻 BABIES

✳ He's been hitting the bottle for years. He'll be two tomorrow.

✳ Why is it nice being a baby?
It's a nappy time.

✳ A team of doctors attended the delivery of quintuplets who were able to walk immediately after the umbilical cords were cut. The senior doctor was asked to explain this unusual occurrence. 'I guess they had a lot of practice,' said the doctor. 'What do you mean, "practice"?' asked a junior colleague. 'They were just born!' The doctor replied, 'Well, it was standing womb only.'

✳ A woman has twins and gives them up for adoption. One of them goes to a family in Egypt and is named 'Amal'. The other goes to a family in Spain; they name him 'Juan'. Years later, Juan sends a picture of himself to his mum. Upon receiving the picture, she tells her husband that she wished she also had a picture of Amal. Her husband responds, 'But they are twins. If you've seen Juan, you've seen Amal.'

✳ A mother found out she was pregnant and told the good news to anyone who would listen. One day when mother and son were shopping, a woman asked the little boy if he was excited about the new baby. 'Yes!' the four-year-old said. 'And I know what we are going to name it, too. If it's a girl we're going to call her Mary, and if it's another boy we're going to call it quits!'

✳ Handy hint: Feed your baby onions so you can find it in the dark.

✳ He was such a big baby that the doctor was afraid to slap him.

✳ He was so ugly when he was born they didn't know whether to buy a cot or a cage.

✳ He used to be a bottle baby, but when he reached the age of ten he pushed the cork out and escaped.

✳ Did you hear about the baby who swallowed a pin? It was OK. It was a safety pin.

✳ Anxiety: Getting up to see why the baby isn't crying.

✳ Our baby looks just like me. But that's OK, as long as he's healthy.

✳ 'Is your baby a boy or a girl?'
'Of course. What else could it be?'

✳ Panic: When your babysitter calls to ask where you keep the fire extinguisher.

* They said the baby looked like me. Until they turned him the right way up.

* When I was born, everyone was so happy. Even the doctor said, 'I think it's a baby.'

* Most babies born today are very young.

balloons

Why did the balloon burst?
Because it saw a lolly pop!

🐻 BATHROOM HUMOUR

* Is reading in the bathroom considered multi-tasking?

* What is a ringleader?
  The first person in the bath.

* Handy hint: Keep your bath in the living room so you won't have so far to walk when the doorbell rings.

* I'd like to give him a gift he needs, but I don't know how to wrap a bathtub.

✹ 'Doctor, doctor, I've got water on the knee, water on the elbow and water on the brain!'
'I suggest you get out of the shower.'

✹ Some days I have to take three or four baths to get the phone to ring.

✹ 'Did you drink carrot juice after the hot bath?'
'No, doctor. I haven't finished the bath yet.'

✹ Why did the robber take a bath?
Because he wanted to make a clean getaway.

✹ Why did the toilet paper roll down the hill?
To get to the bottom.

✹ The only time the world beats a path to your door is if you're in the bathroom.

🦇 BATS

✹ How do bats fly without bumping into anything?
They use their wing mirrors.

✹ Once there were three bats. They lived in a cave surrounded by three castles. One night the bats made a bet to see who could drink the most blood. The first bat comes home one night and has blood dripping off his fangs. The other two bats are amazed and asked how much blood he had drunk. The first bat said, 'See that castle over there? I drank the blood of three people.' The second bat goes out on his night and comes back with blood around his mouth. The other two bats are astonished and ask how many people's blood he had drunk. The bat said, 'See that castle over there? I drank the blood of five people.' The third bat goes out on his night and comes back covered in blood. This was totally amazing to the other two bats. They ask how much blood he drank. The third bat said, 'See that castle over there?' and the other bats nod. 'Well,' says the third bat, 'I didn't.'

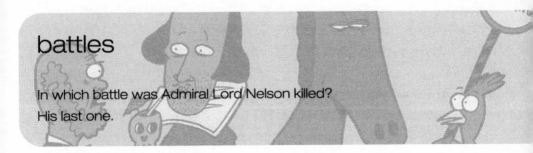

battles

In which battle was Admiral Lord Nelson killed?
His last one.

🦇 BATTLE OF THE SEXES

✳ There were three guys talking in a bar. Two of them talked about the amount of control they had in their marriages, while the third remained quiet. After a while one of the first two turns to the third and says, 'Well, what about you, what sort of control do you have over your wife?' The third fellow says, 'I'll tell you. Just the other night my wife came to me on her hands and knees.' The first two guys were amazed. 'Wow! What happened then?' they asked. The third man took a healthy swallow of his beer, sighed and explained, 'She said, "Get out from under this bed and fight like a man."'

✳ A man and a woman who have never met before find they have to share a two-bunk compartment on a sleeper train. In the middle of the night the man says, 'I'm terribly cold. Could you pass me an extra blanket?' 'I've got a better idea,' says the woman. 'Let's pretend that we're married.' 'I like the sound of that,' says the man. 'So get your own damn blanket.'

✳ I like my men like I like my coffee. Ground up and in the freezer.

✳ I like my women like I like my coffee. Cold and bitter.

✳ A woman gets into bed clutching a duck under her arm. As she pulls the blanket over herself she says, 'This is the pig I'm sleeping with.' Her husband looks at her and says, 'That's not a pig, it's a duck.' The woman replies, 'I think you'll find I was talking to the duck!'

✳ Women who seek to be equal to men lack ambition.

✳ Of all the women in the world, the Iceman has his pick.

✳ Why does the bride always wear white?
Well, aren't all kitchen appliances that colour?

✳ What do women and police cars have in common?
They both make a lot of noise to let you know you did something wrong.

✳ Why is a launderette a bad place to pick up a woman?
Because a woman who can't afford a washing machine will never be able to support you

✳ 'Mummy, am I descended from a monkey?'
'I don't know, dear. I never met your father's family.'

✳ I'm happy to live in a free country where a man can do as his wife pleases.

✳ If a man tells a woman she's beautiful she'll overlook most of his other lies.

✳ Two men were in a pub. One says to his mate, 'My wife is an angel.'
His friend replies, 'You're lucky. Mine is still alive.'

✳ A man and his wife are dining in a plush restaurant, and the husband keeps staring at a drunken lady swigging her drink as she sits alone at a nearby table. The wife asks, 'Do you know her?' 'Yes,' sighs the husband. 'She's my ex-girlfriend. I understand she took to drinking right after we split up seven years ago, and I hear she hasn't been sober since.'

'My God!' says the wife. 'Who would think a person would go on celebrating that long?

✳ Some men think women's hats are funny. Others have to pay for them.

✳ **Element Name**: WOMAN

Symbol: WO

Atomic Weight: (don't even go there!)

Physical Properties: Generally round in form. Boils at nothing and may freeze any time. Melts whenever treated properly. Very bitter if not used well.

Chemical Properties: Very active. Highly unstable. Possesses strong affinity to gold, silver, platinum, and precious stones. Violent when left alone. Able to absorb great amounts of exotic food. Turns slightly green when placed next to a better specimen.

Usage: Highly ornamental. An extremely good catalyst for dispersion of wealth. Probably the most powerful income-reducing agent known.

Caution: Highly explosive in inexperienced hands.

✳ **Element Name**: MAN

Symbol: BY

Atomic Weight: (180 +/- 50)

Physical Properties: Solid at room temperature, but gets bent out of shape easily. Fairly dense and sometimes flaky. Difficult to find a pure sample. Due to rust, ageing samples are unable to conduct electricity as easily as young samples.

Chemical Properties: Attempts to bond with WO any chance it can get. Also tends to form strong bonds with it. Becomes explosive when mixed with Kid (**Element**: Child) for prolonged period of time. Neutralize by saturating with alcohol.

Usage: None known. Possibly good methane source. Good samples are able to produce large quantities on command.

Caution: In the absence of WO, this element rapidly decomposes and begins to smell.

✳ Don't be a sexist; broads hate that.

✳ He took his misfortune like a man. He blamed it on his wife.

✳ It had been many years since the embarrassing day when the young woman, with a baby in her arms, entered his butcher shop. She confronted him with the news that the baby was his and asked what he was going to do about it. After a long discussion, he offered to provide her with free meat until the boy was sixteen. She agreed. He had been counting the years off on his calendar. One day the boy, who had been collecting the meat each week, came into the shop and said, 'I'll be sixteen tomorrow.' 'I know,' said the butcher with a smile. 'I've been counting too. When you take this parcel of meat home, tell your mother that it is the last free meat she'll get. Watch the expression on her face.' When the boy arrived home he told his mother what the butcher had said. She just smiled and said, 'Son, go back to the butcher and tell him I have also had free bread, free milk and free groceries for the last sixteen years and watch the expression on HIS face!'

✳ A visitor, returning to Kuwait for the first time since the Gulf War, was impressed by a sociological change. On previous visits she noted that women customarily walked about five paces behind their husbands. She observed that the men now walked over twenty paces BEHIND their wives! She approached one of the women for an explanation: 'What enabled women here to achieve this marvellous reversal of roles?' 'Land mines,' replied the Kuwaiti woman.

✳ The finalist has been named in the worldwide search for the perfect man. After careful consideration and endless debate, The Perfect Man is ... MR POTATO HEAD. He's tanned, he's cute, he's quiet, he never leaves the toilet seat up, he doesn't stay out all night with the boys, he doesn't demand to hold the remote control, he knows the importance of accessorizing, and if he looks at another girl, you can rearrange his face.

✳ Two men are out on the lake enjoying a couple of beers and fishing when one suddenly says, 'I think I'll divorce my wife. She hasn't spoken to me in six months.' The other replies, 'Better think it over first. Women like that are hard to find.'

✳ A bachelor's life is no life for a single man.

✳ The way to a man's heart is to saw his breastplate open.

✳ How are men like pasta?
They are always in hot water, they lack taste, and they need dough.

✳ What does a man consider to be a seven-course meal?
A hot dog and a six-pack.

✳ Not all men are fools. Some are unmarried.

✳ You can change a man – if he's in nappies.

✳ If they put a man on the moon – they should be able to put them all up there.

✳ All men are idiots, and I married their king.

✳ What are two reasons why men don't mind their own business?
1. No mind. 2. No business.

✳ Even if a man could understand women, he still wouldn't believe it.

✳ A man who refused to fight used to be called a coward. Now he's called a bachelor.

✳ How do men exercise at the beach?
By sucking in their stomachs every time they see a bikini.

✳ What did God say after he created man?
'I can do better than this.'

✳ How do you make a man's eyes light up?
Shine a torch in his ear.

✳ Man cannot live by bread alone, unless he's locked in a cage and that's all you feed him.

✳ He's a man of rare gifts; he hasn't given one in years.

* All men are alike, but they have different faces so you can tell them apart.

* Why is psychoanalysis a lot quicker for men than for women?
  When it's time to go back to his childhood, he's already there.

* A man is driving down a steep, narrow mountain road. A woman is driving up the same road. As they pass each other the woman leans out the window and yells, 'PIG!' The man immediately leans out his window and replies with 'BITCH!' They each continue on their way; as the man rounds the next corner he crashes into a pig in the middle of the road.

* Men are like fine wine. They all start out like grapes, and it's our job to stomp on them and keep them in the dark until they mature into something you'd like to have dinner with.

* Men don't get lost; they discover alternative destinations.

* Why did Dorothy get lost in Oz?
  She had three men giving her directions.

* If man evolved from apes why do we still have apes?

🐻 BEARS

* Where do polar bears vote?
  The North Poll.

✳ Name four animals that live at the North Pole.
Three bears and a seal.

✳ What do you call a bear with no socks on?
Bare-foot.

✳ What's the stupidest animal in the jungle?
The polar bear.

✳ What should you call a bald teddy?
Fred bear!

✳ What animal do you look like when you get into the bath?
A little bear!

✳ What's yellow, comes from Peru, and is completely unknown?
Waterloo Bear, Paddington Bear's forgotten cousin!

✳ What's a teddy bear's favourite pasta?
Tagliateddy!

✳ Why was the little bear so spoiled?
Because its mother panda'd to its every whim.

🐝 BEES

✳ What's the best part of a bee?
Its knees.

✴ What did the bee say to the bluebottle?
I must fly now but I'll give you a buzz later.

✴ Where did Noah keep his bees?
In archives.

✴ What kind of bees hum and drop things?
A fumble bee!

✴ I have an irrational fear of bees. They can fly and I can't, and that's just not fair...

✴ What did one bee say to the other?
None of your buzzness.

✴ What's black, yellow and covered in blackberries?
A bramble bee!

✴ Where do bees go on holiday?
Stingapore!

✴ Why did the bee start quoting poetry?
He was waxing lyrical!

✴ What bee is good for your health?
Vitamin bee!

✴ What's a bee's favourite novel?
The Great Gats-bee!

✳ Why did the bees go on strike?
Because they wanted more honey and shorter working flowers!

✳ What kind of bee can't be understood?
A mumble bee!

✳ Ask to see my tattoo of a rose, but don't ask outside. I'm constantly bothered by bees.

✳ How do bees get to school?
By school buzz!

✳ Why do bees have sticky hair?
They use honey combs.

✳ Where do bees go to the bathroom?
At the BP station!

✳ What kind of bees give milk?
Boobees.

✳ How do you know that bees are happy?
Because they hum while they work.

🦜 BiRDS

✳ Why did the birdie go to the hospital?
To get a tweetment.

✳ Every day, the hummingbird eats its own weight in food. You may wonder how it weighs the food. It doesn't. It just eats another hummingbird.

✳ What do you call a mischievous egg?
A practical yolker.

✳ Birds: The only animal you can eat before they're born and after they're dead.

✳ What do geese watch on TV?
Duckumentaries.

✳ What's a duck's favourite TV programme?
The feather forecast.

✳ How do you know if your cat has eaten a duckling?
It's got that down-in-the-mouth look!

✳ A bird in the hand makes blowing your nose difficult.

✳ Which bird is always out of breath?
A puffin.

✳ Who always succeeds?
A toothless budgie.

✳ How can you tell when a turkey is done?
He flushes the toilet.

✳ What art style is loved by doves?
The Coo-bist Period.

✳ When vultures fly, are they allowed carrion luggage?

✳ A woman brings her budgie to the vet's. It is lying very still and limp.
'I'm afraid it's dead,' says the vet, but the woman refuses to believe
him. 'Please', she says, 'can't you examine it at least?' The vet
goes to the door and whistles. In trots a black Labrador. The vet
points to the budgie, and the dog goes over to the table, puts his
paws up, and gives a good sniff at the little bird, before shaking his
head at the vet and trotting out again. Then a tabby cat comes in. It
jumps on the table, walks over to the budgie, and examines it, flipping it over with its paw. It too shakes its head at the vet and leaves
the room.

'I'm afraid that confirms my diagnosis,' says the vet. 'Your budgie
is unfortunately dead. That will be £500 please.' 'What?' says the
woman. 'That's outrageous. How can it cost so much?' 'Well,' replies
the vet, 'my fee is only £50. But when you include the lab report and
the CAT scan...'

✳ The park ranger was giving a talk explaining the difference between a
crow and a raven. He said the raven has six pinions on each wing
and the crow has five pinions on each wing, making the difference a
matter of a pinion.

✳ A bird in the hand can cause a terrible mess.

✳ A bird in the hand is not good table manners.

✳ A man and a woman were walking along a beach. The man noticed many shorebirds flying in pairs. 'Why do they fly together like that?' he asked the woman. She looked at him thoughtfully and replied, 'Well, you know what they say. One good tern deserves another.'

✳ Why was the pelican kicked out of the hotel?
Because he had a big bill!

✳ Why does a hummingbird hum?
It doesn't know the words!

✳ Which kind of bird picks up heavy things?
A crane!

✳ Which birds steal soap from the bath?
Robber ducks!

✳ What kind of bird opens doors?
A kiwi!

✳ What did the mother turkey say to her disobedient children?
'If your father could see you now, he'd turn over in his gravy!'

✳ What language do birds speak?
Pigeon English!

✳ Where do birds invest their money?
In the stork market!

✷ Where do blind sparrows go for treatment?
The Birds Eye counter!

✷ What kind of birds do you find in church?
Birds of prey.

🐶 BiRTHDAYS

✷ 'I was born via caesarean section. It's never really bothered me but, now and then, when I leave my house, I go out through the window.'
Stephen Wright

✷ He was born on April 2nd – a day too late.

✷ He always remembers his wife's birthday. It's the day after she reminds him of it.

✷ I grew up so poor I didn't celebrate my eighteenth birthday until I was 23.

✷ It's a terrible thing to grow old alone. My wife hasn't had a birthday for four years.

✷ 'Which state were you born in?'
'The nude.'

✷ You know you're old when by the time the last candle is lit on your birthday cake the first one has burnt out.

✳ I'm not saying she's old, but when I tried to count the candles on her birthday cake I was driven back by the heat.

✳ My wife is very economical. She only used 26 candles on her 40th birthday cake.

✳ A family had twin boys whose only resemblance to each other was their looks. If one felt it was too hot, the other thought it was too cold. If one said the TV was too loud, the other claimed the volume needed to be turned up. Opposite in every way, one was an eternal optimist, the other a doom and gloom pessimist. Just to see what would happen, on the twins' birthday their father loaded the pessimist's room with every imaginable toy and game. The optimist's room he loaded with horse manure. That night the father passed by the pessimist's room and found him sitting amid his new gifts crying bitterly. 'Why are you crying?' the father asked. 'Because my friends will be jealous, I'll have to read all these instructions before I can do anything with this stuff, I'll constantly need batteries, and my toys will eventually get broken,' answered the pessimist twin. Passing the optimist twin's room, the father found him dancing for joy in the pile of manure. 'What are you so happy about?' he asked. To which his optimist twin replied, 'There's got to be a pony in here somewhere!'

✳ Her mother decided that her 10-year-old should get something practical for her birthday. 'Suppose we open a savings account for you?' she suggested. 'It's your account, darling,' Susie's mother said as they entered at the bank, 'so you fill out the application.'

The child was doing fine until she came to the space for 'Name of your former bank'. With just a slight hesitation, she put down 'Piggy'.

blindness

What goes tap, tap, tap, boom?
A blind man in a minefield.

If you can see this, you're not blind, which is a very good start.

Can a blind person feel blue?

When the blind lead the blind, get out of the way.

Is it fair to say that there'd be less litter in Britain if blind people were given pointed sticks? *Adam Bloom*

BLONDES

✹ A blonde was sitting on the train reading the newspaper. The headline shouted, '12 Brazilian Soldiers Killed'. She shook her head at the sad news, then turned to the stranger sitting next to her and asked, 'How many is a Brazilian?'

✳ The captain comes on the PA: 'Ladies and gentlemen, we've lost engine number one so we will be arriving 15 minutes late in New York.' A few minutes later, he announces they lost number two engine and now they're looking at one hour late arriving. Wouldn't you know, they lose engine number three. Two hours late now. The blonde turns to her husband and says 'Honey, if we lose the fourth engine we could be up here all night.'

✳ A blonde decides to try horseback riding, even though she has never done it before. She mounts the horse unassisted and it immediately springs into action. It gallops along at a steady and rhythmic pace, but the blonde begins to slip from the saddle. In terror, she grabs for the horse's mane, but cannot seem to get a firm grip. She tries to throw her arms around the horse's neck, but she slides down the side of the horse anyway. The horse gallops along, seemingly ignorant of its slipping rider. Finally, giving up her frail grip, the blonde attempts to leap away from the horse and throw herself to safety. Unfortunately, her foot becomes entangled in the stirrup, and she is now at the mercy of the horse's pounding hooves as her head is struck against the ground over and over.

She starts to lose consciousness, but to her great fortune, Dave, who works at Tesco, sees her and unplugs the horse.

✳ What do you call a blonde hiding in a closet?
The 1987 World Hide and Seek Champion.

✳ Why did the blonde climb the glass wall?
To see what was on the other side.

✳ Why did the blonde crash her plane when landing?
The runway was only 25 ft long, but a mile wide.

✳ How do you drown a blonde?
Tell her there's a mirror at the bottom of the tub.

✳ What is it called when a blonde dies her hair brown?
Artificial intelligence.

✳ What do you call 100 blondes sitting in a circle?
A dope ring.

✳ What do you have when you stand 100 blondes next to each other, shoulder to shoulder? A wind tunnel.

✳ How does a blonde kill a fish?
She drowns it.

✳ A blonde going to New York on a plane. How can you steal her window seat? Tell her the seats that are going to London are all in the middle row.

✳ Why do blondes wear earmuffs?
To avoid the draught.

✳ What is the blonde doing when she holds her hands tightly over her ears?
Trying to hold on to a thought.

✳ How do you plant dope?
Bury a blonde.

✳ What do UFOs and smart blondes have in common?
You keep hearing about them, but never see any.

✳ Why do blondes hate M&Ms?
They're too hard to peel.

✳ How do you know when a blonde has been making chocolate chip cookies?
You find M&M shells all over the kitchen floor.

✳ What's brown and red and black and blue?
A brunette who's told one too many blonde jokes.

✳ Why couldn't the blonde write the number 11?
She didn't know which one came first.

✳ What do you call a blonde with 90 per cent of her intelligence gone?
Divorced.

✳ How did the blonde try to kill the bird?
She threw it off a cliff.

✳ How can you tell if a blonde's been using the computer?
There's Tippex on the screen.

✳ How can you tell if another blonde's been using the computer?
There's writing on the Tippex.

✳ The geometry teacher asked the blonde: 'How many degrees in a circle?' The blonde replied: 'This is a trick question! Did you want Fahrenheit or Celsius?'

✳ A blonde woman was speeding down the road in her little red sports car and was pulled over by a woman police officer who was also a blonde. The blonde cop asked to see the blonde driver's licence. She dug through her handbag and was getting progressively more agitated. 'What does it look like?' she finally asked. The policewoman replied, 'It's square and it has your picture on it.' The driver finally found a square mirror in her purse, looked at it and handed it to the policewoman. 'Here it is,' she said. The blonde officer looked at the mirror, then handed it back saying, 'OK, you can go. I didn't realize you were a cop.'

✳ Why were the blonde's boobs square?
Because she forgot to take the tissue out of the box.

✳ Why did seventeen blondes line up outside the nightclub?
You had to be eighteen to get in.

✳ How can you tell if a blonde is a good cook?
She gets the Pop Tarts out of the toaster in one piece.

✳ A blonde was at the doctor for a check-up, and the doctor said, 'You're getting older, so I need to ask this: Have you ever been incontinent?' The blonde said, 'Yes. I've been to Europe twice.'

✳ Why does a blonde only change her baby's nappy every month? Because it says on it 'suitable for up to 20 lbs'.

✳ How does a blonde high five? She smacks herself in the forehead.

✳ What does a blonde think an innuendo is? An Italian suppository.

✳ What does 'Bones' McCoy say before he performs brain surgery on a blonde? 'Space. The final frontier...'

✳ Why do blondes have more fun? Because they don't know any better. And they're easier to keep amused.

✳ Why do blondes drive BMWs? Because they can spell it.

✳ Why don't blondes double recipes? The oven doesn't go to 700 degrees.

✳ Why don't blondes make good pharmacists? They can't get the bottle into the typewriter.

✳ What's a blonde's favourite wine?
'Daaaady, I want to go to shoppiiiiing!'

✳ If a blonde and a brunette are tossed off a building, who hits the ground first?
The brunette. The blonde has to stop to ask for directions.

✳ What does a blonde owl say?
What, what?

✳ The blonde was at a vending machine with a line forming behind her. She kept putting in change, making her selection, watching the can fall and setting each can on top of the machine. After about fifteen times, a man waiting behind her says, 'Hey, let's keep the line moving.' She replies, 'You'll have to wait. I'm still winning.'

✳ Did you hear about the blonde who, at the bottom of a form where it said 'sign here', wrote 'Pisces'?

✳ A blonde grabbed a large thermos and hurried to a nearby coffee shop. She held up the thermos and the coffee shop worker quickly came over to take her order. 'Is this big enough to hold six cups of coffee?' the blonde asked. The coffee shop worker looked at the thermos, hesitated a few seconds, then finally replied, 'Yeah. It looks like about six cups to me.' 'Oh good!' the blonde sighed in relief. 'Then give me two regular, two black, and two decaf.'

✳ There are three blondes stranded on an island. Suddenly a fairy appears and offers to grant each of them one wish. The first blonde asks to be intelligent. Instantly, she is turned into a brown-haired woman and she swims off the island. The next one asks to be even more intelligent than the previous one, so instantly she is turned into a black-haired woman. The black-haired woman builds a boat and sails off the island. The third blonde asks to become even more intelligent than the previous two. The fairy turns her into a man, and he walks across the bridge!

✳ A girl was visiting her blonde girlfriend when she noticed two dogs. 'What are their names?' she said. 'Timex and Rolex,' said the blonde. Her friend said, 'I've never heard of those names for dogs.' 'Oh,' said the blonde, 'they're watch dogs.'

✳ A blonde is in a car accident and her car is covered in dents. She visits a car repair garage and asks the man how much it would cost to knock them out. It's too expensive for her. 'I do have a solution for you that you can do yourself,' says the mechanic. 'Oh yeah,' says the blonde, 'what's that?' 'You put your mouth over the exhaust pipe and blow really hard. The dents just pop right out.' The blonde went home and tried, but it didn't work. She went to her blonde friend and told her about this. She replied, 'Well of course THAT won't work – you have to roll up the windows first!'

✳ A blonde and her husband are lying in bed one morning when the phone rings. Quick on the draw, the blonde picks up the phone and listens for a moment, then says, 'Well, how the heck should I know, that's like 300 miles from here!' and slams the phone down. The next morning the same happens. Her reply is, 'Like I told you the day before yesterday, I'm not a meteorologist!' and slams the phone down. She comes back to bed and says to her husband: 'I'm getting sick and tired of that woman calling me every morning to ask if the coast is clear.'

✳ A blonde walks into a barber's with headphones on. She tells the barber what cut she wants, but that he has to cut around her headphones. The barber looks a little puzzled but agrees. So, he starts cutting the best he can but accidentally he knocks the headphones off. Within a few seconds the girl dies. Very startled, the man picks up the headphones and hears, 'Breathe in, breathe out.'

✳ What's the definition of paralysis?
Four blondes at a crossroads.

✳ Two blondes are filling their cars at a petrol station. One blonde turns to the other and says, 'Are you as upset as I am about the high price of petrol?' The second blonde replies, 'It doesn't really affect me. I always just put in £10 worth.'

✳ Did you hear about the blonde who got a scarf for Christmas? She returned it – it was too tight.

✳ TO: Boss
FROM: Blonde
RE: Changing Calendars from Y2K
I hope that I haven't misunderstood your instructions because, to be honest, none of this Y to K problem made much sense to me. At any

rate, I have finished the conversion of all of the months on all of the company calendars for this year. The calendars now contain the following new months: Januark, Februark, Mak, Julk. I also changed all the days of each week to: Sundak, Mondak, Tuesdak, Wednesdak, Thursdak, Fridak, and Saturdak.

Now we are now Y to K compliant...

✳ Two tourist groups, one made up of all blondes and one of all brunettes, charter a double-decker bus for a weekend in Vegas. The brunettes ride in the bottom of the bus and the blondes ride on the top level. The brunettes down below are whooping it up and having a great time when one of them realizes she doesn't hear anything from the blondes upstairs. She decides to go up and investigate. When the brunette reaches the top, she finds all the blondes frozen in fear, staring straight ahead at the road and clutching the seats in front of them. The brunette says, 'What is going on up here? We're having a great time downstairs!' One of the blondes says, 'Yeah, but you've got a driver!'

✳ A blonde quickly went out to her mail box, looked in it, closed the door of the box, and went back in the house. A few minutes later she repeated this process by checking her mail again. She did this five more times, and her neighbour, who was watching her, commented: 'You must be expecting a very important letter today the way you keep looking into that mail box.' The blonde answered, 'No, I'm working on my computer, and it keeps telling me that I have mail.'

✳ Why did the blonde have tyre tread marks on her back?
From crawling across the street when the sign said 'DON'T WALK'.

✳ Why did the blonde keep a coat hanger in her back seat?
In case she locked the keys in her car.

✳ One day, I passed a blonde co-worker driving to work. I noticed she had a headlight blown. When I told her that one of her headlights was out, she asked, 'Front or back?'

✳ Why did the blonde stop using the pill?
Because it kept falling out.

✳ Did you hear about the blonde skydiver?
She missed the earth!

✳ What did the blonde say when she looked into a box of Cheerios?
'Oh, look! Doughnut seeds!'

✳ What goes VROOM, SCREECH, VROOM, SCREECH, VROOM, SCREECH?
A blonde going through a flashing red light.

✳ What did the blonde say to the physicist?
'Why, I just love nuclear fission! What do you use for bait?'

✳ Did you hear about the blonde couple that were found frozen to death in their car at a drive-in movie theatre?
They went to see 'Closed For The Winter'.

✳ Did you hear about the blonde who was worried that a mechanic might try to rip her off?
She was relieved when he told her all she needed was indicator-signal fluid.

✳ A blonde is walking down the street with a pig under her arm. She passes a man who asks, 'Where did you get that?' The pig says, 'I won her in a raffle!'

✳ Did you hear about the blonde who went to the library and checked out a book called *How To Hug*?
She got back home and found out it was volume seven of the encyclopaedia.

✳ There was a blonde driving down the road listening to the radio. The announcer was telling blonde joke after blonde joke until the blonde was so mad she turned her radio off. A mile down the road, she saw another blonde out in a corn field in a boat, rowing. The blonde stopped her car, jumped out and yelled, 'You bimbo, it's blondes like you that give us all a bad name. If I could swim I'd come out there and give you what's coming to you!'

✳ A blonde and a redhead are watching the late news. The redhead bets the blonde £50 that the man in the lead story, who is on the ledge of a 40-storey building, will jump.
'I'll take that bet,' the blonde replied. A few minutes later, the newscaster breaks in to report that the man had, indeed, jumped from the building. The redhead, feeling sudden guilt for having bet on such an incident, turns to the blonde and tells her that she does not need to pay the £50. 'No, a bet's a bet,' the blonde replies. 'I owe

you £50.' The redhead, feeling even more guilty, replies, 'No, you don't understand. I saw the six o'clock news, so I knew how it was going to turn out.' 'That's OK,' the blonde replies. 'I saw it earlier too, but I didn't think he'd do it again.'

✳ What do you call 144 blondes?
   Gross ignorance.

✳ A blonde was visiting London for the first time and wanted to see Big Ben. Unfortunately, she was having trouble finding it. Finally she saw a police officer and asked him for directions. 'Well, if you wait at that bus stop right there and get on bus 54, it will take you right there,' explained the officer. 'Thank you,' she cooed, and walked to the bus stop. Five hours later, the police officer was driving by again, and sure enough, the blonde was still standing at the bus stop. The officer stopped and said, 'Excuse me, miss, but I told you that to get to Big Ben, you take the number 54, and it will take you right there. What are you still doing here?' 'Oh, don't worry, officer,' she replied. 'It won't be long now. The 47th bus just went by.'

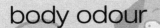

body odour

Did you hear about the man who had BO on one side only?
He bought Right Guard, but couldn't find any Left Guard!

🐶 BODY PARTS

Bottom

✳ If a motorist cuts you off, just turn the other cheek. Nothing gets the message across like a good mooning.

✳ What has a bottom at the top?
Your legs!

✳ Did you hear about the woman that backed into a fan?
No! What happened?
Disassed'er!

Arms

✳ I only use deodorant under one arm, so I know what I would have smelled of.

Brain and mind

✳ Oops. My brain just hit a bad sector.

✳ Out of my mind. Back in five minutes.

✳ I used to have an open mind but my brains kept falling out.

✳ My mind works like lightning. One brilliant flash and it is gone.

Face

✳ Do you look in the mirror after you've washed your face?
No, I look in a towel!

Hands

✳ My hand measures nine inches. Three more and it would've been a foot.

✳ If the palm of your hand itches, you're going to get something. If your head itches, you've already got it.

✳ I asked her father for her hand – he said take the whole girl or nothing.

✳ On the other hand, you have different fingers.

✳ Why is my finger like a lemon pie? Because it's got meringue on it.

✳ Why did the man with one hand cross the road?
To get to the second-hand shop.

✳ If I'm standing at the North Pole, facing the South Pole, and the east is on my left hand, what's on my right hand?
Fingers!

Feet and legs

✳ My wife has a very unusual figure. The seams on her stockings are straight, but her legs are crooked.

✳ Why did the silly kid stand on his head?
His feet were tired!

✳ Did you hear about the woman whose legs had no equal?
They were without parallel.

✳ **Boy 1**: 'My uncle has a cedar chest.'
Boy 2: 'So what? My dad has a wooden leg.'

✳ What disappears when you stand up?
Your lap.

Nose

✳ What is it that even the most careful person overlooks?
His nose!

Eyes

✳ When are eyes not eyes?
When the wind makes them water.

✳ A little boy goes to the optometrist to get his eyes checked. He becomes very confused when he's asked to look at the chart and cover his right eye with his right hand. He also can't figure out how to cover his left eye with his left hand. So the optometrist comes up with the bright idea of covering the kid's head with a paper bag, with a hole cut out for only one eye. At this, the boy bursts into tears. The optometrist whips the bags off and asks, 'What's the matter?!' And the boy whimpers, 'I want wire frames like my brother's!'

✳ I know carrots are good for the eyes, but it nearly makes me blind sticking them in.

✳ 'Your eyes are intoxicating.'
'It must be the eyeballs.'

Breasts

✳ If life gives you lemons, stick them down your shirt and make your boobs look bigger.

✳ An elderly man walks into a lingerie shop to get his wife a fancy bra. The sales woman asks him what size bra she wears. Seven and a half, he replies. 'Seven and a half!' the saleswoman exclaims. 'How did you come up with that size?' 'I used my hat!' he answered.

✳ A friend of mine was telling me about him and his twin brother's early days. They were womb mates and after they were born, were bosom buddies!

✳ A man walked into the ladies department of a Macy's, and walked up to the woman behind the counter and said, 'I'd like to buy a bra for my wife.' 'What type of bra?' asked the clerk. 'Type?' enquires the man. 'There is more than one type?' 'Look around,' said the saleslady, as she showed a sea of bras in every shape, size, colour and material. 'Actually, even with all of this variety, there are really only three types of bras,' replied the sales clerk. Confused, the man asked what the types were. The saleslady replied: 'The Catholic type, the Salvation Army type and the Baptist type. Which one do you need?'

Still confused, the man asked, 'What is the difference between them?' The lady responded, 'It is all really quite simple. The Catholic type supports the masses, the Salvation Army type lifts up the fallen, and the Baptist type makes mountains out of molehills.'

✳ I saw a woman wearing a sweatshirt with 'Guess' on it ... so I said, 'Implants?'

brooms

Why was the broom late?
It over swept!

A boy broom and a girl broom are dating. One day the girl broom says to the boy broom, 'I'm pregnant!' The boy broom replies, 'How is that possible? We haven't even swept together!'

builders

A man phoned the local builders and said to them, 'Can I have a skip outside my house?' The builder said, 'I'm not stopping you!'

bullying

I was bullied at school, called all kinds of different names. But one day I turned to my bullies and said, 'Sticks and stones may break my bones but names will never hurt me,' and it worked! From thereon it was sticks and stones all the way.

🐾 BUMPER STICKERS

✳ Forget world peace. Visualize using your indicators.

✳ If you can read this, I can slam on my brakes and sue you!

✳ If you don't like my driving, don't call anyone. Just take another road. That's why the government made so many of them.

✳ If You Drink, Don't Park – Accidents Cause People.

* Geez if you believe in honkus.

* Who Lit The Fuse On Your Tampon?

* If That Phone Was Up Your Butt, Maybe You Could Drive A Little Better.

* Thank You For Pot Smoking.

* To All You Virgins: Thanks For Nothing.

* Impotence: Nature's Way Of Saying 'No Hard Feelings'.

* If You Can Read This, I've Lost My Trailer.

* Horn Broken ... Watch For Finger.

* It's Not How You Pick Your Nose, But Where You Put The Bogey.

* If You're Not A Haemorrhoid, Get Off My Ass.

* This Would Be Really Funny If It Weren't Happening To Me.

* So Many Pedestrians – So Little Time.

* Cleverly Disguised As A Responsible Adult.

* If We Stop Voting Will They All Go Away?

✳ The Face Is Familiar But I Can't Quite Remember My Name.

✳ Eat Right, Exercise, Die Anyway.

✳ Honk If Anything Falls Off.

✳ Cover Me – I'm Changing Lanes.

✳ He Who Hesitates Is Not Only Lost But Miles From The Next Exit

✳ You! Out Of The Gene Pool!

✳ Where Are We Going And Why Am I In This Handbasket?

✳ Fight Crime: Shoot Back!

✳ If You Can Read This, Please Flip Me Back Over. *Seen upside down on a Land Rover.*

✳ Body By Nautilus; Brain By FisherPrice.

✳ Boldly Going Nowhere.

✳ Cat: The Other White Meat.

✳ Heart Attacks ... God's Revenge For Eating His Animal Friends.

✳ How Many Roads Must A Man Travel Down Before He Admits He Is Lost?

✳ If You Can't Dazzle Them With Brilliance, Riddle Them With Bullets.

✳ Saw It ... Wanted It ... Had A Tantrum ... Got It!

✳ Grow Your Own Dope – Plant A Man.

🐶 CAMELS

✳ The little camel went to his mother and asked, 'Mother, why do we camels have such big eyes?' She looked on him lovingly and replied, 'You see, my son, when we are walking in the desert and the wind starts to blow and there's sand everywhere, we need these big eyes to keep an eye on one another so that we don't get lost.' 'Oh!' he said. 'And why do we have such huge feet?' 'Well,' she said, 'they allow us to walk easily in the desert sands and help us avoid sinking into the dunes.' 'Wow,' he said, 'great equipment. What the heck is this stuff on our backs for?' 'You see,' his mother informed him, 'we can walk for days, even weeks without food or water, so we use it to store fat during those times. But why do you ask me all these obvious questions?' 'Well, Mother,' said the young camel, 'I was just wondering, if we've got all of this great stuff, what are we doing in the zoo?'

🦁 CANNIBALISM

✳ When do cannibals leave the table?
  When everyone's eaten.

✳ What did the cannibal get when he was late for dinner?
  The cold shoulder.

✳ What is a cannibal's favourite game?
  Swallow the leader.

✳ Why did the cannibal decide to become a missionary?
  If you can't eat 'em, join 'em.

✳ Did you hear about the cannibal who loved fast food?
  He ordered a pizza with everybody on it.

✳ Why was the cannibal looking peaky?
  Because he had just eaten a Chinese dog!

✳ Why don't cannibals eat weathermen?
  Because they give them wind!

✳ What do cannibal secretaries do with leftover fingernails?
  They file them!

✳ Two cannibals sat at the fire. One said, 'I really hate my mother-in-law.' The other replied, 'Try the potatoes.'

✹ What do Chinese cannibals eat with?
Chap-sticks.

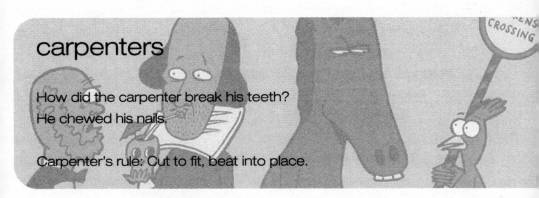

carpenters

How did the carpenter break his teeth?
He chewed his nails.

Carpenter's rule: Cut to fit, beat into place.

🐾 CARTOON CHARACTERS

✹ When confronted by a difficult problem you can solve it more easily by reducing it to the question, 'How would the Lone Ranger handle this?'

✹ What does Speedy Gonzalez use as carpet?
Underlay, underlay.

✹ Even Popeye didn't eat his spinach until he absolutely had to.

✹ What kind of material are the Pink Panther's pants made of?
Denim, denim, denim, denim denim denim denim.

* What did Pooh say to his agent?
  Show me the honey!

* Caution: Cape does not enable user to fly.

* 'I saw Lee Majors, the bionic man, the other day. He looked a million dollars... He's really let himself go.' *Eddie Bannon*

* What does the Invisible Man look like? He's the mirror image of Dracula.

* What do Winnie the Pooh and Jack the Ripper have in common? The same middle name.

* Do you know why there is only one Yogi Bear? Because they made a Boo Boo.

* Who has huge antlers and wears white gloves?
  Mickey Moose.

* Why did Tigger stick his head in the toilet?
  He was looking for Pooh!

* Why is Piglet so smelly?
  Because he plays with Pooh!

* What kind of car does Mickey Mouse's wife drive?
  A Minnie van!

✳ Why did Mickey Mouse take a trip into space?
He wanted to find Pluto!

✳ Why did Goofy put a clock under his desk?
Because he wanted to work over-time!

✳ I'm not normally a praying man, but if you're up there, please save me, Superman!

✳ Well, paint me purple and call me Barney.

✳ What do you call Batman & Robin after they've been run over by a steam roller?
Flatman & Ribbon.

✳ For good, return good. For evil, call Batman.

✳ Why does Snoopy want to quit the comic strip?
He's tired of working for peanuts!

✳ Why did Mickey Mouse get shot?
Because Donald Ducked!

✳ What do you get if you cross the Lone Ranger with an insect?
The Masked-quito!

✳ What do the Honey Monster and Tony the Tiger fear the most?
Cereal killers.

🐱 CATS

✳ Four men were bragging about how smart their cats are. The first man was an engineer, the second man was an accountant, the third man was a chemist, the fourth was a government worker. To show off, the engineer called to his cat, 'T-square, do your stuff.' T-square pranced over to a desk, took out some paper and a pen and promptly drew a circle, a square, and a triangle. Everyone agreed that was pretty smart. But the accountant said his cat could do better. He called his cat and said, 'Spreadsheet, do your stuff.' Spreadsheet went out into the kitchen and returned with a dozen cookies. He divided them into four equal piles of three cookies each. Everyone agreed that was good. But the chemist said his cat could do better. He called his cat and said, 'Measure, do your stuff.' Measure got up, walked over to the fridge, took out a quart of milk, got a ten-ounce glass from the cupboard and poured exactly eight ounces without spilling a drop. Everyone agreed that was good. Then the three men turned to the government worker and said, 'What can your cat do?' The government worker called to his cat and said, 'Coffee Break, do your stuff.' Coffee Break jumped to his feet, ate the cookies, drank the milk, pooed on the paper, bit the other three cats, claimed he injured his back while doing so, filed a grievance report for unsafe working conditions, put in for Workers' Compensation and went home for the rest of the day on sick leave.

✳ Where does a cat go when he loses his tail?
Retail outlet!

✳ What happened when the cat swallowed the penny?
There was money in the kitty.

✳ Did you hear about the cat who drank 5 bowls of water?
He set a new lap record.

✳ 'Cats have nine lives. Which makes them ideal for experimentation.'
Jimmy Carr

✳ St Peter is at his post at the Pearly Gates when a cat shows up. St Peter says, 'I know you! You were a very nice cat on earth and didn't cause any trouble, so I want to offer a gift to you of one special thing you have always wanted.' Cat: 'Well, I did always long to own a nice satin pillow like my master had, so I could lie on it.' St Peter: 'That's easy. Granted. You shall have the satin pillow after you enter in.' Next a group of mice appeared.

St Peter: 'Ah, I remember you. You were such good mice on earth. You didn't steal food and never hurt other animals. Therefore, I want to grant you one special wish you always wanted.' The Chief Mouse replied, 'Well, we always watched the children playing and saw them roller skate, and it was beautiful, and it looked like so much fun, so we'd like some roller skates, if we could?' St Peter: 'Granted. You shall have your wish.' Next day, St Peter is making the rounds inside heaven and sees the cat. 'Well, Cat… Did you enjoy the satin pillow?' Cat: 'Oh, indeed I did. And say … that Meals on Wheels thing was a nice touch, too!'

✳ I can teach my cat any trick he wants to do!

What are cats?

1. Cats do what they want, when they want.
2. They rarely listen to you.
3. They're totally unpredictable.
4. They whine when they are not happy.
5. When you want to play they want to be left alone.
6. When you want to be alone, they want to play.
7. They expect you to cater to their every whim.
8. They're moody.
9. They leave their hair everywhere.
10. They drive you nuts.

Conclusion: Cats are small women in fur coats.

✳ What's the definition of a cat?
An animal that never cries over spilt milk.

✳ Why did the cat join the Red Cross?
It wanted to be a first aid kitty.

✳ 'Have you seen the offices of the RSPCA? It's tiny; you couldn't swing a cat in there.' *Tim Vine*

✳ What do cats eat for breakfast?
Mice Crispies.

✳ A three-year-old boy went with his dad to see a new litter of kittens. On returning home, he breathlessly informed his mother, 'There were two boy kittens and two girl kittens.' 'How did you know that?' his mother asked. 'Daddy picked them up and looked underneath,' he replied. 'I think it's printed on the bottom.'

✳ If you throw a kitten out of a moving car, would it be considered kitty litter?

✳ How is cat food sold?
Usually purr can!

✳ What do cats read at breakfast?
Mewspapers.

✳ What do you call a cat that's eaten a duck?
A duck-filled fatty puss.

✳ Letting the cat out of the bag is a whole lot easier than putting it back in.

✳ She's one bad relationship away from having 30 cats.

✳ I like cats too. Let's exchange recipes.

✳ What do you get if you cross a cat with a canary?
Shredded tweet!

✳ What is white, sugary, has whiskers and floats on the sea?
A catameringue!

✳ On what should you mount a statue of your cat?
A caterpillar!

✳ Why did the cat eat cheese?
So he could sit by the mousehole with baited breath.

✳ What do you get if you cross a cat with a lemon?
A sourpuss.

✳ What do you get if you mix a cat with a ball of wool?
Mittens.

✳ Whatever happened to that guy that made those great bird sounds?
The cat ate him.

✳ What are cat-erpillars afraid of?
Dog-erpillars.

✳ What is the difference between a cat and a comma?
One has the paws before the claws and the other has the clause before the pause.

🐾 CENTIPEDES

✳ Why was the centipede late?
Because he was playing 'This Little Piggy' with his friends!

✳ What is worse than a giraffe with a sore throat?
A centipede with chilblains!

✳ What do you call a guard with 100 legs?
A sentrypede!

✳ What do you get if you cross a centipede and a chicken?
Enough drumsticks to feed an army!

✳ What did one centipede say to the other centipede?
You've got a lovely pair of legs, you've got a lovely pair of legs,
you've got a lovely pair of legs, you've got a lovely pair of legs, you've
got a lovely pair of legs, you've got a lovely pair of legs...

chat-up lines

I need someone really bad. Are you really bad?

Are you wearing lipstick? Well, mind if I taste it?

🐷 CHAVS

✳ What do you call a Chav in a box?
Innit.

✳ What do you call a Chav in a filing cabinet?
Sorted.

* What do you call a Chav in a box with a lock on it?
  Safe.

* What do you call an Eskimo Chav?
  Innuinnit.

* Why are Chavs like slinkies?
  They have no real use but it's great to watch one fall down a flight of stairs.

* What do you call a Chavette in a white tracksuit?
  The bride.

* You're in your car and you see a Chav on a bike. Why should you try not to hit him? It might be your bike.

* What's the difference between a Chav and a coconut?
  One's thick and hairy, the other's a coconut.

* What's the first question at a Chav quiz night?
  'What you lookin' at?'

* How do you get 100 Chavs into a phone box?
  Paint three stripes on it.

* Two Chavs in a car without any music. Who's driving?
  The police.

✳ What do you call a Chav with 9 GCSEs?
A liar.

✳ What do you say to a Chav with a job?
'Can I have a Big Mac, please?'

✳ What do you say to a Chav in a suit?
'Will the defendant please stand.'

✳ What do you call a knife in Chav-ville?
Exhibit A.

✳ Why is three Chavs going over a cliff in a Nova a shame?
A Nova seats four.

✳ What do you call a 30-year-old Chavette?
Granny.

✳ What do you call 100 Chavs at the bottom of a river?
A start.

✳ How many Chavs does it take to clean a floor?
One: 'That's some uvver bleeder's job innit.'

✳ Why did the Chav take a shower?
He didn't mean to, he just forgot to close the Nova's window in the car wash.

✳ Why did the Chav cross the road?
To start a fight with a random stranger for no reason whatsoever.

✳ What do you call a Chav at college?
The cleaner.

✳ A bus full of Chavs was driving through Wales. As they were approaching Llanfgogogferrinfourasoch they started arguing about the pronunciation of the town's name. They argued back and forth until they stopped for lunch. As they stood at the counter, one Chav asked the blonde employee, 'Before we order, could you settle an argument for us? Would you please pronounce where we are very slowly?' The blonde girl leaned over the counter and said, 'Burrrrrrrr-gerrrrrrr-Kiiiiing.'

🐔 CHICKENS

✳ What do you get if you cross a cement mixer with a chicken?
A bricklayer.

✳ What do you call a chicken in a shellsuit?
An egg!

✳ If an egg floated down the Thames, where would it have come from?
A chicken!

✳ Why did the chicken run away from home?
It was tired of being cooped up.

✳ What happened to the chicken whose feathers were all pointing the wrong way?
She was tickled to death!

✳ What do you get if you cross a poodle with a chicken?
Pooched eggs.

✳ Why did the chicken cross the road, roll in the dirt, and cross the road again?
Because he was a dirty double-crosser.

✳ What do you get if you cross a nun and a chicken?
A pecking order!

✳ Why did the punk cross the road?
Because he was stapled to the chicken's back.

✳ What kind of bird lays electric eggs?
A battery hen!

✳ Why does a rooster watch TV?
For hentertainment!

✳ What do you get from a drunk chicken?
Scotch eggs!

✳ Did you hear about the chickens who lived in a cement mixer?
They laid scrambled eggs.

✳ What do you call a scary chicken?
A poultrygeist.

✳ What goes cluck, cluck, BANG!?
A chicken in a minefield.

✳ If a rooster lays an egg on the middle of a slanted roof, on which side
will it fall?
Neither side. Roosters don't lay eggs!

✳ What did the sick chicken say?
I've got people-pox!

✳ Why didn't the chicken cross the road?
He was a chicken.

✳ Why did the starstruck chicken cross the road?
To see Gregory Peck!

✳ Why did the dirty chicken cross the road?
For some fowl purpose!

✳ Which dance do suicidal chickens do?
The foxtrot!

✳ It was so hot, the chickens were laying hard-boiled eggs.

🐨 CHILDREN AND YOUNG PEOPLE

✳ Teach a child to be polite and courteous, and when he grows up, he'll never be able to edge his car onto a motorway.

✳ A woman had five children. One day she was talking to a friend about how she had changed as a mother from the first child to the last. In fact, she told her friend, she had mellowed a lot over the years. 'When my oldest coughed or sneezed, I called the ambulance for her. When my youngest swallowed a coin, I just told him it was coming out of his pocket money.'

✳ A little girl asked her mother, 'Can I go outside and play with the boys?' Her mother replied, 'No, they're too rough.' The little girl thought for a moment and asked, 'If I can find a smooth one, can I play with him?'

✳ Fred came home from his first day at school. 'Nothing exciting happened,' he told his mother, 'except the teacher didn't know how to spell cat so I told her.'

✳ A man was walking through the park pushing his son in a buggy. The child was crying at the top of his voice and try as he might, his father could not calm him down. On the verge of despair he said, 'Calm down, Billy, it'll eventually be OK.' A woman passing stopped to remark, 'How nicely you treat Billy. You are such a sweet man. It's very obvious that you love your son very much.' The startled man replied, 'Madam, I am Billy.'

✳ In infant class, the teacher explained the difference between a watch and a clock.

She told the students that when it was a large timepiece on a wall and not attached to your body, it was called a clock. When it was worn on your body, it was called a watch.

A few days later, there was a power outage, and the classroom clocks had not been reset. The teacher asked Peter, who was wearing a wristwatch, for the time. Peter looked at his wrist, and then confidently announced, 'It is exactly ten o'watch.'

✳ How did the boy feel after being caned?
Absolutely whacked!

✳ If a mute kid swears does his mother wash his hands with soap?

✳ A man called his kids together, held up a toy and asked them who should get it.

'Who never talks back to Mother and does everything she says?' Three small voices answered in unison. 'OK, Dad, you can have it.'

✳ We have enough youth: how about a fountain of 'smart'?

✳ Did you hear about the two kids arrested yesterday? One was drinking battery acid, the other eating fireworks. They charged one and let the other off.

✳ I was the sort of child my mother warned me not to play with.

✳ I'm not saying he's a difficult boy, but since he was eight his parents have been pleading with him to run away from home.

* He's at that awkward age: too old to cry, too young to swear.

* Learn from my parents' mistake. Don't have kids!

* Children should be seen and not had.

* Most children eat spinach so they'll grow up big and strong enough to refuse it.

* A child is growing up when it stops asking where it came from and refuses to tell you where it's going.

* The average income of the modern teenager is about 2 a.m.

* One thing you can say about kids – they don't go around showing you snapshots of their grandparents.

* My kids have a pet name for me: Bias. Buy us this, buy us that.

* What stories do the ship captain's children like to hear?
Ferry tales!

* Children certainly brighten up a home – they never turn off the lights.

* Why did the little boy put lipstick on his head?
He wanted to make up his mind!

* Did you hear about the contortionist who married a fortune teller?
They had a child who could foresee its own end.

✳ After tucking their three-year-old son in bed one night, his parents heard sobbing coming from his room. Rushing back in, they found him crying hysterically. He managed to tell them that he had swallowed a penny and he was sure he was going to die. No amount of talking helped. His father, in an attempt to calm him down, palmed a penny from his pocket and pretended to pull it from his ear. The little boy was delighted.

In a flash, he snatched it from his father's hand, swallowed it, then cheerfully demanded, 'Do it again, Dad!'

✳ You can't scare me, I have children.

✳ It is not what a teenager knows that bothers his parents. It's how he found out.

✳ There are three ways to get things done: do it yourself, hire someone to do it, or tell your kids not to do it.

✳ An adolescent is someone who acts like a baby when they aren't treated like an adult.

✳ My parents put us to sleep by tossing us in the air. Of course, you have to have low ceilings for this method to work.

✳ The best way to keep children at home is to make the home atmosphere pleasant, and let the air out of their tyres.

✳ A man was laying a new concrete path. No sooner was his back turned than a crowd of children came running by, leaving unsightly footmarks all over the hardening surface.

The man started to swear. A neighbour who heard him said to him, 'I'm surprised, Sam. You told me you liked kids.' 'I like them – in the abstract, but not in the concrete.'

* The difference between in-laws and outlaws? Outlaws are wanted.

* To stop your children being spoiled, keep them in the fridge.

* At the age of four, I was left an orphan. I ask you: what could I do with an orphan?

* 'Why did you kick your brother in the stomach?'
'Because he turned around.'

* Eve to Adam: 'What do you mean the kids don't look like you?'

* Today's children would be less spoiled if we could spank parents.

* A seven-year-old girl admitted calmly to her parents that a boy had kissed her after class.
    'How did that happen?' gasped her mother. 'It wasn't easy,' admitted the child. 'Three girls had to help me catch him!'

* Little Johnny went to the police claiming he was constantly beaten by his parents. Social Services looked into it and found the whole family had abuse problems going back generations. The judge didn't know what to do! Finally, he found the perfect solution. He gave Johnny to Tottenham Hotspur. They never beat anyone.

✳ What do Mr Razzi's children call him?
Papa Razzi.

Children's books from hell

You Were an Accident

You Are Different and That's Bad

The Boy Who Died From Eating All His Vegetables

Dad's New Wife Robert

Fun Four-letter Words to Know and Share

Hammers, Screwdrivers and Scissors: An I-Can-Do-It Book

The Kids' Guide to Hitchhiking

Kathy Was So Bad Her Mom Stopped Loving Her

Curious George and the High-Voltage Fence

All Cats Go to Hell

The Little Sissy Who Snitched

That's It, I'm Putting You Up for Adoption

Grandpa Gets a Casket

The Magic World Inside the Abandoned Refrigerator

The Pop-Up Book of Human Anatomy

Whining, Kicking and Crying to Get Your Way

Things Rich Kids Have, but You Never Will

Pop! Goes the Hamster … and Other Great Microwave Games

Your Nightmares are Real

Eggs, Toilet Paper, and Your School

Places Where Mommy and Daddy Hide Neat Things

Daddy Drinks Because You Cry

Oh, the Places You'll Scratch and Sniff

Strangers Have the Best Candy

Some Kittens Can Fly!

Getting More Chocolate on Your Face

Where Would You Like to Be Buried?

The Attention Deficit Disorder Association's Book of Wild Animals of North Europe – Hey! Let's Go Ride Our Bikes!

When Mommy and Daddy Don't Know the Answer, They Say 'God Did It'

Garfield Gets Feline Leukaemia

What Is That Dog Doing to That Other Dog?

Why Can't Mr Fork and Ms Electrical Outlet Be Friends?

Testing Homemade Parachutes Using Only Your Household Pets

Babar Meets the Taxidermist

Start a Real-Estate Empire with the Change from Your Mom's Purse

The Care Bears Maul Some Campers and are Shot Dead

How to Become the Dominant Military Power in Your Elementary School

Controlling the Playground: Respect through Fear

Children's lexicon

FEEDBACK: The inevitable result when the baby doesn't appreciate the strained carrots.

FULL NAME: What you call your child when you're angry at him.

GRANDPARENTS: The people who think your children are wonderful even though they're sure you're not raising them right.

HEARSAY: What toddlers do when anyone mutters a dirty word.

INDEPENDENT: How we want our children to be as long as they do everything we say.

OUCH: The first word spoken by children with older siblings.

PUDDLE: A small body of water that draws other small bodies wearing dry shoes into it.

SHOW-OFF: A child who is more talented than yours.

STERILIZE: What you do to your first baby's dummy by boiling it, and to your last baby's dummy by blowing on it and wiping it off.

TOP BUNK: Where you should never put a child wearing Superman pyjamas.

TWO-MINUTE WARNING: When the baby's face turns red and she begins to make those familiar grunting noises.

VERBAL: Able to whine in words.

WHODUNNIT: None of the kids that live in your house.

🐻 CHRISTMAS

✳ What goes oh oh oh?
Santa walking backwards.

✳ Be naughty – save Santa the trip.

✳ Why does Christmas come when the shops are always so crowded?

✳ Santa Claus: The only man to be interested in an empty stocking.

✳ What do you get if you cross Father Christmas with a detective?
Santa Clues!

✳ Every time I see a fireplace, I think of Santa Claus and am ashamed.

✳ What does an electrician get for Christmas?
Shorts.

✳ Husband: A man who buys his football tickets four months in advance and waits until 24 December to do his Christmas shopping.

✳ Who sings 'White Christmas' and explodes?
Bang Crosby.

✳ The Bermuda Triangle got tired of warm weather. It moved to Finland. Now Santa Claus is missing.

✳ What do you call someone who is afraid of Santa?
A Clausterphobic.

✳ What do you call Santa's helpers?
Subordinate Clauses.

✳ What do you call a bunch of Grandmasters of chess bragging about their games in a hotel lobby?
Chess nuts boasting in an open foyer!

✳ Why did the elf push his bed into the fireplace?
He wanted to sleep like a log.

✳ Why did Santa spell Christmas N-O-E?
Because the angel had said, 'No L!'

✳ What goes Ho, Ho, Swoosh, Ho, Ho, Swoosh?
Santa caught in a revolving door!

✳ Why does Santa Claus go down the chimney on Christmas Eve?
Because it 'soots' him!

✳ Why does Scrooge love Rudolph the Red-Nosed Reindeer?
Because every buck is dear to him.

✳ How come you never hear anything about the tenth reindeer 'Olive'?
Yeah, you know, 'Olive the other reindeer, used to laugh and call him names.'

✳ Why is Christmas just like a day at the office?
You do all the work and the fat guy with the suit gets all the credit.

✳ What was so good about the neurotic doll the girl was given for Christmas?
It was wound up already.

✳ What's a good Christmas tip?
Never catch snowflakes with your tongue until all the birds have gone south for the winter.

✳ Three men die in a car accident on Christmas Eve. They all find themselves at the Pearly Gates waiting to enter heaven. On entering they must present something relating to or associated with Christmas. The first man searches his pocket, and finds some mistletoe, so he is allowed in. The second man presents a cracker, so he is also allowed in. The third man pulls out a pair of stockings. Confused at this last gesture, St Peter asks, 'How do these represent Christmas?' Answer: 'They're Carol's.'

✳ A mafioso's son sits at his desk writing a Christmas list to Jesus. He first writes, 'Dear baby Jesus, I have been a good boy the whole year, so I want a new...' He looks at it, then crumples it up into a ball and throws it away. He gets out a new piece of paper and writes again, 'Dear baby Jesus, I have been a good boy for most of the year, so I want a new...' He again looks at it with disgust and throws it away. He then gets an idea. He goes into his mother's room, takes a statue of the Virgin Mary, puts it in the closet, and locks the door. He takes another piece of paper and writes, 'Dear baby Jesus. If you ever want to see your mother again...'

✳ In a small southern town in Texas there was a nativity scene that showed great skill and talent had gone into creating it. One small feature stood out. The three wise men were wearing firemen's helmets. Totally unable to come up with a reason or explanation, a visitor decided to ask a local what it meant. At a shop on the edge of town, he asked the lady behind the counter about the helmets. She exploded into a rage: 'People these days never do read the Bible!' The visitor assured her that he did, but simply couldn't recall anything about firemen in the Bible. She jerked her Bible from behind the counter and ruffled through some pages, and finally jabbed her finger at a passage. Sticking it in his face she said, 'See, it says right here, "The three wise man came from afar."'

✳ Father Christmas wins a saucepan in a competition. Now that's what you call pot luck!

✳ What do the reindeer sing to Father Christmas on his birthday? Freeze a jolly good fellow!

✳ What do you call a man who claps at Father Christmas? Santapplause!

✳ Who delivers presents to baby sharks at Christmas? Santa Jaws!

✳ What does Father Christmas call his money? Iced lolly!

✷ What's Father Christmas called when he takes a rest while delivering presents?
Santa Pause!

You know Santa hates your kids when...

✷ Kid's letter to North Pole comes back stamped, 'Dream on.'

✷ Kid asks for new bike, gets pack of cigarettes.

✷ Along with presents, Santa leaves hefty bill for shipping and handling.

✷ By the time he gets to your house, all he has left is foam packing.

✷ Christmas Day, your kid wakes up with a reindeer head in his bed.

✷ Instead of 'Naughty' or 'Nice', Santa has him on the 'Stupid' list.

✷ Labels on all your kid's toys read 'Straight from Craptown'.

✷ Four words: 'Off my lap, Tubby!'

✷ What Christmas song is this: ABCDEFGHIJK MNOPQRSTUVWXYZ?
No L!

✷ Why did the police arrest Santa?
Because he was out all night sleighing.

✳ What do elves learn in school?
The elf-abet!

✳ Why was Santa's little helper depressed?
Because he had low elf-esteem.

✳ Why does Santa have three gardens?
So he can hoe-hoe-hoe.

✳ What do you get when you cross an archer with a gift-wrapper?
Ribbon Hood.

✳ What was wrong with the boy's brand new toy electric train set he received for Christmas?
Forty feet of track – all straight!

✳ How does Tony Blair's household keep Christmas politically correct?
On Christmas morning, they give the presents TO the tree.

✳ What do you call a cat on the beach at Christmas time?
Sandy Claus!

✳ What nationality is Santa Claus?
North Polish.

✳ Why does Santa's sled get such good mileage?
Because it has long-distance runners on each side.

CLOTHES

❋ What bow can't be tied?
A rainbow!

❋ What happens when you throw a jacket and trousers into a river?
You get a wet suit.

❋ If you don't feel very well, what do you probably have?
A pair of gloves on.

❋ Why doesn't the Gingerbread Man wear shorts?
Because he has crummy legs.

❋ What kind of button won't unbutton?
A bellybutton!

❋ What kind of coat can be put on only when wet?
A coat of paint.

❋ I got some new underwear yesterday. Well, it was new to me.

❋ What did the tie say to the hat?
'You go on ahead and I'll hang around!'

❋ A cardboard belt would be a waist of paper.

❋ What has twenty pairs of legs but can't walk?
Ten pairs of trousers.

✳ I went to buy some camouflage trousers the other day but I couldn't find any.

✳ 'That suit fits you like a glove.'
'That's the trouble – it's supposed to fit like a suit.'

✳ Did you hear about the woman who had five legs?
Her knickers fitted her like a glove.

✳ I bought my wife a complete fur outfit – two steel traps and a rifle.

✳ 'Excuse me, you look like Helen Green.'
'I look worse in pink.'

clowns

What has orange hair, big feet, and comes out of a test tube?
Bozo the clone.

Is it true that cannibals won't eat clowns because they taste funny?

competitions

One man says to the other, 'Hey, how did you rate in the spitting contest?' The other guy replies, 'Oh, I never entered. I didn't expectorate.'

compliments

A pat on the back is only a few centimetres from a kick in the pants.

CONFUSiON

✳ I had amnesia once, maybe twice.

✳ Am I ambivalent? Well, yes and no.

✳ The following statement is true. The previous statement is false.

✳ I'm as confused as a baby in a topless bar.

✳ When you don't know what you are doing, do it neatly.

✳ If you can't convince them, confuse them.

conservation/countryside

Save a tree – eat a beaver.

A bunch of city dwellers go to the country, where a sign in a national park urges them to 'Keep still and listen to the silence'. After a while one turns to his wife and asks, 'I can't hear anything, can you?'

cookery

Cookbooks can be exciting, what with all the stirring chapters.

I longed to ride the range, but it kept burning my trousers.

Darling, what's this on my plate? In case I have to describe it to the doctor.

My wife's cooking melts in your mouth. I wish she'd defrost it first.

COURTS / JUDGES

* What did the judge say when the skunk walked in the courtroom? 'Odour in court.'

* Several women appeared in court, each accusing the other of the trouble they were having in the apartment building where they lived. The judge, with Solomon-like wisdom, decreed, 'I'll hear the oldest first.' The case was closed for lack of evidence.

* A man was sued by a woman for defamation of character. She charged that he had called her a pig. The man was found guilty and fined. After the trial he asked the judge, 'Does this mean that I cannot call Mrs Johnson a pig?' The judge said that was true. 'Well, does this mean I cannot call a pig Mrs Johnson?' the man asked. The

judge replied that he could indeed call a pig Mrs Johnson with no fear of legal action. The man turned, looked directly at Mrs Johnson and said, 'Good afternoon, Mrs Johnson.'

cowboys

So this cowboy walks into a German car showroom and he says, 'Audi!'

What's the nearest thing to silver?
The Lone Ranger's bottom!

Why did the cowboy die with his boots on?
Because he didn't want to stub his toe when he kicked the bucket!

CHICKENS CROSSING

COWS

✳ What do you get if you cross a camel and a cow?
Lumpy milkshakes.

✳ Who was the first to see a cow and think, I wonder what will happen if I squeeze these dangly things and drink whatever comes out?

✳ From what animal do you get dragon milk?
A cow with short legs.

* What do you call a cow eating grass in a garden?
A lawn mooer.

* Where do cows go on holiday?
Moo York.

* What do you call a bull who tells jokes?
Laugh-a-bull!

* What do you get if you cross a cow with a duck?
Cream quackers.

* How do you count cows?
With a cowculator.

* What do you call cows with a sense of humour?
Laughing stock.

* What happens if you walk under a cow?
You get a pat on the head.

* Milking a cow is easy. Any jerk can do it.

* It was so cold the farmer milked for twenty minutes before he realized he was shaking hands with himself.

* Where do cows go for fun?
To the moooovies.

✳ What has one horn and gives milk?
A milk lorry.

✳ An Englishman, Irishman and a Scotsman were walking through a field when they met a cow. 'That's an English cow,' said the Englishman. 'No,' said the Irishman, 'that's definitely an Irish cow.' 'You're both wrong,' said the Scotsman, 'it's a Scottish cow – look, it's got bagpipes underneath.'

✳ A farmer says to his friend, 'I can't decide whether to buy a bicycle or a new cow.' His friend replies, 'You'd look pretty silly riding a cow.' 'I'd look even sillier trying to milk a bicycle,' retorts the farmer.

✳ Two cows are in a field. One goes, 'Moooooo!' The other cow turns to her: 'I was going to say that.'

✳ What do you call a man with cow droppings all over his feet?
An incowpoop!

✳ Why did the bull rush?
Because it saw the cow slip!

✳ What do you get from a pampered cow?
Spoiled milk.

✳ What kind of things does a farmer talk about when he is milking cows?
Udder nonsense!

✳ What's a cow's favourite vegetable?
A cowat!

✳ I was told that cow tongue is a delicacy, but I have a hard time tasting something that is tasting me back.

✳ Knock knock.
Who's there?
The interrupting cow.
The interrupting cow wh-
MOO!

✳ To err is human; to moo, bovine.

✳ Déjà moo: The feeling that you've heard this bull before.

✳ What does a cow with buck teeth say?
Moooof!

✳ What kind of maths do cows do best?
Moooo-tiplication.

✳ Two cows standing next to each other in a field. Daisy said to Dolly, 'I was artificially inseminated this morning.' 'I don't believe you,' said Dolly. 'It's true, straight up no bull!'

The two-cow explanation of the world...

A CHRISTIAN: You have two cows. You keep one and give one to your neighbour.

A SOCIALIST: You have two cows. The government takes one and gives it to your neighbour.

A TORY: You have two cows. Your neighbour has none. So what?

A LIBERAL: You have two cows. Your neighbour has none. You feel guilty for being successful. You vote people into office who tax your cows, forcing you to sell one to raise money to pay the tax. The people you voted for then take the tax money and buy a cow and give it to your neighbour. You feel righteous.

A COMMUNIST: You have two cows. The government seizes both and provides you with milk.

A FASCIST: You have two cows. The government seizes both and sells you the milk. You join the underground and start a campaign of sabotage.

DEMOCRACY, AMERICAN STYLE: You have two cows. The government taxes you to the point you have to sell both to support a man in a foreign country who has only one cow, which was a gift from your government.

CAPITALISM, AMERICAN STYLE: You have two cows. You sell one, buy a bull, and build a herd of cows.

BUREAUCRACY: You have two cows. The government takes them both, shoots one, milks the other, pays you for the milk, then pours the milk down the drain.

AN AMERICAN CORPORATION: You have two cows. You sell one, and force the other to produce the milk of four cows. You are surprised when the cow drops dead.

A FRENCH CORPORATION: You have two cows. You go on strike because you want three cows.

A JAPANESE CORPORATION: You have two cows. You redesign them so they are one-tenth the size of an ordinary cow and produce twenty times the milk.

A GERMAN CORPORATION: You have two cows. You re-engineer them so they live for 100 years, eat once a month, and milk themselves.

AN ITALIAN CORPORATION: You have two cows but you don't know where they are. You break for lunch.

A RUSSIAN CORPORATION: You have two cows. You count them and learn you have five cows. You count them again and learn you have 42 cows. You count them again and learn you have twelve cows. You stop counting cows and open another bottle of vodka.

A MEXICAN CORPORATION: You think you have two cows, but you don't know what a cow looks like. You take a nap.

A SWISS CORPORATION: You have 5,000 cows, none of which belong to you. You charge for storing them for others.

A BRAZILIAN CORPORATION: You have two cows. You enter into a partnership with an American corporation. Soon you have 1,000 cows and the American corporation declares bankruptcy.

AN INDIAN CORPORATION: You have two cows. You worship them.

✳ What did the farmer call the cow that would not give him any milk? An udder failure!

comparisons

I was busier than a beaver in a coffee lake.

He was more nervous than a ceiling-fan seller with a comb-over.

He was more tense than Mick Jagger on Father's Day.

🐵 CRIME

✳ A pickpocket was up in court for a series of petty crimes. The judge said, 'Mr Banks, you are hereby fined £100.' The lawyer stood up and said, 'Thanks, my lord. My client only has £75 on him at this time, but if you'd allow him a few minutes in the crowd…'

✳ A judge went to court to hear the pleas of a woman that her husband be released from the prison. 'What was he convicted of?' asked the judge gently. 'Stealing a loaf of bread,' replied the offender's wife, shifting nervously in her chair. 'Is he a good husband?' 'No,' she replied frankly, blushing a bit. 'He beats me when he gets drunk. He bullies our children. He's unfaithful, and he's really not much good at all.' 'It sounds to me as though you're better off without him,' said the judge. 'Why on earth do you want him out of jail?'

'Well,' she explained, 'we're out of bread again.'

✳ What's the most common crime committed by transvestites?
Male fraud.

✳ Crime doesn't pay. Does that mean my job is a crime?

✳ Work off excess energy. Steal something heavy.

✳ A woman was caught stealing a can of peaches. Her husband accompanies her to the trial. 'How many peaches were in the can?' asks the judge. 'Six,' she confesses. 'Then I must sentence you to six years in prison, one for every peach you stole,' says the judge.

Her husband stands up and says, 'Judge. She also stole a bag of peas.'

✳ What happened to the kleptomaniac's daughter?
She took after her mother.

✳ I'm proud to say that my kids have proved time and again that they're reliable and trustworthy. Not once have they ever jumped bail.

✳ Why did the cashier steal money from the till?
She thought the change would do her good.

✳ Don't steal a police car unless you're prepared to floor it all the way to Mexico.

✳ Don't tell any big lies today. Small ones can be just as effective.

✳ The truth will set you free, but a good lie can always break you out.

✳ Have you heard about the three-fingered thief? All he steals is bowling balls.

✳ Who was the world's greatest thief?
Atlas, because he held up the whole world!

✳ Crime doesn't pay, but at least you're your own boss.

✳ Did you hear about the young man who was let off by the judge after stealing a petticoat? It was because it was his first slip.

✳ **Judge**: 'Did you strike that man in the excitement?'
Defendant: 'No, your honour. I hit him in the stomach.'

✳ **Judge**: 'Do you realize, young lady, that you are facing the electric chair?'
Defendant: 'I don't mind facing it, your honour. It's the sitting down in it I could do without.'

✳ What would you call theft in Peking?
A Chinese takeaway!

✳ Assassins do it from behind.

✳ What kind of robbery is least dangerous?
A safe robbery.

✳ If you didn't get caught, did you really do it?

✳ If you try and don't succeed, cheat. Repeat until caught. Then lie.

✳ A poor man slipped into confession on Christmas Eve. 'Forgive me, Father, for I have sinned. I stole this turkey to feed my family. Would you take it and assuage my guilt?'

   'Certainly not,' said the priest. 'As penance, you must return it to the one from whom you stole it.' 'I tried,' the man sobbed, 'but he refused. Oh, Father, what should I do?' 'If what you say is true, then it is all right for you to keep it for your family.' Thanking the priest, the man hurried off. When confession was over, the priest returned to his house. When he walked into the kitchen, he found that someone had stolen his turkey.

cross-dressing

CHICKENS CROSSING

A wealthy man and his wife are going to a function, so they decide to give the butler the night off. However, a couple of hours later the wife is bored, so she leaves the party and goes home, only to find the butler sitting alone at the table. She orders the butler upstairs to her bedroom, where she locks the door. 'Jeeves,' she commands, 'take off my hat.' Jeeves promptly obeys. 'Now, Jeeves,' she says, 'take off my dress.' He obeys. 'Now, Jeeves, please remove my underwear.' Breaking into a nervous sweat, Jeeves complies. 'Now, Jeeves,' the wife says, 'if I should ever catch you wearing my clothes again...'

crocodiles

Did you hear about the guy combining an abalone and a crocodile? He wanted to call it an abodile. I think it's a crock of baloney.

Never insult an alligator until after you have crossed the river.

CUCKOOS

✳ **Teacher**: Can you name a bird that doesn't build its own nest?
Darren: Yes, sir. The cuckoo.
Teacher: Well done. And how did you know that?
Darren: Everyone knows that. Cuckoos live in clocks.

🐸 DANCiNG

✳ My best friend became addicted to country and western line dancing. It got so bad he had to enter a two-step programme.

✳ Dancing cheek to cheek is really a form of floor play.

✳ Why couldn't the butterfly go to the dance? Because it was a moth-ball.

✳ How do you make a tissue dance? Put a little boogey in it!

✳ What do cars do at the disco? Brake dance.

✳ I'm busier than a one-legged Riverdancer.

✳ Dancing is like a shower: one wrong turn and you're in hot water.

✳ Where did the butcher dance?
At the meatball!

✳ Did you hear about the Irishman who went to the country to see a barn dance?

✳ Why don't dogs make good dancers?
Because they have two left feet!

✳ Why do ballerinas stand on their toes? Can't they just get taller women?

✳ There's no future in hula dancing: it's a shaky business.

✳ I don't mind you dancing on my feet; it's the continual jumping off and on that gets me.

✳ Why do mice have small balls?
Not that many know how to dance.

✳ 'Darling, I want to dance like this for ever!'
'What, you don't want to improve?'

✳ 'Until I met you life was like a big desert.'
'Is that why you dance like a camel?'

✳ Where did the computer go to dance?
To a disc-o.

✴ I went to a nightclub the other day. It was so crowded I had to dance cheek to cheek with the girl behind me.

✴ Did you hear about the man who was tap dancing? He broke his ankle when he fell into the sink.

🐺 DAYS OF THE WEEK

✴ What are the strongest days of the week? Saturday and Sunday. All the rest are weak days!

✴ What two days of the week start with the letter 'T'?
Today and Tomorrow!

✴ Remember, you should always give 100% at work: 12% Monday; 23% Tuesday; 40% Wednesday; 20% Thursday; 5% Friday.

✴ 'It's gone for ever – for ever, I tell you!'
'What has?'
'Yesterday!'

✴ If you think today isn't such a great day – try missing it.

✴ A calendar's days are numbered.

🐻 DEAFNESS

✳ What kind of fish will help you hear better?
A herring aid!

✳ My grandfather is hard of hearing. He needs to read lips. I don't mind him reading lips, but he uses one of those yellow highlighters.

✳ An elderly couple were attending a church service. About halfway through, she leans over and says, 'I just had a silent fart – what do you think I should do?' He replies, 'Put a new battery in your hearing aid.'

✳ An elderly gentleman was telling his friend about his new hearing aid. He said, 'This hearing aid is so good that I can hear a pin drop to the floor 60 feet away.' The friend said, 'What kind is it?' The old man looked at his watch and said, 'It's 2.30.'

🐻 DEATH

✳ A couple lived near the coast. One morning, the wife said she was going sailing in the bay. The husband told her to be careful. When she didn't return that night, he called the authorities, who searched the bay. They next day, two policemen appeared at his door. 'We have some bad news for you, some good news, and some great news.' 'What's the bad news?' asked the husband, steeling himself. 'Your wife drowned in the bay.' 'What's the good news?' he asked. 'When we pulled her up, there were a dozen king crabs and eight lobsters clinging to her.' 'What's the great news?' 'We're pulling her up again tomorrow!'

✳ Two widows were in the lounge of the Seniors' Centre. 'Well,' one said, 'Margaret has just cremated her third husband.' 'Yeah, that's the way it goes,' replied the other widow. 'Some of us can't find a husband, and others have husbands to burn!'

✳ 'They sent flowers to the funeral. And I couldn't help thinking, if you'd sent them before, she'd have pulled through her illness.' *Reginald D. Hunter*

✳ A dying businessman called his best friend to his deathbed. 'I want you to promise me that when I die you will have my remains cremated.' 'And what,' his friend asked, 'do you want me to do with your ashes?' The businessman said, 'Just put them in an envelope and mail them to the Inland Revenue. Write on the envelope, "Now you have everything."'

✳ An old woman is upset at her husband's funeral. 'You have him in a brown suit and I wanted him in a blue suit.' The mortician says, 'We'll take care of it, ma'am,' and yells back, 'Ed, switch the heads on two and four!'

✳ 'My dad's dying wish was to have his family around him. I can't help thinking he would have been better off with more oxygen.' *Jimmy Carr*

✳ A man gets a call from the family doctor. The doctor says, 'I have good news and bad news. The bad news is your wife is a complete vegetable and will need constant care and nursing for the rest of her life.' The physician goes on to say that he will even be required to assist his wife with her bodily functions and have to wipe her rear end. The man says, in horror, 'Well, what could possibly be the good news?' The doctor says, 'The good news is I was kidding. Your wife is dead.'

✳ Did you hear about the man who drowned at work in a vat of varnish. A terrible end, but a beautiful finish!

✳ He died a natural death – he was hit by a car.

✳ A football fan has got a hallowed ticket to the cup final and takes his seat excitedly, seconds before kick-off. To his disbelief, despite the place being packed to the rafters, next to him is a solitary empty seat. He leans over to an old fella who is sitting quietly on the other side of the spare and explains his amazement. The old fellow stares out at the pitch and slowly responds: 'Actually, the empty seat is mine. My beloved wife passed away last week and this is the first ever cup final I have been to without her sitting by my side.' The man is truly saddened by this and replies: 'I'm really sorry to hear that, mate, I'm really very sorry. Were you unable to pass on the ticket to a family member to come and accompany you for the day?' The old fella shakes his head sorrowfully. 'Naah, I asked and no one would come with me.' 'Really?' the man says with surprise. 'Not even a friend or a colleague offered to join you?' 'Naah, not one of 'em,' the old fella reiterates. 'They're all at her funeral.'

✴ Did you hear about the Irishman who was condemned to hang, but saved himself by dying in prison?

✴ Where do undertakers go in October?
The hearse of the year show!

✴ 'I saw that show, *50 Things To Do Before You Die.* I would have thought the obvious one was "Shout For Help".' *Mark Watson, Rhod Gilbert*

✴ The only difference between a rut and a grave is the depth.

✴ If you can survive death, you can probably survive anything.

✴ A manager walks into his office and sees a blonde crying. He approaches her and asks why she's crying. She tells him she just found out her mother died. The manager tells her to take the rest of the day off and not to worry about work. Later, the manager calls the blonde to see how she's doing. The blonde is crying harder than before. He tries to console her, but he can't. The blonde says, 'I was calling everyone to let them know about my mother's death and I found out something horrible.' 'What?' the manager asks. 'I found out my sister's mum died too!'

✴ Life is the process of losing our illusions, until we finally lose the illusion that we are alive.

✴ My grandpa used to say, 'You know, one of these days I'm going to wake up dead.' He was right.

✳ **Doctor**: Did that medicine I gave your uncle straighten him out?
Man: It certainly did. We buried him yesterday.

✳ What do you get if you lean a corpse against a doorbell?
A dead ringer.

✳ If Elvis were alive right now, he'd be scratching at the inside of his coffin.

✳ It isn't the cough that carries you off. It's the coffin they carry you off in.

✳ What happens when plumbers die?
They go down the drain!

✳ These days, I spend a lot of time thinking about the hereafter – I go somewhere to get something and then wonder what I'm here after.

✳ It used to be only death and taxes were inevitable. Now, of course, there's shipping and handling, too.

✳ The idea is to die young as late as possible.

✳ He was deader than a shrunken head at a hacky sack festival.

✳ Death is hereditary.

✳ Don't take life too seriously: you won't get out alive.

* Bombs don't kill people, explosions kill people.

* Entropy isn't what it used to be.

* I intend to live for ever – so far so good.

* Capital punishment isn't for making examples, it's for making bad people dead.

* Should crematoriums give discounts for burn victims?

* Death to all fanatics!

* Life's a bleach and then you dye.

* I'd like to leave this world like I came into it: screaming, naked and covered in someone else's blood.

* How can you tell if a corpse is angry?
  It flips its lid!

* Life: No one gets out alive.

* How many men do you need for a mafia funeral?
  Only one. To slam the car boot shut.

decorating

I was doing some decorating, so I got out my step-ladder. I don't get on with my real ladder.

A homeowner was delighted with the job the painter had done on his house. 'You did such a great job,' he said as he handed the man money. 'There's an extra £80 in there to take the missus out to dinner and a film.' Later that night, the doorbell rang. The homeowner went to the door and found the painter standing on the porch. 'What's the matter?' he asked. 'Did you forget something?' 'Nope,' replied the painter. 'I'm just here to take your missus out to dinner and a film like you said.'

🦫 DEFiNiTiONS

❋ *Abdicate* (v), to give up hope of ever having a flat stomach.

❋ *Adult* (n), a person who has stopped growing at both ends and is now growing in the middle.

❋ *Balderdash* (n), a rapidly receding hairline.

❋ *Beauty parlour* (n), a place where women curl up and dye.

✳ *Circular Definition* (adj), see Definition, Circular.

✳ *Circumvent* (n), the opening in the front of boxer shorts.

✳ *Coffee* (n), a person who is coughed upon.

✳ *Deja Fu* (adj), the feeling that somehow, somewhere, you've been kicked in the head like this before.

✳ *Dust* (n), mud with the juice squeezed out.

✳ *Egotist* (n), someone who is usually me-deep in conversation.

✳ *Embarrassment* (adj), when two eyes meet through a keyhole.

✳ *Esplanade* (v), to attempt an explanation when drunk.

✳ *Flabbergasted* (adj), appalled over how much weight you have gained.

✳ *Flatulence* (n), the emergency vehicle that picks you up after you are run over by a steamroller.

✳ *Frisbeetarianism* (n), the belief that, when you die, your soul goes up on the roof and gets stuck there.

✳ *Gargoyle* (n), an olive-flavoured mouth wash.

✳ *Handkerchief* (n), cold Storage.

* *Inflation* (n), cutting money in half without damaging the paper.

* *Lymph* (v), to walk with a lisp.

* *Mosquito* (n), an insect that makes you like flies better.

* *Negligent* (adj), describes a condition in which you absentmindedly answer the door in your nightie.

* *Oyster* (n). a person who sprinkles his conversation with Yiddish expressions.

* *Pokémon* (n), a Jamaican proctologist.

* *Raisin* (n), grape with a sunburn.

* *Rectitude* (n), the formal, dignified demeanour assumed by a proctologist immediately before he examines you.

* *Secret* (n), something you tell to one person at a time.

* *Testicle* (n), a humorous question in an exam.

* *Tomorrow* (n), one of the greatest labour saving devices of today.

* *Toothache* (n), the pain that drives you to extraction.

* *Willy-nilly* (adj), impotent.

✳ *Wrinkles* (n), something other people have. You have character lines

✳ *Yawn* (v), an honest opinion openly expressed.

🦷 DENTISTS

✳ **First tramp**: I see my dentist twice a year.
Second tramp: Really?
First tramp: Yes, once for each tooth.

✳ Why did the Irishman save his old magazines?
He wanted to be a dentist.

✳ What time is it when you must go to the dentist?
Tooth-hurty.

✳ Why are dentists artistic?
Because they are good at drawing teeth.

✳ How did the dentist become a brain surgeon?
His drill slipped.

✳ Do you swear to pull the tooth, the whole tooth and nothing but the tooth?

✳ Why did the tree go to the dentist?
To get a root canal.

✳ Why did the king go to the dentist?
To get his teeth crowned.

✳ What did the tooth say to the dentist?
'Fill 'er up.'

🦁 DEVIL

✳ Why do ghouls and demons hang out together?
Because demons are a ghoul's best friend.

✳ What do demons have on holiday?
A devil of a time!

✳ I am an agent of Satan, but my duties are largely ceremonial.

✳ A priest came to a dying man to read him his last rites. 'Do you reject the devil?' asked the priest. 'This is no time to be making enemies,' replied the man.

✳ What do you get when you cross Elvis with the devil?
Memphistopheles.
Where would he live?
Fall from grace-land.

dictionaries

Dictionaries: If you've read one, you've read them all.

Dictionaries: The only place where success comes before work, and divorce comes before marriage.

Did you hear about the drama being written about the dictionary? It's a play on words.

DiNOSAURS

* Hearing about a dinosaur alive in the rainforests of South America, a professor launches a scientific expedition. After several weeks he stumbles upon a little man wearing a loincloth, standing near a 300-foot-long dead dinosaur. The scientist can't believe his eyes. 'Did you kill this dinosaur?' he asks. 'Yep,' replies the rainforest native. 'But it's so big and you're so small! How did you kill it?' 'With my club,' the primitive fellow answers. 'How big is your club?' 'Well, there are about a hundred of us...'

* What are prehistoric monsters called when they sleep?
A dinosnore!

* 'God creates dinosaurs. God kills dinosaurs. God creates man. Man kills God. Man creates dinosaurs. Dinosaurs eat man... Woman inherits the earth.' *Jurassic Park*

✳ What do you get when you cross a dinosaur and a pig?
Jurassic pork!

✳ Why can't you hear a pterodactyl go to the toilet?
Because it has a silent P.

diplomacy

Diplomacy is the art of saying good doggie while looking for a bigger stick.

A diplomat is someone who can tell you to go to hell in such a way that you will look forward to the trip.

CHICKEN CROSSING

🐶 DOGS

✳ What do you get if you cross a sheepdog and a jelly?
Colliewobbles.

✳ Who is a dog's favourite comedian?
Growlcho Marx.

✳ What happens to a dog that keeps eating bits off of the table?
He gets splinters in his mouth.

✳ Outside of a dog, man's best friend is a book. Inside of a dog, it is very dark.

✳ You can say any foolish thing to a dog, and the dog will give you a look that says, 'You're right! I never would've thought of that!'

✳ What has two legs and bleeds easily?
Half a dog.

✳ Ever notice that when the doorbell rings, the dog's the first one to the door, but it's never for him?

✳ What do you get if you cross a Rottweiler with a Labrador?
A dog that scares you then runs off with the toilet roll.

✳ Why do dogs bury bones in the ground?
Because you can't bury them in trees!

✳ A guy walks into a bar with his dog. They get to drinking, and after a while the dog passes out. Soon the man gets up to leave and the bartender says, 'Hey, you can't leave that lyin' there.' The guy turns and says, 'It's not a lion, it's my dog.'

✳ Why did the poor dog chase his own tail?
He was trying to make both ends meet.

✳ What do you get if you cross a Rottweiler and a hyena?
I don't know but join in if it laughs.

✳ What do you get if you cross a dog with a blind mole?
A dog that keeps barking up the wrong tree.

✳ What dog loves to take bubble baths?
A shampoodle.

* Sorry – my karma ran over your dogma.

* His dog's called Camera as it's always snapping.

* How do you catch a runaway dog?
  Hide behind a tree and make a noise like a bone!

* What dogs are best for sending telegrams?
  Wire-haired terriers!

* What did the cowboy say when he saw a bear eat Lassie?
  'Well, doggone!'

* What do you get if you cross a dog and a skunk?
  Rid of the dog!

* What do you get if you cross a dog with a kangaroo?
  A dog that has somewhere to put its own lead!

* What do you get if you cross a dog with a vegetable?
  A Jack Brussel.

* Did you hear about the blind man who went bungee jumping?
  Scared the hell out of the dog.

* Which dog can jump higher than a building?
  Any dog. Buildings can't jump.

* Where does a Rottweiler sit in the cinema?
  Anywhere it wants to!

✳ What do you do if your dog eats your pen?
Use a pencil instead!

✳ Dear God, help me to be the person my dog thinks I am.

✳ What do you call a dog with no hind legs and a tail of steel?
Sparky.

✳ There once was a dog named Tax. I opened the door and income Tax.

✳ Where do you find a dog with no legs?
Right where you left him.

✳ What did the dog say when he sat on the sandpaper?
Rough.

✳ A dog has an owner. A cat has a staff.

✳ Why didn't the Texan dog speak to his foot?
Because it's not polite to talk back to your paw!

✳ When I'm feeling down, I like to whistle. It makes the neighbour's dog run to the end of his chain and gag himself.

✳ My neighbour was bitten by a rabid dog. I went to see how he was and found him writing frantically. I told him rabies could be cured and he didn't have to worry about a will. He said, 'Will? What will? I'm making a list of the people I want to bite.'

✳ What happened to the dog that ate nothing but garlic?
His bark was much worse than his bite!

✳ What dog wears contact lenses?
A cock-eyed spaniel!

✳ I bought a lap dog, but I had to get rid of it. Every time I sat on its lap it bit me.

✳ One dog said to another: 'What happened to me shouldn't happen to a man.'

✳ Did you hear about the Irish watchdog? It's very vigilant. Every time there's a suspicious noise his owner wakes it and it starts barking.

✳ We've got a great watchdog. Last week it watched a burglar while he broke in and stole all our silver.

✳ Some dogs are pointers: mine's a nudger. He's too polite to point.

✳ When is the most likely time that a stray dog will walk into your house?
When the door's open!

✳ I bought a gun dog, but he's useless. He never hits the target.

✳ Dogma: A dog with puppies.

✳ What do you get if you take a really big dog out for a walk?
A Great Dane out!

✳ **Teacher**: This essay you wrote about a dog is a word-for-word copy of your brother's.
  Pupil: That's right. It's the same dog.

✳ **Phil**: Why is your dog staring at me like that?
  Dave: Probably because that's his bowl you're eating from.

✳ Two men are talking about animals. One says to the other: 'I know of a dog worth £10,000!' 'Really?' replies the other. 'Who would have thought a dog could save so much.'

✳ If you think you're a person of some influence, try ordering somebody else's dog around.

✳ When is a black dog not a black dog?
  When it's a greyhound!

✳ Why do dogs run in circles?
  Because it's hard to run in squares!

✳ How did the little Scottish dog feel when he saw a monster?
  Terrier-fied!

✳ What do you get if you cross a gun dog with a telephone?
  A golden receiver!

✳ What do you get if you cross a Beatle and an Australian dog?
  Dingo Starr!

✳ Walking past a veterinary clinic, a woman noticed a small boy and his dog waiting outside. 'Are you here to see Dr Meyer?' she asked. 'Yes,' the boy said. 'I'm having my dog put in neutral.'

✳ **Man 1**: I've just got a new dog. Would you like to come and see him?
Man 2: Does he bite?
Man 1: Dunno. That's why I want you to come round, to help me find out.

✳ Did you hear about the dog that was so lazy that when his owner was watering the garden he never lifted a leg to help him.

✳ A man, a monkey, and a dog were washed up on a deserted island after being shipwrecked. The days and months passed, and they became resigned to their fate of being alone together for the rest of their lives. Their existence fell into a routine: they would collect firewood together, get water from the stream and go on trips to gather food. For relaxation they got into the habit of going to the beach every evening to watch the sun go down. The evenings were perfect, the sky red and gold with beautiful clouds as the sun set, the breeze warm and gentle. As they sat there, night after night, the man was painfully aware of his loneliness. Eventually, he leaned over to the monkey and put his arm around its waist. The dog immediately became jealous, growling fiercely until the man took his arm away. After that, the three of them continued to enjoy the sunsets together, but there was no more cuddling. A few weeks passed by, when there was another shipwreck. The only survivor was a beautiful young woman, the most beautiful woman the man had ever seen. She was in a bad state when they rescued her, and slowly they nursed her back to good health. When the young woman was well enough, they introduced her to their evening beach ritual. It was another beautiful evening: red sky, golden sunset, a warm and gentle breeze, perfect for a night of romance. The man tried to fight his surging emotions, but in the end he gave in. He leaned over to the young woman and whispered in her ear, 'Would you mind taking the dog for a walk?'

✳ A local business was looking for office help. They put a sign in the window, stating the following: 'HELP WANTED. Must be able to type, must be good with a computer and must be bilingual. We are an Equal Opportunity Employer.' A short time afterwards, a dog trotted up to the window, saw the sign and went inside. He looked at the receptionist and wagged his tail, then walked over to the sign, looked at it and whined. Getting the idea, the receptionist got the office manager. The office manager looked at the dog and was surprised to say the least. However, the dog looked determined, so he led him into the office. Inside, the dog jumped up on the chair and stared at the manager. The manager said, 'I can't hire you. The sign says you have to be able to type.' The dog jumped down, went to the type-writer and proceeded to type out a perfect letter. He took out the page and trotted over to the manager with it, then jumped back on the chair.

The manager was stunned, but then told the dog, 'The sign says you have to be good with a computer.' The dog jumped down again and went to the computer. The dog proceeded to enter and execute a perfect programme that worked flawlessly the first time. By this time the manager was totally dumbfounded! He looked at the dog and said, 'I realize that you are a very intelligent dog and have some interesting abilities. However, I still can't give you the job.' The dog jumped down and went to a copy of the sign and put his paw on the sentences that told about being an Equal Opportunity Employer. The manager said, 'Yes, but the sign also says that you have to be bilingual.' The dog looked at the manager calmly and said, 'Miaow!'

✳ What do you give a dog with a fever?
Mustard – it's the best thing for a hot dog!

✳ A dog thinks: Hey, these people I live with feed me, love me, provide me with a nice warm, dry house, pet me, and take good care of me... They must be gods!

A cat thinks: Hey, these people I live with feed me, love me, provide me with a nice warm, dry house, pet me, and take good care of me... I must be a god!

dolphins

What is a dolphin's favourite TV show?
Whale of Fortune!

Why was the dolphin trainer depressed?
He had no porpoise.

How do you wash a dolphin?
With an all-porpoise cleaner.

🐺 DRINKING

✳ A man walks into a bar with his Golden Retriever. 'Hey, can I get a drink on the house if my dog talks for you?' The barman laughs, 'Dogs can't talk, pal. But if you can prove to me yours does, I'll give you a drink. If not, you're barred.' 'OK,' says the guy. He turns to his dog. 'OK, fella. Tell me, what is on top of your doghouse?' 'Roof!' The man turns and smiles at the barman. 'THAT ain't talking! Any dog can bark!' 'OK, boy. Tell me, how does sandpaper feel?' 'Ruff!' 'What the hell are you tryin' to pull, mister?' 'OK, OK,' says the man. 'One more question, please. OK, buddy, tell me, who is the greatest ball player who ever lived?' 'Ruth.' The barman beats the hell out of the guy and throws him onto the pavement outside of the bar, then throws the dog out next to him. The dog stands up and looks at his owner. 'Geez. D'ya think I shoulda said DiMaggio?'

✳ A bloke walks into a pub and sees Van Gogh standing at the bar. 'Hi Van, can I get you a drink?' 'No, thanks, I got one ear.'

✳ John Wayne enters a bar. Everybody stops drinking and an uneasy silence fills the room. They are all aware that the fastest hand in the West has entered the room and they all get out of his way. John sits at the bar and orders a whisky. The cowboy next to him tries to play it cool and not attract attention. John looks at him and says: 'Two plus two?' The guy is so scared he can barely talk. He manages to say: 'What?' John fixes his glare on him and repeats: 'Two plus two. Answer me NOW!' The guy is now completely terrified, but realizes he had better answer. He starts thinking really hard and does his best to add the two numbers. He comes up with the answer: 'Five?' A few seconds later he is dead from a shot to the head. John puts his gun back and orders another whisky. The barman, shocked, manages to ask: 'Excuse me, Mr Wayne, but why did you shoot him?' John drinks his whisky, looks at the barman and says: 'The man knew too much.'

❋ A very short painter walks into a Parisian bar and offers to buy his friend a drink. His friend, rushing out of the door, shouts, 'Can't stop now, no time Toulouse.'

❋ David Hasselhoff walks into a bar, and says to the barman, 'I want you to call me David Hoff.' 'Sure,' says the barman. 'No hassle.'

❋ Count Dracula has finished at a swanky restaurant and decides to hit the town, and spends the night drinking Bloody Marys in various clubs and biting on unsuspecting women's necks. Later on he is heading for home, wandering along the street sometime before sunrise. Suddenly he is hit on the back of the head. He looks round and sees nothing. He looks down and sees a small sausage roll. Mmmm, he thinks. What's going on here? A few yards further on and … BANG! Smacked on the back of the head again! He whirls round as quick as he can, but nothing. Again he looks down and there is a small triangular sandwich lying on the ground. How odd! A few yards further along the street and … crash! Smacked on the back of the head again! He whirls round as quick as he can, but nothing. He's getting really angry now. Again he looks down and there is a cocktail sausage lying on the ground. He stands and peers into the darkness of the night. Nothing. He walks a few yards further on when he gets a tap on the shoulder. With a swirl of his cape and a cloud of mist he turns as fast as he can. He feels a sharp pain in his heart. He falls to the ground clutching his chest, which is punctured by a small cocktail stick laden with a chunk of cheese and a pickle. On the ground dying, he looks up and sees a young female. With his dying breath he gasps, 'Who are you'? She replies, 'I'm Buffet, the Vampire Slayer.'

* A man goes into a bar. As he waits to get served, a regular sitting next to him calls out, 'I'll have another waterloo.' The barman gives the regular a tall, ice-cold drink and asks the first man what he would like. The thirsty man points to the man next to him and says, 'I guess I'll have what he's having, a waterloo.' So the barman brings the newcomer a tall, ice-cold drink. The man takes a long deep drink and calls out, 'HEY! This isn't any good. It tastes just like water!' The regular bar sitting next to him says, 'It is water. That's all I drink.' He turns to the bartender and says, 'Right, Lou?'

* A man walks into a bar and orders a drink and some peanuts. While drinking, he hears funny voices, but thinks nothing of it. Again, he hears the funny voices and asks the barman what they are. The barman points to the peanuts and says, 'Don't worry about them. They are complimentary nuts.'

* A duck walks into a pub and heads straight for the bar. He asks the barman, 'Have you got any bread?'
'No sorry, we don't sell bread.'
'Have you got any bread?'
'No, I just told you, we don't have any bread.'
'Aw, right then. What about bread? Do you have any bread?'
'NO! WE'VE GOT NO BREAD.'

'Got any bread?'

'Look, you stupid duck, we don't have any bread! And if you ask me again, I'll nail your beak to the bar!'

'Have you got any nails?'

'No.'

'Got any bread?'

✳ A man walks into a bar near a concert hall with an octopus under his arm and says, 'I'll bet any of you that my octopus can play any instrument that you give him.' Two men bet £50 each that the octopus can't play their instruments. The first man hands over his French horn and the octopus starts to play it. The second man hands over his tuba and sure enough the octopus starts to play it. The bartender then walks into the back room and comes back five minutes later with a set of bagpipes and bets all the money in the drawer that the octopus won't be able to play it. He hands over the bagpipes to the octopus and waits. After about a minute of watching the octopus run its tentacles over the bagpipe, the owner of the octopus says, 'Come on now! Play it!' The octopus replies, 'What do you mean play it?! If I can figure out how to get the plaid pyjamas off it, I'm gonna make love to it!'

✳ A white horse goes into a bar, and orders a pint of bitter. 'Blimey,' the barman says, 'we sell a whisky named after you.' 'What, Eric?' says the horse.

✳ An Irishman walks into a bar and orders a martini. The barman brings his drink, and the Irishman fishes the olive out and puts it in a jar. He orders another, and does exactly the same thing. The Irishman repeats this until he has a pile of olives in his jar on the bar. 'Excuse me,' says the barman, 'but is there something wrong with the drink?' 'Oh no,' says the Irishman. 'The wife sent me out to get a jar of olives.'

✷ An Irishman goes into a bar and orders three pints of Guinness. When they arrive he lines them up, taking a sip from each in turn. The barman watches him for a bit, and, unable to contain his curiosity, asks him what he's doing. 'Well,' he says, 'I have two brothers, one in Australia, one in America, while I stayed here in Dublin. When they left we all agreed that we'd drink this way to remember all the times we drank together.' The barman is touched by this story, and the man becomes a regular in the pub. One day he comes in, and only orders two pints. The barman puts two and two together. 'I'm very sorry about the loss of one of your brothers.' 'Eh?' says the Irishman. 'What are you talking about?' 'Well, you've only ordered two pints,' says the barman. 'Oh,' says the Irishman, 'it's not them, it's me. I've given up drinking.'

✷ Dave eventually persuades Phil to come to a bar he's been going to for years. They're drinking together when someone yells '34', followed by mass laughter. A little while later someone else shouts '21', and again there is a big laugh. 'What's going on?' Phil asks Dave. 'Well,' says Dave, 'we've all been coming here so long that we've all heard the same jokes so many times. So we've numbered them to save time. If you want to tell a joke, just shout out a number.' Phil decides to give it a try. '420,' he shouts. There is a massive roar of laughter. 'What's going on?' says Phil. 'Oh,' says Dave, 'we hadn't heard that one before.'

✳ A drunk goes into a bar. 'Drinks for everyone, and one for you too,' he says to the barman. The barman serves everyone, including himself. 'That'll be fifty pounds, please.' 'I don't have any money,' says the drunk. The barman takes him outside and beats him up. The next day the drunk comes back. 'Drinks for everyone, including the barman.' The barman thinks to himself, he wouldn't be so stupid to do the same thing again – he must have money this time, so he serves the drinks. But when he asks him to pay, the drunk tells him that he doesn't have any money again. The barman takes him outside and gives him a savage beating. The next night, the same drunk comes in and tells the barman to get a round for everyone. 'And not one for me tonight?' asks the barman. 'Nah,' says the drunk. 'You get mean when you drink.'

✳ A man had always ordered his drink by simply saying, 'A Coke, please.' However, the waitress always responded, 'I'm sorry, we don't have Coke. We have Pepsi, Diet Pepsi, Dr Pepper, 7 Up.' Tired of listening to the long list of soft drinks, the man decided to make life easier. So one day he simply asked the barman at his local for a 'dark, carbonated beverage'. The young man behind the counter looked up and said, 'And would you like a cylindrical plastic sucking device with that?'

✳ A man and his wife have a child born who has no arms, legs or torso. Nonetheless, they love their son dearly, and raise him as well as they can. When he turns eighteen, his dad decides to take him to the pub for his first taste of adult life. He proudly orders his son his first pint, and the whole pub looks on as he takes his first sip of alcohol. Unbelievably, as soon as he takes a drink, a torso suddenly pops out under his head. The barman shakes his head in wonder, while the whole pub whoops in joy. The father, shocked, begs his son to drink again. He takes another drink, and the whole pub is overjoyed to see two arms pop out. Only the barman shakes his head in dismay. 'Take another drink,' chant the punters, while the father looks on with tears of wonder running down his face. The boy drinks again, as the barman watches aghast. Two legs sprout, and the now tipsy young man downs the last of the pint. The father falls to his knees in amazement as his son leaps up and runs round the pub. He then bounds out of the door, straight into the path of an oncoming car, and is instantly killed. A terrible silence falls. Then the barman speaks: 'The boy should have quit while he was a head.'

✳ A bear walks into a pub, and takes a huge bite out of the bar. 'Get out!' shouts the barman. 'We don't serve druggies.' 'But I'm not a druggie,' replies the puzzled bear. 'Yeah? Then what about the bar bit you ate?'

✳ A man was sitting in a bar and noticed a group of people using sign language. He also noticed that the bartender was using sign language to speak to them. When the bartender returned to him, the man asked how he had learned to use sign language. The bartender explained that these were regular customers and had taught him to speak in sign. The man thought that was great. A few minutes later, the man noticed that the people in the group were waving their hands around wildly. The bartender looked over and signed, 'Now cut that out! I warned you!' and threw the group out of the bar. The man asked why he had done that and the bartender said, 'If I told them once I told them 100 times – NO SINGING IN THE BAR!'

✳ A drunken sailor fell into a big mud puddle in the street and was looking for something there. Soon two other sailors came over and asked him: 'Hey, what are you looking for?' 'You better give me a hand, men,' said the drunk. The new arrivals walked into the puddle too and set about searching for something unknown. At last the first drunk got out of the puddle and exclaimed: 'I've found it!' 'What did you find?' 'The shore!' he exclaimed.

✳ Two drunks are walking along. One drunk says to the other, 'What a beautiful night... Look at the moon.' The other drunk stops and looks at his drunk friend. 'You are wrong. That's not the moon, that's the sun.' They started arguing for a while when they came upon another drunk walking, so they stopped him. 'Sir, could you please help settle our argument? Tell us what that thing is up in the sky that's shining. Is it the moon or the sun?' The third drunk looked at the sky and then looked at them and said, 'Sorry, I don't live around here.'

✳ I had eighteen bottles of whisky in the cellar, and my wife insisted I empty the contents of each bottle down the sink, or else. After careful consideration, I reluctantly agreed and finally proceeded with the unpleasant task. I withdrew the cork from the first bottle and poured the contents down the sink with the exception of one glass, which I drank. Then I withdrew the cork from the second bottle and did likewise with it, with the exception of one glass, which I drank. I then withdrew the cork from the third bottle and poured the whisky down the sink, which I drank. I pulled the cork from the fourth bottle down the sink and poured the bottle down the glass, which I drank. I pulled the bottle from the cork of the next and drank one sink out of it, and threw the rest down the glass. I pulled the sink out of the next glass and poured the cork down the bottle. Then, I corked the sink with the glass, bottled the drink and drank the pour. When I had everything emptied, I steadied the house with one hand, counted the glasses, corks, bottles and sinks with the other, which were twenty-nine, and as the houses came by I counted them again, and finally I had all the houses in one bottle, which I drank. I'm not under the affluence of incohol as some tinkle peep I am. I'm not half as thunk as you might drink. I fool so feelish I don't know who is me, and the drunker I stand here, the longer I get.

✳ A Texan, a New Yorker and a New Jersey resident were drinking their favourite beverage in a bar. The Texan drained his glass of tequila, threw the half-full bottle up in the air, drew and fired his pistol, shattering the bottle. The other two were shocked at his ruining perfectly good tequila. The Texan, however, simply drew himself up and announced: 'Where I come from, we have plenty of tequila.' The New Yorker, not to be outdone, drained his glass of wine, threw the half-full wine bottle into the air, drew and fired his pistol, also shattering his bottle. Looking over at the other two with an air of superiority characteristic of New Yorkers, he announced: 'Where I come from, we have plenty of fine wine and the best of everything!' The New Jersey resident drained his bottle of Bud, threw it up in the air, drew his pistol and shot the New Yorker dead. He then caught the bottle on the way down and showed it to the Texan. 'Where I come from,' he said slowly, 'we recycle bottles AND we have too many New Yorkers.'

✳ After the Great Britain Beer Festival in London, all the brewery presidents decided to go out for a beer. The guy from Corona sits down and says, 'Hey, señor, I would like the world's best beer, a Corona.' The bartender dusts off a bottle from the shelf and gives it to him. The guy from Budweiser says, 'I'd like the best beer in the world. Give me "The King Of Beers", a Budweiser.' The bartender gives him one. The guy from Coors says, 'I'd like the only beer made with Rocky Mountain spring water. Give me a Coors.' He gets it. The guy from Guinness sits down and says, 'Give me a Coke.' The bartender is a little taken aback, but gives him what he ordered. The other brewery presidents look over at him and ask, 'Why aren't you drinking a Guinness?' The Guinness president replies, 'Well, if you guys aren't drinking beer, neither will I.'

✳ A Texan walks into a pub in Ireland and clears his voice to the crowd of drinkers. He says, 'I hear you Irish are a bunch of hard drinkers. I'll give 500 American dollars to anybody in here who can drink ten pints of Guinness back to back.' The room is quiet and no one takes up the Texan's offer. One man even leaves. Thirty minutes later the same gentleman who left shows back up and taps the Texan on the shoulder. 'Is your bet still good?' asks the Irishman. The Texan says yes and asks the bartender to line up ten pints of Guinness. Immediately the Irishman tears into all ten of the pint glasses, drinking them all back to back. The other pub patrons cheer as the Texan sits in amazement. The Texan gives the Irishman the $500 and says, 'If ya don't mind me askin', where did you go for that 30 minutes you were gone?' The Irishman replies, 'Oh … I had to go to the pub down the street to see if I could do it first.'

✳ A man comes to a bar and yells: 'QUICK!!!! Give me a glass of beer!!! Before IT gets started!!!' A bartender goes: 'What started?! What are you talking about?!' 'No questions. Just give me the beer, faster!!!' He drinks the beer and screams again: 'One more, hurry up!!! Before it gets started!!!' 'What started?!' 'Never mind!!! Give me my beer!!!' He drinks the second glass and continues: 'Third glass!!! Faster!!! Before it gets started!!! Do it!!!' Finally, the bartender asks: 'Hey, pal. Are you gonna pay?!' And the man goes: 'Damn! It's started…'

✳ A feminist walks into a bar that has a sign marked: 'For Men Only.' 'I'm sorry, ma'am,' says the bartender. 'We only serve men in this place.' 'That's OK,' she says. 'I'll take two of them.'

✳ Two men are sitting around drinking. One guy says to the other, 'I bet I could gross you out right now.' The other guy says, 'No way you could gross me out, whatever you do I could top.' So the first guy looks at the second guy and sticks his fingers down his throat and vomits all over the table. The second guy looks at him and says, 'Nice try,' then pulls out a straw…

✳ An angry wife was complaining about her husband spending so much time at the pub. So, one night he took her along. 'What'll you have?' he asked. 'Oh, I don't know. The same as you, I suppose,' she replied. The husband ordered a couple of whiskies and drank his in one gulp. His wife watched him, then took a sip from her glass and immediately spat it out. 'Yuck, that's nasty poison!' she sputtered. 'I don't know how you can drink this stuff!' 'Well, there you go,' cried the husband. 'And all this time you thought I was enjoying myself every night!'

Bar staff

✳ A bartender is just a pharmacist with a limited inventory.

✳ What a barman! When I asked for something tall, cold and full of gin, he called his wife out.

Beer

✳ Beer – the reason I wake up every afternoon.

✳ Beauty is in the eye of the beer holder.

✳ Beer: It's not just for breakfast any more.

✳ I can't spell and beer doesn't help.

✳ I drink beer to celebrate major events, such as the fall of communism, or the fact that our refrigerator is still working.

🐻 DRUNKENNESS

✳ A distressed-looking man had drunk several drinks in rapid succession before the barman asked him, 'Are you trying to drown your sorrows, mate?' 'You could say that,' the man replied. 'It usually doesn't work, you know,' said the barman. 'No,' agreed the man. 'I can't even get her anywhere near the water.'

✳ I'd rather have a bottle in front of me than a frontal lobotomy.

✳ What do you call a group of men found drowned in a wine vat?
The Grape-full Dead!

✳ Two drunks were walking home along the railway tracks. The first drunk says, 'There's a hell of a lot of steps here.' The second drunk says, 'I'll tell you what's worse, this hand rail is low down.'

✳ Alcohol is not the answer, it just makes you forget the question.

✳ Scientists have located the gene for alcoholism. They found it at a party, talking way too loudly.

✳ Patrick left the pub after having too much to drink. He was taking the underground home. As he started to get on the escalator, he read the sign: 'Dogs must be carried on the escalator.' He shouted, 'Now where I am to find a dog after midnight?'

✳ Don't drink and drive. You might hit a bump and spill your drink.

✳ What do you call an alcoholic dog?
A whino!

✳ What's the difference between a drunk and an alcoholic?
Drunks don't have to go to the meetings.

✳ A man, very drunk, staggers home one night. Climbing the stairs to the bedroom he shares with his wife, he loses his balance and falls over the banister. He lands on his bum, which is made even more painful by the whisky bottle he is carrying in his back pocket. In agony, he hobbles to the hall mirror and takes down his trousers to examine the sorry state of his rump. His lacerated and bleeding cheeks obviously need attention, so he finds a packet of plasters and proceeds to patch himself up, sticking a plaster wherever he sees blood. The next morning, his wife confronts him. 'You must have been totally drunk,' she says. 'Never,' says the man. 'Why do you say that?' 'Well,' she answers. 'For a start your trousers stink of whisky. There are bloodstains all over the hall. But what really gives it away are the sticking plasters all over the mirror.'

* A drunk is sitting on a park bench staring disconsolately at a bottle of beer. A man passes and asks him what the matter is. 'I don't know what to do,' says the drunk. 'My heart says yes, my mind says no, and I haven't heard from my liver in two days.'

Alcohol warnings

* The government is considering additional warnings on beer and alcohol bottles, such as:

Warning: Consumption of alcohol may make you think you are whispering when you are not.

Warning: Consumption of alcohol is a major factor in dancing like an idiot.

Warning: Consumption of alcohol may cause you to tell the same boring story over and over again until your friends want to smash your head in.

Warning: Consumption of alcohol may cause you to they sings like thish.

Warning: Consumption of alcohol may lead you to believe that ex-lovers are really dying for you to telephone them at four in the morning.

Warning: Consumption of alcohol may leave you wondering what the hell happened to your pants.

Warning: Consumption of alcohol is the leading cause of inexplicable rug burns on the forehead.

Warning: Consumption of alcohol may create the illusion that you are tougher, handsomer and smarter than some really, really big guy named Killer.

Warning: Consumption of alcohol may lead you to believe you are invisible.

Warning: Consumption of alcohol may lead you to think people are laughing with you.

Warning: Consumption of alcohol may cause an influx in the time-space continuum, whereby small (and sometimes large) gaps of time may seem to disappear.

Warning: Consumption of alcohol may actually cause pregnancy.

✳ She only drinks to forget she drinks.

✳ A drunk man's words are a sober man's thoughts.

✳ Liquor may be a slow poison, but who's in a hurry?

✳ After spending a happy evening drinking together, two acquaintances promise to meet again in ten years at the same bar, same time. Ten years later, the first guy walks in, looks around, and sure enough, there is his friend on a bar stool. He clasps the old friend's hand and cries, 'The day we left, I didn't think I'd really see you here!' The friend looks up, stares, sways slightly and asks, 'Who left?'

✳ Sometimes when I reflect back on all the beer I drink I feel ashamed. Then I look into the glass and think about the workers in the brewery and all of their hopes and dreams. If I didn't drink this beer, they might be out of work and their dreams would be shattered. Then I say to myself, 'It is better that I drink this beer and let their dreams come true than be selfish and worry about my liver.'

✳ Two young Irishmen were getting ready to go on a camping trip. The first one said, 'I'm taking along a bottle of whisky just in case of rattlesnake bites. What are you taking?' The other one said, 'Two rattlesnakes!'

✳ A rather drunk man was walking along the street one day. He was staggering quite a bit and made two nuns that were approaching him very nervous. The two nuns split apart and one walked to the man's left and one walked to the man's right. After the nuns were past the man, he turned around and said, 'Now how in the hell did she do that?'

✳ This small skinny chap walks up to the bar and starts to sit on a bar stool. A big biker on the next stool says, 'That seat's taken!' The little man sits down anyway. The biker grabs him and whacks him several times with the back of his hand and tells the bartender, 'When he wakes up, tell him that was Judo from Japan.' Next day the little man returns. Before the big biker gets a chance to hit him, the little man hits him several times and the biker falls to the floor. The little man tells the bartender, 'Tell that sucker when he wakes up, that was a monkey wrench from B&Q.'

✳ A car sped off the highway, went through the guardrail, rolled down a cliff, bounced off a tree and finally shuddered to a stop. A passing motorist, who had witnessed the entire accident, helped the miraculously unharmed driver out of the wreck. 'Good Lord, mister,' he gasped. 'Are you drunk?' 'Of course,' said the man, brushing the dirt from his suit. 'What the hell do you think I am ... a stunt driver?'

✳ It's people that give drinking a bad name.

✳ A completely inebriated man was stumbling down the street with one foot on the kerb and one foot in the gutter. A policeman pulled up and said, 'I've got to take you in, pal. You're obviously drunk.' The man asked, 'Ociffer, are you absolutely sure I'm drunk?' 'Yeah, I'm sure,' said the copper. 'Let's go.' Breathing a sigh of relief, the wino said, 'Thank goodness, I thought I was lame.'

✳ There is a man sitting in a bar who is really, really drunk. When the bar closes he gets up to go home. He stumbles and falls a couple of times and finally manages to get out of the door. As he gathers himself, he sees a nun passing by. He stumbles over to her and starts punching her in the face. The nun is shocked beyond belief, but before she can say anything, he leans over and punches her again. This time the nun hits the pavement. The drunk stumbles over to her, kicks her in the butt, picks her up and throws her against the wall. By now the nun is very weak and can barely move. He leans over her, grabbing her by the collar of her habit and says, 'Not feeling too STRONG tonight, ARE YOU, BATMAN!'

✳ This guy goes into a bar and sees a man downing shots of bourbon as fast as the bartender can pour them. He watches for a while then finally goes up to the drunk. 'What kind of a way is that to drink good bourbon?' he asks. 'It's the only way I can drink it since my accident,' the man replies, throwing down two more shots in fast order. 'What kind of accident was that?' The man guzzles another shot, shudders and then answers, 'I once knocked over a drink with my elbow.'

✳ A man with a wooden eye was sitting at a bar one night. He glanced across the room and noticed a very attractive woman with just one flaw – she had a very large nose. He was very self-conscious about his eye but got up the nerve to ask her for a dance. 'Would you like to dance with me?' he asked. She replied, 'Would I!' 'No need to be rude, big nose.'

✳ A herd of buffalo can only move as fast as the slowest buffalo, much like the brain can only operate as fast as the slowest brain cells. The slowest buffalo are the sick and weak so they die off first, making it possible for the herd to move at a faster pace. Like the buffalo, the weak, slow brain cells are the ones that are killed off by excessive beer drinking and socializing, making the brain operate faster. The moral of the story: Drink more beer, it will make you smarter.

✳ Bill sat in the local pub, bragging about his athletic prowess. None of the regulars challenged him, but a visitor piped up, 'I'll bet you 50 quid that I can push something in a wheelbarrow for one block and you can't wheel it back.' Bill looked over the skinny stranger and decided it wasn't much of a challenge. 'I'll take you on,' he said. The two men and a number of regulars borrowed a wheelbarrow and took it to the corner. 'Now let's see what you're made of,' taunted Bill. 'OK,' said the challenger. 'Get in.'

✳ Two executives, James and Bill, staggered out of their company's Christmas party in London. Bill crossed the street, while Gary stumbled into a tube entrance. When Bill reached the other side, he noticed Gary emerging from the station stairs. 'Where've you been?' Bill slurred. 'I don't know,' replied Gary, 'but you should see the train set that guy has in his basement!'

✳ Where does an Irish family go on holiday?
A different bar.

✳ Good advice for cocktail parties: If you can't say something nice about someone, just hold your drink and listen to others who can't either.

✳ What would you call a drunk who works at an upholstery shop?
A recovering alcoholic.

✳ Two friends were out drinking when suddenly one lurched backward
off his barstool and lay motionless on the floor. 'One thing about Jim,'
his buddy said to the bartender. 'He knows when to stop.'

✳ There was a man who had at least four to five drinks of whisky every
day of his adult life. When he died, they cremated him, and it took
two days to put out the fire!

✳ I drink so much alcohol I'm afraid to smoke.

✳ I can tell when my wife drinks. Her face gets blurred.

✳ He drank so much beer that when he ate a peanut you could hear
the splash.

✳ A man who goes into the pub optimistically often comes out misty
optically.

✳ You know someone's drinking too much when you offer them wine,
beer and whisky and they say 'yes'.

✳ They say whisky and petrol don't mix. They do, but it doesn't taste
nice.

🐺 DRUGS

✳ Three students are sitting in a room smoking cannabis. After a few spliffs they run out. One of the men stands up and says, 'Look, we've got loads more tobacco, I'll just nip into the kitchen and make one of my speciality joints.' Off he goes into the kitchen where he takes some cumin, turmeric and a couple of other spices from the spice rack, grinds them up and rolls them into a joint. On his return he hands it to one of his smoking partners, who lights it and takes a long drag. Within seconds he passes out. Ten minutes go by and he's still out cold, so they decide to take him to the hospital. On arrival he is wheeled into intensive care. The doctor returns to his friends and asks, 'So what was he doing then? Cannabis?' 'Well, sort of,' replies one of the guys, 'but we ran out of drugs, so I made a home-made spliff.' 'Oh,' replies the doctor, 'so what did you put in it?' 'Um, a bit of cumin, some turmeric and a couple of other spices.' The doctor sighs. 'Well, that explains it.' 'Why, what's wrong with him?' demands one of the students. The doctor replies, 'He's in a korma.'

✳ Police recently arrested a man on drug charges. The suspect allegedly had been selling pills he claimed would give you eternal youth. When going through their files, police discovered it was the fourth time the man had been charged. His earlier arrests were in 1612, 1800 and 1928.

✳ Drugs may lead to nowhere, but at least it's the scenic route.

* Acid: Better living through chemistry.

* 'My parents are from Glasgow which means they're incredibly hard, but I was never smacked as a child ... Well, maybe one or two grams to get me to sleep at night.' *Susan Murray*

* The price of Prozac doubled last year. When Prozac users were asked what they thought about the increase, they said, 'Whatever.'

* Good news: Pete Doherty has entered a twelve-step programme. The bad news is that he lives twelve steps from a crack house.

* Viagra: A whole new concept of recreational drugs.

* Drugs: Accomplish your dreams.

* I used to have a drug problem, but now I have more money.

* Have you heard about the pill which is half aspirin and half glue? It's for splitting headaches.

* Why did the man tiptoe into the chemist's? He didn't want to wake the sleeping pills.

* Did you hear about the man who complained to the pharmacist that he had given his wife arsenic instead of sleeping pills? The pharmacist charged him another £10.

* Reality is a crutch for people who can't handle drugs.

🦆 DUCKS

✳ What do you get if you put a duck in an area of geological activity?
An earthquack.

✳ What is a duck's favourite dance?
The quackstep!

✳ Why don't ducks tell jokes when they're flying?
Because they would quack up.

✳ How do you turn a duck into a soul singer?
Put it in a microwave until its Bill Withers.

✳ Would you like a duck egg for tea?
Only if you quack it for me!

✳ What kind of doctor treats ducks?
A quack!

✳ What happens to ducks before they grow up?
They grow down.

✳ Why do ducks have webbed feet?
To put out fires.

✳ Why do elephants have flat feet?
To put out burning ducks.

✳ Three old friends passed away together in an accident and went to heaven. When they arrived, St Peter said, 'We have only one rule here in heaven... Don't step on the ducks.' So they entered heaven and, sure enough, there were ducks all over the place. It was almost impossible not to step on a duck, and although they tried their best to avoid them, one of the friends accidentally stepped on one. Along came St Peter with the ugliest woman the man had ever seen. St Peter chained them together and said, 'Your punishment for stepping on a duck is to spend eternity chained to this ugly woman!' The next day, the second friend accidentally stepped on a duck and along came St Peter, who doesn't miss a thing, and with him was another extremely ugly woman. He chained them together with the same admonishment as for the first friend. The third friend observed all this and not wanting to be chained for all eternity to an ugly woman, was very, VERY careful where he stepped. He managed to go months without stepping on any ducks but one day St Peter came up to him with the most gorgeous woman he had ever laid eyes on... a very tall, tanned, curvaceous, sexy blonde. St Peter chained them together without saying a word. The man asked, 'I wonder what I did to deserve being chained to you for all eternity?' The woman replied, 'I don't know about you, but I stepped on a duck.'

🐶 DYSLEXIA

✳ Why did the dyslexic cow join a yoga class? Because all he could say was 'Ommm'.

✳ There's a new organization called DAM: Mothers Against Dyslexia.

✳ Did you hear about the dyslexic lawyer? He studied all year for the bra exam.

✳ If you're cross-eyed and have dyslexia, can you read perfectly?

✳ Did you hear about the paranoid dyslexic? He always thought he was following someone.

✳ 'I realized I was dyslexic when I went to a toga party dressed as a goat.' *Marcus Brigstocke*

🐸 EARTH

✺ Earth first! (We'll strip-mine the other planets later.)

✺ Earth is a great big funhouse without the fun.

✺ There is no gravity. The earth sucks.

✺ It's a small world, but I wouldn't want to paint it.

✺ The Earth Is Full – Go Home.

earthquakes

What did the ground say to the earthquake?
You crack me up!

What did one earthquake say to another?
It's not my fault.

EATING OUT

* A prosperous-looking gentleman ate a fine meal at an expensive restaurant and topped it off with some very expensive brandy. He summoned the head waiter. 'Do you recall,' he asked pleasantly, 'how a year ago, I ate just such a repast here and then, because I couldn't pay for it, you had me thrown into the gutter like a common bum?' 'I'm very sorry, sir,' began the contrite head waiter. 'Oh, it's quite all right,' said the guest, 'but I'm afraid I'll have to trouble you again...'

* A customer was continually bothering the waiter in a restaurant. First, he asked that the air conditioning be turned up because he was too hot, then he asked for it to be turned down because he was too cold, and so on for about half an hour. Surprisingly, the waiter was very patient, walking back and forth and never once getting angry. Finally, a second customer asked why they didn't just throw out the pest. 'Oh, I don't mind,' said the waiter with a calm smile. 'We don't even have air conditioning.'

* The customer in the Italian restaurant was so pleased with his meal he asked to speak to the chef. The owner proudly led him into the kitchen and introduced him to the chef.

    'Your pasta quattro formaggi was superb!' the customer said. 'I just spent a month in Italy, and yours is better than any I had over there.' 'Naturally,' the chef said. 'Over there, they use domestic cheese. Ours is imported!'

✳ A guy goes into a restaurant, sits down at a table and says to the waiter, 'Bring me some turtle soup, and make it snappy.'

✳ A lady walks into an ice-cream shop and asks for a chocolate cone. The man says, 'I'm sorry, but we don't have chocolate. But I'll give you a second scoop of a different flavour for free.' So the lady thinks for a moment and says, 'I'll have chocolate.' The man behind the counter is fed up and says, 'Spell VAN in Vanilla.'
'V-A-N.'
'Spell STRAW in Strawberry.'
'S-T-R-A-W?'
'Spell STINK in chocolate.'
'There is no stink in chocolate.'
'That's what I've been trying to tell you!'

✳ The tourist wandered into a gourmet food shop in Mayfair. He picked out two apples and a pear. 'That will be £8.00,' the owner said. The tourist gave him a ten-pound note and walked away. 'Wait! Don't you want your change?' 'Forget it. I stepped on a grape on my way in.'

✳ This greasy spoon restaurant was so bad, on the menu there were even flies in the pictures.

✳ What's a bacteria?
The rear entrance to a cafeteria.

✳ Have you ever seen a man-eating tiger?
No, but in the café next door I once saw a man eating chicken!

✴ A wealthy businessman choked on a fish bone at a restaurant. Fortunately a doctor was seated at a nearby table. Springing up, the doctor skilfully removed the bone and saved his life. As soon as the fellow had calmed himself and could talk again, he thanked the surgeon enthusiastically and offered to pay him for his services. 'Just name the fee,' he croaked gratefully. 'OK,' replied the doctor. 'How about half of what you'd have offered when the bone was still stuck in your throat?'

✴ Never go into the water after a heavy meal. You won't find it there.

✴ A couple decide to go for a meal on their anniversary and after some deliberation decide on their local Chinese restaurant. They peruse the menu and finally agree to share the chef's special chicken surprise. The waiter brings over the meal, served in a lidded cast-iron pot. Just as the wife is about to start on the meal, the lid of the pot rises a tiny amount and she briefly sees two beady little eyes looking around before the lid slams back down. 'Did you see that?' she asks her husband. He hasn't so she asks him to look in the pot. He reaches for it and again the lid rises, and he sees two beady little eyes looking around before it firmly slams back down. Rather perturbed, he calls the waiter over, explains what is happening and demands an explanation. 'Well, sir,' says the waiter. 'What did you order?' 'We both chose the same,' he replies. 'The chicken surprise.' 'Oh, I do apologize, this is my fault,' says the waiter. 'I've brought you the Peking duck.'

✴ A young man walks into a seedy café in Mexico. He sits at the counter and notices an old cowboy with his arms folded staring blankly at a full bowl of chilli. After fifteen minutes of just sitting there staring at it, the young cowboy bravely asks the old man, 'If you ain't gonna eat that, mind if I do?' The older cowboy slowly turns his head towards him and says, 'Nah, go ahead.' Eagerly, the young man reaches over and slides the bowl to his place and starts spooning it in with delight. He gets nearly down to the bottom and notices a dead mouse in the chilli. The sight is shocking and he immediately pukes up the chilli into the bowl. The old cowboy quietly says, 'That's as far as I got too.'

★ What did one plate say to the other plate?
Dinner's on me.

★ I'm so busy that if you see me eating at a table I'm on holiday!

★ I don't know what to do. I went out to dinner at a Chinese restaurant last night, and my fortune cookie contradicted my horoscope.

★ A man had invited the vicar and his wife for dinner, and it was little Billy's job to set the table. But when it was time to eat, Billy's mother said with surprise, 'Why didn't you give Mrs Brown a knife and fork, dear?' 'I didn't think I needed to,' Billy explained. 'I heard Daddy say she always eats like a horse.'

EDUCATION

★ If you haven't much education you must use your brain.

★ What is a forum?
Two-um plus two-um!

* Murphy's Law: If you are given an open-book exam, you will forget your book. If you are given a take-home test, you will forget where you live.

* Written on a toilet roll in a public lavatory: 'Sociology Degrees, please take one.'

* Why did the boy study in the aeroplane?
  He wanted a higher education!

* **Father**: Son, what are your results in the end of term examination?
  Son: Underwater.
  Father: What do you mean, underwater?
  Son: Below 'C' level.

School

* Why did the jellybean go to school?
  Because he wanted to be a smarty.

* What's a mushroom?
  The place they store the school food!

* A kid gets home from his first day at school. 'Mum, everyone is saying I'm too hairy!' The mother, frightened, yells to her husband: 'Quickly! The dog is talking!'

* What's big and yellow and comes in the morning to brighten a mother's day?
  The school bus!

✳ A blonde comes home from school one day and says to her mum, 'Mummy, we learnt the alphabet today. The other kids can only go to C but I can go to K.' The mother says, 'Well done, dear.' Girl says, 'Mummy, is that because I'm blonde?' and the mother replies, 'Yes, dear.' The next day the blonde arrives home from school and says to her mum, 'Mummy, we learnt numbers today. The other kids can only go to three but I can go to ten.' The mother says, 'Well done, dear.' The girl asks, 'Mummy, is that because I'm blonde?' Her mother replies, 'Yes, dear.' The next day the blonde arrives home from school and says, 'Mummy, today we went swimming and I noticed I am the only one in my class with breasts. Is that because I'm blonde?' The mother replies, 'No, dear, it's because you are 25 years old.'

✳ All work and no play is the average school day.

✳ What did the inflatable teacher say to the inflatable boy who took a pin into the inflatable school?
You've let me down, you've let the school down but, above all, you've let yourself down.

✳ **Pupil:** I don't think I deserve zero for this work.
Teacher: Me neither, but it was the lowest I could give.

✳ Our son brought home a note from school. They wanted to have a written excuse for his presence.

✳ I failed geometry because I refused to believe that pie are squared.

✳ Today in English we learned absolutely nothing about killing mocking-birds.

✳ I think I'll skip English tomorrow. There are just certain aspects of Moby I don't want to know about.

✳ Our school is very poor; our physics book is so out of date the last chapter deals with combustion.

✳ The school governors decided to remove speech and debate from the curriculum; there was no argument.

✳ $7/5$ of all school children do not understand fractions.

✳ What's a snake's favourite school subject?
Hiss-story.

✳ In what school do you learn how to greet people?
In hi school!

✳ The class assignment in composition was to write about something unusual that happened during the past week. Little Irving got up to read his. 'Papa fell in the well last week,' he began. 'Good heavens,' shrieked Mrs Kroop, the teacher. 'Is he all right now?' 'He must be,' said little Irving. 'He stopped yelling for help yesterday.'

✳ Where does ice cream go to learn?
Sundae school.

✳ Fred was saying his prayers as his father passed by his bedroom door. 'God bless Mummy, and God bless Daddy, and please make

Calais the capital of France.' 'Fred,' said his father, 'why do you want Calais to be the capital of France?' 'Because that's what I wrote in my geography test!'

✳ Why was the maths book sad?
It had so many problems.

✳ What does an elf do after school?
Gnome work.

✳ As long as there are exams, schools will still have prayers.

✳ Why did the boy eat his homework?
Because his teacher said it was a piece of cake!

✳ What mostly don't you hear in school?
The H.

✳ Did you hear about the boy in love with two schoolbags?
He's bisatchel.

University

✳ Lecturer: Someone who talks in other people's sleep.

✳ I studied to be a bone specialist. My tutors said I had the head for it.

✳ I didn't go to university. I slept at home.

✳ What key went to college?
Yale!

✳ 'But officer, I am a university graduate.'
'Ignorance is no excuse.'

✳ New medical students were made to take a difficult class in physics. One day the lecturer was discussing a particularly complicated concept. A student rudely interrupted to ask, 'Why do we have to learn this stuff?' 'To save lives,' the lecturer responded quickly and continued. A few minutes later, the same student spoke up again. 'So how does physics save lives?' he persisted. 'It keeps idiots like you from graduating,' replied the lecturer.

✳ A professor is lecturing his class one day. 'In English,' he announces, 'a double negative forms a positive. In some languages, however, like Russian, a double negative is still a negative. However, there is no language where a double positive can form a negative.' A voice from the back piped up: 'Yeah, right.'

✳ What's the difference between an American student and an English student?
About 3,000 miles!

✳ A pompous and smug businessman is addressing a class of students. For hours he drones on about his successes and achievements. 'I'm a self-made man,' he proudly concludes. A voice goes up from the back of the hall: 'We accept your apology.'

✳ The graduate with a science degree asks: 'Why does it work?'
The graduate with an engineering degree asks: 'How does it do that?'
The graduate with an accounting degree asks: 'How much does it cost?'
The graduate with the arts degree asks: 'Do you want fries with that?'

✳ What's black and white all over and difficult?
An exam paper.

🐺 EGYPT

✳ *Although they had no first aid class,*
Egyptians were not dummies.
They knew the art of bandaging,
They learned it from their mummies.

✳ One day, the captain of the 40-oared royal barge goes down to speak to the slaves in the hold of his ship. 'Men, I have some good news and some bad news. The good news is, the Pharaoh will be joining us today for a trip up the Nile.' The men cheered and rattled their chains. 'The bad news is, he wants to go water skiing.'

✳ Why was the Egyptian girl worried?
Because her daddy was a mummy!

✳ Did they play tennis in ancient Egypt?
Yes, the Bible tells how Joseph served in Pharoah's court!

＊ Why do Egyptians who eat beans have the same pharaoh?
They all have toot-in-common.

electricity

All power corrupts, but we do need the electricity.

Did you hear about the Irishman who wanted some current literature? He bought a book on electricity.

🐘 ELEPHANTS

＊ Why did the elephant eat the candle?
He wanted a light snack!

＊ What do you get when you cross an elephant and a skin doctor?
A pachydermatologist.

＊ What's the difference between an elephant and a flea?
An elephant can have fleas but a flea can't have elephants.

＊ Why did the elephant put his trunk across the path?
To trip up the ants!

✳ How do you get down from an elephant?
You don't. You get down from a duck.

✳ What ant is even bigger than an elephant?
A giant!

✳ What's the best way to see a charging herd of elephants?
On TV!

✳ Why don't elephants like playing cards in the jungle?
Because of all the cheetahs!

✳ What do you call an elephant that never washes?
A smellyphant!

✳ What's a jumbo jet?
A flying elephant.

✳ When two elephants went to the seaside, why could only one of them go swimming?
They only had one pair of trunks.

✳ Why have elephants got big ears?
Because Noddy won't pay the ransom.

✳ How does an elephant climb an oak tree?
It sits on an acorn and waits till it grows.

✳ How does an elephant get down from a tree?
It sits on a leaf and waits for autumn.

＊ Burying a dead elephant is a huge undertaking.

＊ Where do you buy an old elephant?
A mammoth sale.

＊ What do you give a manic elephant?
Trunkquillizers.

＊ What do you call an elephant with a TV in its stomach?
An eletubby.

＊ Why did the elephant leave the zoo?
It was fed up with working for peanuts.

＊ She has a memory like an elephant, and a body to match.

＊ Elephants are found in Africa, although they're so big they rarely get lost.

＊ Why aren't elephants allowed on the beach?
They always have their trunks down!

＊ What's big and grey and wears a mask?
The Elephantom of the Opera!

＊ What's big and grey with horns?
An elephant brass band!

＊ What's yellow on the outside and grey on the inside?
An elephant disguised as a banana!

＊ Why do elephants do well in school?
Because they have a lot of grey matter!

＊ What do you call an elephant that's small and pink?
A failure!

＊ What do you call an elephant creeping through the jungle in the middle of the night?
Russell!

＊ What animals were last to leave the ark?
The elephants as they had to pack their trunks!

＊ Why do elephants paint the souls of their feet yellow?
So they can hide upside-down in bowls of custard.
Have you ever found an elephant in your custard?
Must work then.

＊ How do you get four elephants in a red Mini?
Two in the front and two in the back.

＊ How can you tell if an elephant has been in your fridge?
There's one set of footprints in the butter.

＊ How can you tell if two elephants have been in your fridge?
There's two set of footprints in the butter.

＊ How can you tell if four elephants have been in your fridge?
There's a red Mini parked outside.

✴ What do you call an elephant that can't do sums?
Dumbo!

✴ What's grey, carries grapes and flowers, and cheers you up when you're ill?
A get wellephant!

✴ What weighs four tons and is bright red?
An elephant holding its breath!

✴ What's grey and highly dangerous?
An elephant with a machine gun!

✴ What's grey, has a wand, huge wings and gives money to elephants?
The tusk fairy!

✴ What has three tails, four trunks and six feet?
An elephant with spare parts!

✴ What's grey, beautiful and wears glass slippers?
Cinderelephant!

🐵 ENGINEERS

✴ Five surgeons were taking a coffee break. The first surgeon said, 'Accountants are the best to operate on because when you open them up, everything inside is numbered.' The second surgeon said, 'Nah, librarians are the best. Everything inside them is in alphabetical order.' The third surgeon responded, 'Try electricians, man! Everything inside them is colour coded.' Then the fourth doctor interceded: 'I prefer lawyers. They're heartless, spineless, gutless and their heads and their butts are interchangeable.' To which the fifth surgeon, who had been quietly listening to the conversation, added, 'I like engineers. They always understand when you have a few parts left over at the end.'

✳ Three engineers were standing at the urinals. The first engineer finished and walked over to the sink to wash his hands. He then proceeded to dry his hands very carefully. He used paper towel after paper towel and ensured that every single spot of water on his hands was dried. Turning to the other two engineers, he said, 'At Hewlett Packard, we are trained to be extremely thorough.' The second engineer finished his task at the urinal and proceeded to wash his hands. He used a single paper towel and made sure that he dried his hands using every available portion of the paper towel. He turned and said, 'At Lockheed-Martin, not only are we trained to be extremely thorough, but we are also trained to be extremely efficient.' The third engineer finished and walked straight for the door, shouting over his shoulder, 'At Apple Computer, Inc., we don't pee on our hands.'

escalators, stairs and lifts

What goes up and down but never moves?
Stairs.

What did one elevator say to the other elevator?
I think I'm coming down with something!

ETHNIC

* How does every ethnic joke start?
  With a look over your shoulder.

American

* What do people do with broken-down cars in West Virginia?
  Build a house next to them.

* Why are there only 49 contestants in the Miss Black America this year?
  They couldn't find a girl willing to wear a sign that said 'I-da-ho'.

* America is like a melting pot. The people at the bottom get burned, and the scum floats to the top.

* Why did Eve want to move to New York?
  She fell for the Big Apple!

* In America, anybody can be president. That's one of the risks you take.

* Once we had Clinton, Johnny Cash and Bob Hope. Now we have Bush, no Cash and no Hope.

* George Bush has been working hard, 24/7, 24 hours a week, 7 months a year.

✳ A Frenchman was explaining the red, white and blue French flag to an American.

'Our flag is symbolic of our taxes. We get red when we talk about them, white when we get our tax bills, and blue after we pay them.' The American nodded. 'It's the same in the USA only we see stars too!'

✳ Detroit: Where the weak are killed and eaten.

✳ Three prisoners are captured in the war. They are asked what they wish to have for their last meal. The Italian asks for and receives a pepperoni pizza. The Frenchmen requests and receives a filet mignon. The American requests a plate of strawberries. The captors are surprised and reply, 'Strawberries?' 'Yes, strawberries.' 'But they are out of season!' 'That's OK. I'll wait…'

Australian

✳ What is the Australian for foreplay?
Brace yourself, Sheila!

✳ A Texan farmer goes to Australia for a vacation. There he meets an Aussie farmer and gets talking. The Aussie shows off his big wheat field and the Texan says, 'Oh! We have wheat fields that are at least twice as large.' Then they walk around the ranch a little, and the Aussie shows off his herd of cattle. The Texan immediately says, 'We have longhorns that are at least twice as large as your cows.' The conversation has almost died when the Texan sees a herd of kangaroos hopping through the field. He asks, 'And what are those?' The Aussie replies with an incredulous look, 'Don't you have any grasshoppers in Texas?'

Chinese

✳ 'Apparently, one in five people in the world are Chinese. And there are five people in my family, so it must be one of them. It's either my mum or my dad. Or my older brother Colin. Or my younger brother Ho-Cha-Chu. But I think it's Colin.' *Tim Vine*

✳ I thought about how mothers feed their babies with tiny little spoons and forks so I wondered what do Chinese mothers use? Toothpicks?

Chinese phrasebook

Ai Bang Mai Ne	I bumped into the coffee table
Ar U Wun Tu	A gay liberation greeting
Chin Tu Fat	You need a face lift
Dum Gai	A stupid person
Gun Pao Der	An ancient Chinese invention
Hu Flung Dung	Which one of you fertilized the field?
Hu Yu Hai Ding	We have reason to believe you are harbouring a fugitive

Kum Hia	Approach me
Lao Ze Sho	*Emmerdale*
Lao Zi	Not very good
Lin Ching	An illegal execution
Moon Lan Ding	A great achievement of the American space programme
Ne Ahn	A lighting fixture used in advertising signs
Shai Gai	A bashful person
Tai Ne Bae Be	A premature infant
Tai Ne Po Ne	A small horse
Ten Ding Ba	Serving drinks to people
Wan Bum Lung	A person with TB
Wa Shing Kah	Cleaning an automobile
Wai So Dim	Are you trying to save electricity?
Wai U Shao Ting	There is no reason to raise your voice

Eskimo

★ Did you hear about the man who took six months to learn to sing 'Night And Day'?
He was an Eskimo.

★ There was this Eskimo girl who spent the night with her boyfriend and next morning found out that she was six months pregnant.

* What do you call an Eskimo cow?
  An Eskimoo!

* What does an Eskimo keep his house together with?
  Iglue!

* Why do Eskimos eat whale meat and blubber?
  You'd blubber too if you had to eat whale meat.

* How often do Eskimos lose their snow trousers?
  Once in a blue moon.

French

* The French have launched their own version of Google called Quaero. You just type in the subject you're interested in, and Quaero refuses to look it up for you.

* Having finally committed to sending troops to Iraq, the French have ordered a new national flag. It's a white cross on a white background.

* Did you hear about the new French tank? It has fourteen gears. Thirteen go in reverse, and one goes forward in case the enemy attacks from behind.

* How many Frenchmen does it take to defend France?
  Don't know, never been tried.

✳ The trouble with the French is that they have no word for entrepreneur.

✳ What is the guillotine?
A French chopping centre.

German

✳ What do Germans use for birth control?
Their personalities!

✳ What do you get if you cross an Irishman with a German?
A man who's too drunk to follow orders!

✳ What did the German clockmaker say to the clock that only went 'tick, tick, tick'?
'Ve haff vays of making you tock!'

✳ A sailor got into trouble off the German shore. In desperation he radioed in to the coastguard: 'Mayday, Mayday, we are sinking, we are sinking!!!' With great relief he heard the radio crackle into life: 'Und vhat are you sinking about?'

✳ How do you say 'brassiere' in German?
'Keipsemfrumfloppin.'

✳ Why are there so many tree-lined streets and leafy lanes in France?
Germans like to march in the shade.

Iraqi

✳ Did you hear that Saddam Hussein won the coin toss?
He elected to receive.

✳ What is Iraq's national bird?
Duck.

✳ How is Saddam like Fred Flintstone?
Both look out their windows and see rubble.

✳ Why does the Iraqi navy have glass-bottom boats?
So they can see their air force.

✳ What is the best Iraqi job?
Foreign ambassador.

Irish

✳ Two IRA men were driving with a bomb in their car. 'Don't drive so fast! You may set off the bomb!' cautioned one. To which the other Paddy replied, 'Don't worry, we have a spare bomb in the boot.'

✳ What do you call an Irishman who steals your pint?
Nick McGuinness.

✳ Why did the Irishman swallow razor blades?
To sharpen his appetite.

✳ Two Irishmen went hunting. They saw a sign that said 'Bear left', so they went home.

✳ Why don't they have ice cubes in Ireland?
The lady with the recipe died.

✳ What do you call an Irishman hanging from the ceiling?
Sean DaLeer.

✳ What do you call an Irishman bouncing off walls?
Rick O'Shay.

✳ Why did the Irishman run outside with his wallet open?
He'd heard there was going to be a change in the weather.

✳ Shaun was visited at his deathbed by his two good Irish friends, Pat and John. Shaun asked his friends to grant his final wish. 'Anything, Shaun, you just name it,' said Pat. Shaun asked that when he was gone his friends would pour a bottle of the best Irish whisky over his grave. 'Of course,' replied Pat, 'but would you give us one last favour?' 'What might that be?' asked Shaun. 'Would you mind if we kind of filtered that whisky through our kidneys first?'

✳ The scene: An Irish pub in Boston on Saint Paddy's day. The only customer is drinking a pint of Guinness at the bar. A second patron walks in, orders a drink, and sidles up to the next stool. The late arrival turns to the other and makes small talk. 'Where ye from?' he asks in a thick Irish accent. 'Ah'm from Ireland!' the first man replies. 'Ah, me too! Let's drink to Ireland!' 'To Ireland!' The two men down their pints and order another round. 'Whut part of Oireland are ye from?' 'Ah'm from Dublin!' 'Ah, me too!' 'A drink to Dublin!' The two men down another pint and order more drinks. 'What school did ye attend?' 'St Margaret's.' 'Ah, me too.' 'A drink to St Margaret's, our old school!' More drinks are dispatched. 'What year did ye graduate?' 'Eh, 1965.' 'Me too. This is a coincidence. A drink to the great class o' 1965!' The two men continue their animated conversation, slapping each other on the back and downing more pints. A local walks in during this scene and hears the carousing. He calls to the barman. 'What the hell are those two on about?' The barman replies, 'Ah, the O'Malley twins are drunk again.'

✳ Two Irishmen walked out of a bar. Well, it COULD happen.

✳ A German man, a Japanese man and an Irishman are naked in a sauna. Suddenly there is a beeping sound, which stops when the German presses his forearm. The others look at him. 'That's my pager,' he explains. 'I have a microchip implanted under the skin.'

A few minutes later a phone rings. The Japanese man lifts his palm to his ear and listens. When he has finished he says to his companions, 'That was my phone, which is implanted under my skin.' The Irishman is feeling very low-tech, but determined not to be outdone. He leaves the sauna and goes into the toilets. He returns a few minutes later with a long piece of toilet paper hanging from his backside. 'Whaddaya know!' he exclaims. 'Someone's sending me a fax.'

✳ Did you hear about the Irish cryptologist who cracked the highway code?

✳ Two Irishmen are sitting in a pub having a beer and watching the brothel across the street. They spy a Baptist minister walk into the brothel, and one of them says, 'Aye, 'tis a shame to see a man of the cloth goin' bad.' Then they see a rabbi enter the brothel, and the other Irishman says, 'Aye, 'tis a shame to see that the Jews are fallin' victim to temptation as well.' Then they see a Catholic priest enter the brothel, and one of the Irishmen says, 'What a terrible pity ... one of the girls must be dying.'

✳ Did you hear about the Irishman who bought an electric car? He was unhappy with its performance, so he rang up the garage to complain. 'My car will only go ten metres,' he said to the salesman. The sales-man ran through some checks with him. 'Is the battery charged up? Are the brakes off? Is it in gear?' The Irishman confirmed that every-thing seemed to be working fine. The salesman was baffled. 'Why do you think it only goes ten metres?' he asked the Irishman. 'Because that's as far as the lead will stretch to the plug,' he replied.

✳ Did you hear about the Irishman who got a puncture?
He didn't see the fork in the road.

✳ Mick and Paddy are out in the country shooting rabbits. Suddenly, right in front of his friend Paddy, Mick falls to the ground, throws a quick spasm, then lies perfectly still. He doesn't seem to be breath-ing, his eyes are rolled back in his head. In fact, he looks pretty well dead. Quick as a flash, a horrified Paddy whips out his mobile and calls 999. He gasps breathlessly to the operator. 'Mick just fell to the ground right here in front o' me! He's not breathing. He has no heartbeat! I think he's dead! What can I do?' Well accustomed to this sort of situation, the emergency operator responds with her most soothing tone. 'OK, Paddy, you must try to stay calm. If there's anything can be done, we'll do it. But you will have to keep your cool, then we can take it one step at a time. OK now?' 'Sure! Sure! Of course, you're right. I'm fine. Just tell me what I must do,' Paddy replies. 'Great! Now first of all, let's make sure he's dead,' says the operator. The line goes silent, then a shot is heard by the operator. BANG! Paddy's voice comes back on the phone. 'OK! What next?'

✳ Pat gets a call from his Irish friend, Mick. 'I've got a problem,' says Mick. 'What's the matter?' asks Pat. 'Well, I've bought this jigsaw puzzle, but it's just too hard. None of the pieces fit together and I can't find any edges.' 'What's the picture of?' asks Pat.

　'It's a picture of a big rooster,' replies Mick. 'All right,' says Pat, 'I'll come over and have a look.' He goes over to Mick's house. He leads Pat into his kitchen and shows him the jigsaw puzzle on the kitchen table. Pat looks at the jigsaw, frowns, then turns to Mick and says, 'For Pete's sake, Mick, put the cornflakes back in the box!'

✳ Did you hear about the Irishman who was thrown out of the submarine corps?
He slept with the windows open.

✳ Did you hear about the Irishman who stayed up all night studying for a blood test?

✳ After digging to a depth of 100m last year, Russian scientists found traces of copper wiring dating back 1,000 years, and came to the conclusion that their ancestors already had a telephone network 1,000 years ago. So as not to be outdone, in the weeks that followed, American scientists dug 200m, and headlines in the US newspapers read: 'US scientists have found traces of 2,000-year-old optical fibers, and have concluded that their ancestors already had advanced high-tech digital telephone 1,000 years earlier than the Russians.' One week later, the Irish press reported the following: 'After digging as deep as 500m, Irish scientists have found absolutely nothing. They have concluded that 5,000 years ago, their ancestors were already using mobile phones.'

✳ A woman is dancing happily down the railroad tracks, singing to herself: '21... 21... 21...' After a little while, an Irish woman walks up to her. She observes for a minute and then asks, 'What are you doing?' The woman does not answer and keeps singing. '21... 21 ... 21...' So the Irish woman jumps on the tracks and follows her dancing and starts singing. '21... 21... 21 ..' A little later a train comes down the tracks. The woman jumps off, but the Irish woman keeps dancing and singing to herself and gets hit by the train.

   The woman gets back on the track and starts dancing and singing again. '22... 22... 22...'

✳ An angry Irish female runs into a local police station. 'Somebody has stolen my car!' she proclaims loudly. The officer at the desk replies, 'Settle down, madam. Everything is going to be OK. Now, did you get a description of the suspect?' 'No,' the young woman replies. 'But I did get the licence plate number.'

✳ An Irishman reported for his university final examination which consisted of 'yes/no' type questions. He took his seat in the examination hall and stared at the question paper for five minutes. In a fit of inspiration, he took his wallet out, removed a coin and started tossing the coin and marking the answer sheet: Yes for Heads and No for Tails. Within half an hour he was all done, whereas the rest of the class was still sweating it out. During the last few minutes, he was seen desperately throwing the coin, muttering and sweating. The moderator, alarmed, approached and asked what was going on. His reply was, 'I finished the exam in half an hour, but I'm rechecking my answers.'

✳ Did you hear about the Irishman who joined the navy to see the world and spent four years in a submarine?

✳ Did you hear about the Irishman who put cotton wool in his ears when he bathed so he wouldn't hear the ring around the tub?

✳ There were eleven people hanging onto a rope that came down from a plane. Ten were Irish, and one was a university professor. They all decided that one person should get off because if they didn't then the rope would break and everyone would die. No one could decide who should go, so finally the professor said, 'I'll get off.' After a really touching speech from the professor saying she would get off, all of the Irish people started clapping.

✳ How would you know the Irishman on an oil rig?
He would be the one throwing bread to the helicopters.

✳ What did the Irishman do when he tried to do Riverdance?
He drowned.

✳ What happened to the Irishman who was ironing the curtains?
He fell out the window.

✳ Did you hear about the Irish farmer who packed up and went to live in the city when he heard the country was at war?

✳ Did you hear about the Irishman who took his mothballs back to the shop?
He said he hadn't managed to hit a single one.

Japanese

✳ What colour is the sky over Japan?
Brew.

✳ What is a crick?
The noise a Japanese camera makes.

Jewish

✳ A plane takes off, with a Jewish pilot and Chinese co-pilot. There is a frosty atmosphere in the cockpit until eventually the Jewish pilot speaks. 'I don't like the Chinese,' he says. 'Why is that?' asks the co-pilot. 'You bombed Pearl Harbor,' says the captain. 'That's why I don't like the Chinese.' 'No, you've got it wrong. It was the Japanese who bombed Pearl Harbor,' explains the co-pilot. The captain replies: 'Japanese, Chinese, Vietnamese... It doesn't matter, they're all alike.'

Silence falls in the cockpit. Finally the co-pilot says, 'I don't like Jews.' 'Why not?' asks the captain. 'Because they sunk the *Titanic*,' replies the Chinese co-pilot. 'No, no, no,' the captain corrects him. 'Jews did not sink the *Titanic*. It was an iceberg.' 'Iceberg, Goldberg, Rosenberg… It doesn't matter to me,' replies the co-pilot.

✳ An older Jewish couple was starting on a vacation, but it soon became obvious that their habit of arguing over everything was not taking a break. 'It's "Hawaii", I'm telling you!' she shouted. 'Oy! I never KNEW someone so stubborn! It's pronounced "Havaii"!' he replied. And so it went all the way to the airport and for the long flight. As they got off the airplane, the husband abruptly stopped his wife and turned to a man standing at the airport gate. 'Now that we're on the island, you can settle an argument between my wife and I. Is this Hawaii or Havaii?' The man smiled and said, 'This is Havaii.' 'Ha!' the husband said, turning to his wife. 'See, didn't I tell you never to argue with me? I'm always right!' As they began to walk away, he turned and gave the man a hearty 'Thank you!' The man responded: 'You're velcome!'

✳ A rabbi and his young son are walking on the seashore one summer day. Without warning, a huge wave comes along and washes the son into the sea. The rabbi, in tears, kneels down and prays: 'Oh Lord, why have you taken my only son from me? I keep kosher, I read the Torah every day, I give charitably and I have brought up my only son on my own since his mother died.' At that a huge wave washes the son back onto the shore. The rabbi looks up at the sky and says: 'Oh COME ON! He had a hat!'

✳ The children of Israel wandered around the desert for 40 years. Even in biblical times, men wouldn't ask for directions.

Mexican

✳ A stranded driver in Mexico had walked for almost an hour to get help when a cloud of dust in the distance offered some hope. The man quickened his pace and soon discovered that a yard full of playing children was the source of the disturbance. The man called out to an old woman on the front porch, 'Madam, do you have a monkey wrench?' 'Theese no monkey ranch, theese my children!' the woman replied with indignation.

Scottish

✳ A young English boy finds a kilt and tries it on for a laugh. He goes to show his mum, saying, 'Look, Mum, I'm Scottish.' Outraged, she slaps him hard on the cheek, and shouts, 'Go tell your granny what you just said.' The boy finds his grandma and shows her his kilt. 'Look, Granny, I'm Scottish.' A look of rage crosses the old lady's face, and she slaps the boy hard on the other cheek. 'I can't believe you just said that!' she shouts. 'Go and repeat it to your father.' Bawling, the kid finds his dad. 'Look, Dad, I'm Scottish.' His dad says nothing, but picks up a stick and gives him a sound thrashing. 'What do you have to say for yourself now?' asks his dad when he's finished. The kid yells back at him: 'I've only been Scottish for five minutes and already I hate all you English!'

✳ A Scotsman gets injured watching a football match and decides to sue. That night in the pub he is looking sorry for himself. 'Did you lose your case?' asks the barman. 'Aye,' he replies. 'The judge said the club cannae be held responsible.' 'How did you hurt yourself?' the barman says. 'Och, I fell out of the tree,' replies the Scotsman.

✳ What's the difference between a Scotsman and a coconut?
You can get a drink out of a coconut.

✳ What do you call a Scottish cloakroom attendant?
Angus McCoatup.

✳ What do Scotsmen eat?
Tart'n'pie!

Welsh

✳ What is the Welsh for foreplay?
Are you awake, Gwen?

✳ Now that Catherine Zeta-Jones-Douglas has become firmly established in Hollywood, the Welsh film industry is to receive additional funding to step up production. They are going to remake many well-known films, but this time with a Welsh flavour. The following are planned for release next year:

9½ Leeks

The Sheepshag Redemption

Trefforest Gump

Cwmando

The Lost Boyos

An American Werewolf in Powys

Huw Dares Gwyneth

Dai Hard

The Wizard of Oswestry

Cool Hand Look-you

Sheepless in Seattle

The Eagle has Llandudno

The Magnificent Severn

Haverfordwest Was Won

Austin Powys

The Magic Rhonddabout

Independence Dai

The Llanfairpwllgwyngyllgogerychwyrndrobwllllantysiliogogogoch That Time Forgot

Welsh Connection

Welsh Connection II

The Bridge on the River Wye

Lawrence of Llandovery

A Beautiful Mind-you

The Welsh Patient

The King and Mair

Breakfast at Taffynys

Look You Back in Bangor

Evans Can Wait

A Fishguard Called Rhondda

Where Eagles Aberdare

Dial M For Merthyr

A-Rhondda the World in 80 Days

Look-you Who's Talking

Swansea of Love

Dai Another Day

Merthyr on the Orient Express

The Empire Strikes Bach

Ponty Python's Life of Bryn

Caerphillydelphia

✳ How do Welsh people eat cheese?
Caerphilly!

failure

If at first you don't succeed, failure may be your style.

If at first you don't succeed, give up, no use being a damn fool.

If at first you don't succeed, look in the bin for the instructions.

If everything seems to be going right, you obviously don't know what the hell is going on.

FAMILIES

✳ A married couple was in a terrible accident where the woman's face was severely burned. The doctor told the husband that they couldn't graft any skin from her body because she was too skinny. So the husband offered to donate some of his own skin. However, the only skin on his body that the doctor felt was suitable would have to come from his buttocks. The husband and wife agreed that they would tell no one about where the skin came from, and requested that the doctor also honour their secret. After all, this was a very delicate matter. After the surgery was completed, everyone was astounded at the woman's new beauty. She looked more beautiful than she ever had before! All her friends and relatives just went on and on about her youthful beauty. One day, she was alone with her husband, and she was overcome with emotion at his sacrifice. She said, 'Dear, I just want to thank you for everything you did for me. There is no way I could ever repay you.'

'My darling,' he replied, 'think nothing of it. I get all the thanks I need every time I see your mother kiss you on the cheek.'

✳ I don't think my parents liked me. I asked for a bath toy and they gave me a piranha.

✳ What's different about an illegitimate Rice Krispy?
Snap, Crackle, But No Pop.

✳ Big noses usually run in families.

✳ Our family is so ugly, we keep the negatives in the photograph album.

✳ My sister used to go out with a mushroom harvester – apparently he used to be a fun guy to be with!

✳ If Mr and Mrs Bigger had a baby, who would be the biggest of the three?
The baby, because he's a little Bigger!

✳ Someone has described heaven as a family reunion that never ends. What could hell possibly be like? Home videos of the same reunion?

✳ It's sad how whole families are torn apart by simple things, like wild dogs.

✳ Two kids are talking to each other. One says, 'I'm really worried. My dad works twelve hours a day to give my family a nice home and plenty of food. My mum spends the whole day cleaning and cooking for me. I'm worried sick!' The other kid says, 'What have you got to worry about? Sounds to me like you've got it made!' The first kid says, 'What if they try to escape?'

✳ This morning I woke up to the unmistakable scent of pigs in a blanket. That's the price you pay for letting the relatives stay over.

✳ How do you make antifreeze?
Steal her pyjamas.

✳ Success is relative. The more success, the more relatives.

🐫 FARMERS

✳ What did the farmer say to the cow on his roof?
Get off.

✳ An old farmer decided to visit a pond at the back of his property that
he had not visited for a long time. As he neared the pond, he heard
voices shouting and laughing with glee. As he came closer, he
discovered a bunch of young women were skinny dipping in his
pond. He politely made the women aware of his presence, and they
all went to the deep end. One of the women shouted to him, 'We're
not coming out until you leave!' The farmer replied, 'I didn't come
down here to see you skinny dipping. I'm just here to feed the
alligator.'

✳ A farmer in Alabama was driving across a bridge in his pickup truck
when he noticed a man standing on the rail of the bridge ready to
jump to his death in the river below.

The Alabama farmer stopped his truck, ran up to the man and
said, 'Hey, why are you doing this?' The man replied, 'Well, I have
nothing to live for.' The Alabama man replied, 'Well, think of your wife
and children!' The jumper replied, 'I have no wife or children.'

'Well, then think of your mother and father!' The man replied,
'Mom and Dad passed on many years back.' The Alabama man then
said, 'Well, think of General Robert E. Lee!'

The would-be jumper replied, 'Who?' With that the Alabama man
said, 'Jump, you damn Yankee, jump!'

✳ Did you hear about the farmer who tried fish farming, but had to give it up when his tractor kept getting stuck in the lake?

✳ A chicken farmer buys 2,000 baby chicks. He goes back to the salesman in a week and says he needs 2,000 more baby chicks. He comes back a week later needing 2,000 more. The salesman asks what the problem is. The chicken farmer says, 'Well, I don't know if I'm planting 'em too deep or too close together.'

✳ How did the farmer mend his pants?
With cabbage patches!

✳ A man bought several acres of wasteland and, within a year, had turned it into a thriving produce farm. The local vicar stopped by and complimented the man on his progress. Then he added, 'Wondrous things can surely happen when man and God work together.'
'Amen,' said the man, 'but you should've seen the place when God was running it alone.'

✳ What's the difference between a love story reader and a farmer?
One reads it and weeps, the other weeds it and reaps.

✳ How did the cows hurt the farmer?
They trod on his corn.

✳ Did you hear about the farmer who ploughed his field with a steam-roller?
He wanted to grow mashed potatoes!

✳ What did the neurotic pig say to the farmer?
You take me for grunted.

✳ When is a farmer like a magician?
When he turns his cow to pasture.

✳ Why did the farmer call his pig 'Ink'?
Because it was always running out of the pen.

✳ An aged farmer and his wife were leaning against the edge of their pigpen when the old woman wistfully recalled that the next week would mark their golden wedding anniversary. 'Let's have a party,' she suggested. 'Let's kill a pig.' The farmer scratched his grizzled head. 'Well, Doris,' he finally answered, 'I don't see why the pig should take the blame for something that happened fifty years ago.'

✳ A rural police officer attended a farm where a farmer had lost 2,025 pigs. Later, entering the details onto the computer back at the station, the policeman decided to check the facts. He called the farmer directly: 'Is it true, Mr Giles, that you lost 2,025 pigs?' he asked. 'Yeth,' lisped the farmer. Satisfied, the policeman hung up and typed: 'Subject lost two sows and 25 pigs.'

✳ The farmer's son was returning from the market with the crate of chickens his father had entrusted to him, when all of a sudden the box fell and broke open. Chickens scurried off in different directions, but the determined boy walked all over the neighbourhood scooping up the wayward birds and returning them to the repaired crate. Hoping he had found them all, the boy reluctantly returned home, expecting the worst. 'Pa, the chickens got loose,' the boy confessed sadly, 'but I managed to find all twelve of them.' 'Well, you did real good, son,' the farmer beamed. 'You left with seven.'

✹ Could crop circles be the work of a cereal killer?

✹ A very zealous soul-winning young preacher recently came upon a farmer working in his field. Being concerned about the farmer's soul, the preacher asked the man: 'Are you labouring in the vineyard of the Lord, my good man?' Not even looking at the preacher and continuing his work, the farmer replied, 'Naw, these are soybeans.' 'You don't understand,' said the preacher. 'Are you a Christian?' With the same amount of interest as his previous answer, the farmer said, 'Nope, my name is Jones. You must be lookin' for Jim Christian. He lives a mile south of here.' The determined preacher tried again, asking the farmer, 'Are you lost?' 'Naw! I've lived here all my life,' answered the farmer. 'Are you prepared for the resurrection?' the frustrated preacher asked. This caught the farmer's attention and he asked, 'When's it gonna be?' Thinking he had accomplished something, the young preacher replied, 'It could be today, tomorrow, or the next day.' Taking a handkerchief from his back pocket and wiping his brow, the farmer remarked, 'Well, don't mention it to my wife. She don't get out much and she'll wanna go all three days.'

✹ A fire started on a farm. The fire station from the nearby town was called to put the fire out, the firemen arrived in a dilapidated old fire engine. They drove straight towards the fire and stopped in the middle of the flames. The firemen jumped off the truck and frantically started spraying water in all directions. Soon they had snuffed out the centre of the fire, breaking the blaze into two easily controllable parts. The farmer was so impressed with their work and so grateful that his farm had been spared that he presented the fire department with a cheque for £1,000. A local news reporter asked the fire captain what the department planned to do with the funds. 'That should be obvious,' he responded. 'The first thing we're doing is getting the brakes fixed on that stupid fire engine.'

* A retiring farmer, in preparation for selling his land, needed to rid his farm of animals. So he went to every house in his town. To the houses where the man is the boss, he gave a horse. To the houses where the woman is the boss, a chicken was given. He got towards the end of a street and saw a couple outside, gardening. 'Who's the boss around here?' he asked. 'I am,' said the man. 'I have a black horse and a brown horse,' the farmer said, 'which one would you like?' The man thought for a minute and said, 'The black one.' 'No, no, no, get the brown one,' the man's wife said. 'Here's your chicken,' said the farmer.

* A clergyman walking down a country lane sees a young farmer struggling to load hay back onto a cart after it has fallen off. 'You look hot, my son,' says the cleric. 'Why don't you rest a moment, and I'll give you a hand?' 'No thanks,' says the young man. 'My father wouldn't like it.' 'Don't be silly,' the minister says. 'Everyone is entitled to a break. Come and have a drink of water.' Again the young man protests that his father would be upset. Losing his patience, the clergyman says, 'Your father must be a real slave driver. Tell me where I can find him and I'll give him a piece of my mind!' 'Well,' replied the young farmer, 'he's under the load of hay.'

✳ A man had always dreamed of owning his own cattle ranch, and finally made enough money to buy himself the spread of his dreams. 'So, what did you name the ranch?' asked his best friend when he flew out to visit. 'We had a heck of a time,' admitted the new cowboy. 'Couldn't agree on anything. We finally settled on the Double R Lazy L Triple Horseshoe Bar-7 Lucky Diamond Ranch.' 'Wow!' His friend was impressed. But looking around he saw no cattle. 'So ... where are all the cows?' 'None of 'em survived the branding.'

✳ A farmer was milking his cow. He was just starting to get a good rhythm going when a bug flew into the barn and started circling his head. Suddenly, the bug flew into the cow's ear. The farmer didn't think much about it, until the bug squirted out into his bucket. It went in one ear and out the udder.

✳ A farmer and his brand new bride were riding home from the chapel in a wagon pulled by a team of horses, when the older horse stumbled. The farmer said, 'That's once.' A little further along, the poor old horse stumbled again. The farmer said, 'That's twice.' After a little while, the poor old horse stumbled again. The farmer didn't say anything, but reached under the seat, pulled out a shotgun and shot the horse. His brand new bride yelled, telling him, 'That was an awful thing to do.' 'That's once.'

fear

I'm not afraid of the dark, as long as the light's on.

🐶 FIGHTING

✳ We're inseparable. In fact, it takes six people to pull us apart.

✳ 'All right, break it up. What's this fight about?'
'He called me a dirty number, warden.'

✳ I was a war baby. My parents took one look at me and started fighting.

✳ 'I'm ashamed of you,' the mother said. 'I don't want you fighting!' 'He threw a stone at me!' the boy said. 'So I threw one back at him.' 'You should have come and got me instead,' his mother said. 'Why? Your aim is terrible!'

✳ Some people say, 'If you can't beat them, join them.' I say, 'If you can't beat them, beat them,' because they will be expecting you to join them, so you will have the element of surprise.

✳ What do you get if you're hit on the head with an axe?
A splitting headache.

🐶 FILMS

✳ Auntie Em, hate you, hate Kansas, taking the dog. Dorothy.

✳ Which fly makes films?
Stephen Spielbug!

✳ If Spielberg makes a sequel to *ET* will he call it *ETC*?

✳ I went to the pictures the other day, and saw an extremely explicit love scene. It was only after an hour that I realized I was facing the wrong way.

✳ I went to see a film the other day, and found it extremely refreshing. I felt like a new man when I woke up.

✳ Have you seen the movie *Constipated*?
No, it hasn't come out, yet.

✳ Two men are talking in the pub. 'You look familiar,' says one. 'I'm an actor. You might have seen me in the movies,' replies the other. 'Oh, where do you sit?' says the first man.

✳ I went to the local video shop and I said, 'Can I take out *The Elephant Man*?' He said, 'He's not your type.' I said, 'How about *Batman Forever*?' He said, 'No, you'll have to bring it back tomorrow.'

✳ Who is in cowboy films and always broke?
Skint Eastwood!

✳ Coarse and violent nudity. Occasional language.

✳ Viewer discretion may be advised, but it's never really expected.

🦁 FIRE

✳ If you're trying to start a fire by rubbing two sticks together, make sure one of them is a match.

✳ One day Billy was at home playing with matches even though his mother had told him not to. He accidentally set the house on fire, and he and his mother fled outside. As the house was burning down, his enraged mother said, 'Boy, is your dad going to spank you when he gets home.' But Billy just laughed; he knew his dad had come home early for a nap.

✳ A man found his house was on fire, so he called the fire station and told them, 'Hey, my house is on fire.' The fireman asked, 'How do we get there?' 'Don't you still drive those big red trucks?' he asked.

✳ Build a man a fire and he'll be warm for a day. Set a man on fire and he'll be warm for the rest of his life.

✳ Did you hear about the wife who made her husband resign from the fire service?
She felt he spent too much time with old flames.

✳ I walked into the living room the other day to find my son in front of a roaring fire. This was disturbing, as we don't have a fireplace.

✳ An Irishman had two wooden legs. One day his house caught on fire. The firemen saved the house, but he burned to the ground. He took the insurance company to court but they said he didn't have a leg to stand on.

✴ What kind of crackers do firemen like in their soup?
Firecrackers!

✴ What did the fireman's wife get for Christmas?
A ladder in her stocking!

✴ What did the big firecracker say to the little firecracker?
My pop is bigger than yours.

✴ Who invented fire?
Some bright spark!

✴ How do you get five donkeys on a fire engine?
Two in the front, two in the back, and one on the roof going EE-AW-EE-AW.

🐟 FISH AND SEA CREATURES

✴ What did the fish say when he swam into the wall?
Dam!

✴ How could the dolphin afford to buy a house?
He prawned everything!

✳ Why are goldfish red?
The water turns them rusty!

✳ There was a murder at the local fish market. A woman killed a gentleman just for the halibut. He was hard of herring, it was later found.

✳ What's brown and lies on the seabed?
An oyster egg.

✳ Why did the lobster blush?
Because he saw the ocean's bottom!

✳ What did the fisherman say to the magician?
'Pick a cod, any cod.'

✳ Which fish can perform operations?
A sturgeon.

✳ We are all prawns in the game of life.

✳ Why do mermaids wear seashells?
Because they are too big for the B-shells and too small for the D-shells.

✳ What do fish sing to each other?
'Salmon-chanted Evening.'

✳ Do fish get thirsty?

✳ What do you get if you cross an abbot with a trout?
Monkfish!

✳ What bit of fish doesn't make sense?
The piece of cod that passeth all understanding.

✳ What is dry on the outside, filled with water and shoots through buildings?
A fish tank!

✳ What was the Tsar of Russia's favourite fish?
Tsardines!

✳ What do you get if you cross a trout with an apartment?
A flat fish.

✳ What happened to the cold jellyfish?
It set!

✳ What's the difference between a fish and a piano?
You can't tuna fish!

✳ Why are sardines the stupidest fish in the sea?
Because they climb into tins, close the lid and leave the key outside!

✳ What kind of money do fishermen make?
Net profits.

✳ What is a chameleon's motto?
A change is as good as a rest.

✳ What kind of fish goes well with ice cream?
Jellyfish.

✳ What did the boy fish say to his girlfriend?
'Your plaice or mine.'

✳ Why are fish boots the warmest ones to wear?
Because they have electric 'eels.

✳ What fish do road-menders use?
Pneumatic krill.

✳ What happens when sharks take their clothes off?
They go sharkers!

✳ What game do fish like playing the most?
Name that tuna!

✳ Why do sharks live in salt water?
Because pepper water would make them sneeze.

✳ Why are fish clever?
Because they travel in schools.

✳ Which part of a fish weighs the most?
The scales.

✹ How do you communicate with a fish?
Drop him a line!

✹ What does a shark eat with peanut butter?
Jellyfish!

✹ Where do shellfish go to borrow money?
To the prawn broker!

✹ What do you call a big fish who makes you an offer you can't refuse?
The Codfather.

✹ What happened to the shark who swallowed a bunch of keys?
He got lockjaw.

✹ Where do fish wash?
In a river basin!

✹ What fish only swims at night?
A starfish.

✹ How do fish go into business?
They start on a small scale.

✹ Which fish go to heaven when they die?
Angelfish.

✹ What do you get when you put a fish and an elephant together?
Swimming trunks.

✳ Why does an oyster never give away its pearl?
Because its shellfish.

✳ What kind of noise annoys an oyster?
A noisy noise annoys an oyster.

✳ **1st kipper**: Smoking's bad for you.
2nd kipper: It's OK, I've been cured.

✳ What kind of fish is useful in freezing weather?
Skate.

✳ What lives in the ocean, is grouchy and hates neighbours?
A hermit crab.

✳ What do you get from a bad-tempered shark?
As far away as possible!

✳ Why are some fish at the bottom of the ocean?
Because they dropped out of school.

fleas

What do you call a cheerful flea?
A hoptomist.

How do you find where a flea has bitten you?
Start from scratch.

How do fleas travel around?
By itch-hiking.

What time is it when a fly and a flea pass each other?
Fly past flea.

FLiES

* If there are two flies in the kitchen, which one is the cowboy?
  The one on the range.

* How do you make a butterfly?
  Flick it out of the butter dish with a knife!

* Once there was a woman who was such a bad cook that the flies took up a collection to fix the screen door.

* So just what are time flies, and why do they like an arrow?

* A little boy goes into the school's bathroom and sees a fly on the side of the sink. 'Oh,' he thinks, 'I'll pull off his wings.' And he pulls them right off. And off to class he goes. The next little boy comes in to use the same bathroom and sees the same fly by the sink. 'Oh, I think I'll pull off its legs.' Legs off, he rushes to class. Third little boy pulls off the fly's head. Fourth little boy comes in and says, 'Yum! A raisin!'

* No one suspects the butterfly!

* Where do flies go in winter?
  To the glass foundry to be turned into bluebottles.

* How do fireflies start a race?
  Ready, steady, glow!

* If there are five flies in the kitchen, how do you know which one is the American football player?
  The one in the sugar bowl!

* What did one firefly say to the other?
  'Got to glow now!'

* What goes 'snap, crackle and pop'?
  A firefly with a short circuit!

* How do stones stop moths eating your clothes?
  Because rolling stones gather no moths!

* What do insects learn at school?
  Mothmatics.

* What's the biggest moth in the world?
  A mammoth!

* Some days you are the fly, some days you are the windscreen.

✳ What's pretty, delicate and carries a sub-machine gun?
A killer butterfly.

✳ How do you know when a moth farts?
It flies straight for an instant.

✳ What do you get if you cross a firefly and a moth?
An insect that can find its way around a dark wardrobe.

✳ How can a woman rid her flat of cockroaches?
Ask them for a commitment.

✳ Why did the firefly keep stealing things?
He was light-fingered.

✳ Why were the flies playing football in a saucer?
They were playing for the cup.

✳ What is the difference between a fly and a bird?
A bird can fly but a fly can't bird.

✳ What is green, sooty and whistles when it rubs its back legs together?
Chimney Cricket!

🐵 FLOWERS

✳ What do you send a sick florist?

✳ Some girls are like flowers. They grow wild in the woods.

✳ What kind of dog sniffs out new flowers?
A bud hound!

✳ I used to wear a flower in my lapel, but I had to stop. The pot kept bumping on my belt.

✳ Always take time to stop and smell the roses ... and sooner or later, you'll inhale a bee.

✳ What flower grows on your face?
Tulips.

✳ What sort of children does a florist have?
Either budding geniuses or blooming idiots.

✳ What do you get if you cross a crocodile with a flower?
I don't know, but I'm not going to smell it!

✳ What gloves can be held but not worn?
Foxgloves.

✳ I'm not saying he's vain, but he goes into the garden so the flowers can smell him.

🦁 FLYING

☀ Take-offs are optional. Landings are mandatory.

☀ A passenger jet was suffering through a severe thunderstorm. The passengers were being bounced around by the turbulence. A young woman turned to a minister sitting next to her and, with a nervous laugh, asked, 'Reverend, you're a man of God, can't you do something about this storm?' To which he replied, 'Lady, I'm in sales, not management.'

☀ 'At the airport they asked me if anybody I didn't know gave me anything. Even the people I know don't give me anything.' *George Wallace*

☀ If God meant man to fly, He'd have given him more money.

☀ The knack of flying is learning how to throw yourself at the ground and miss.

☀ Gravity never loses. The best you can hope for is a draw.

☀ If you push the stick forward, the houses get bigger, if you pull the stick back, they get smaller. (Unless you keep pulling the stick back – then they get bigger again.)

☀ Flying is not dangerous; crashing is dangerous.

✳ It's better to be down here wishing you were up there, than up there wishing you were down here.

✳ The propeller is just a big fan in the front of the plane to keep the pilot cool. Want proof? Make it stop; then watch the pilot break out into a sweat.

✳ Speed is life, altitude is life insurance. No one has ever collided with the sky.

✳ It's best to keep the pointed end going forward as much as possible.

✳ The only time you have too much fuel is when you're on fire.

✳ Did you hear about the stupid Kamikaze pilot?
He flew 57 missions!

✳ Flying is the second greatest thrill known to man... Landing is the first.

✳ Everyone already knows the definition of a 'good' landing is one from which you can walk away. But very few know the definition of a 'great landing'. It's one after which you can use the plane another time.

✳ The probability of survival is equal to the angle of arrival.

✳ You know you've landed with the wheels up when it takes full power to taxi.

* A helicopter is a collection of rotating parts going round and round and reciprocating parts going up and down – all of them trying to become random in motion. Helicopters can't really fly – they're just so ugly that the earth immediately repels them.

* There are three simple rules for making a smooth landing. Unfortunately, no one knows what they are.

* A photographer for a national magazine was assigned to get photos of a great forest fire. Smoke at the scene was too thick to get any good shots, so he frantically called his home office to hire a plane. 'It will be waiting for you at the airport!' he was assured by his editor. As soon as he got to the small, rural airport, sure enough, a plane was warming up near the runway. He jumped in with his equipment and yelled, 'Let's go! Let's go!' The pilot swung the plane into the wind and soon they were in the air. 'Fly over the north side of the fire,' said the photographer, 'and make three or four low-level passes.' 'Why?' asked the pilot. 'Because I'm going to take pictures! I'm a photographer, and photographers take pictures!' said the photographer with great exasperation. After a long pause the pilot said, 'You mean you're not the instructor?'

* An airliner experienced an unusually bumpy landing. After they had taxied to the terminal, the sheepish pilot took his regular station at the door, telling the passengers, 'Thanks for flying with us.' In light of his bad landing, he was fully prepared to grin and bear it should anyone make a comment. But no one had, and the only passenger left coming down the aisle was a little old lady walking with a cane. She stopped at the door and turned to him. 'Captain, mind if I ask you a

question?' 'Why, no, madam,' said the pilot. 'What is it?' 'Were we shot down?'

✳ The only thing worse than a captain who never flew as co-pilot is a co-pilot who once was a captain.

✳ A thunderstorm is never as bad on the inside as it appears on the outside. It's worse.

✳ It's easy to make a small fortune in aviation. You start with a large fortune.

✳ Passengers were waiting to board the flight to Dublin when they announced that the flight was full. The airline was looking for volunteers to give up their seats. In exchange, they'd give you a £100 voucher for your next flight and a first-class seat in the plane leaving an hour later. About eight people ran up to the counter to take advantage of the offer. It was only about fifteen seconds later that all eight of those people sat down grumpily as the lady behind the ticket counter announced, 'If there is anyone else OTHER than the flight crew who'd like to volunteer, please step forward...'

✳ A male pilot is a confused soul who talks about women when he's flying, and about flying when he's with a woman.

✳ Try to keep the number of your landings equal to the number of your take-offs.

✳ There are old pilots, and there are bold pilots, but there are no old, bold pilots!

🐺 FOOD AND DRINK

✳ What do you call artificial spaghetti?
Mockaroni!

✳ What's green and writes underwater?
A ballpoint gherkin.

✳ What's yellow and goes slam, slam, slam, slam?
A four-door banana.

✳ Where does okra come from?
Okrahoma!

✳ Why did the orange stop in the middle of the road?
Because it ran out of juice.

✳ The older you get, the better you get. Unless you are a banana.

✳ What came after the Stone Age and the Bronze Age?
The sausage!

✳ I'm not saying she's a bad cook, but when we have something different for lunch we get food.

✳ What do you call a woman who sells herself for lasagne?
A pastatute!

✳ Instant human! Just add coffee.

✳ Ham and eggs: A day's work for a chicken, a lifetime commitment for a pig.

✳ I bought a box of Animal Crackers and it said on it, 'Do not eat if seal is broken.' So I opened up the box, and sure enough… *Brian Kiley*

✳ How was pasta invented?
Someone used their noodle.

✳ Did you hear about the man who got vinegar in his ear?
Now he suffers from pickled hearing.

✳ Want to hear my tortilla joke? I must warn you, it's really corny.

✳ A guy walks down the road with a fried egg on his head. Another guy asks him why he has a fried egg on his head. The guy replies, 'Well, if it was boiled it'd roll off.'

✳ When I come home and smell a delicious meal cooking in the kitchen, I know I've gone into the wrong house.

✳ 'I bought some bread this morning.'
'Ciabatta?'
'No, it was a fixed price.'

✴ As the strongman said on his way to the beach: I'm mussel-bound.

✴ Our kitchen is so small we can only use condensed milk.

✴ 'Mummy, why can't we get a waste disposal unit?'
   'Be quiet and keep chewing.'

✴ What did the grape do when it got stepped on?
   It let out a little wine!

✴ What happens to cows during an earthquake?
   They give milk shakes!

✴ What did the hungry Dalmatian say when he had a meal?
   That hit the spots!

✴ Why did the jelly wobble?
   Because it saw the milk shake!

✴ What did baby corn say to mama corn?
   Where's popcorn?

✴ What would you call two banana skins?
   A pair of slippers.

✴ Chocolate makes your clothes shrink.

✴ How can you pick out Ronald McDonald in a nudist colony?
   He's the one with sesame seed buns.

✳ Drink your coffee; there are people in India sleeping.

✳ Cole's Law: Thinly sliced cabbage.

✳ What's the difference between bogeys and broccoli?
Kids don't eat broccoli.

✳ What's green then yellow then green then yellow then green?
A banana with a night job as a pickle.

✳ To get a very soft boiled egg, only put it in hot water for one second.

✳ The walls in my apartment are so thin, when I peel onions the neighbours cry.

✳ We were so poor when I was young all we ate was scrambled eggs. Mother would put one egg on the table and we'd all scramble for it.

✳ What do you call a gingerbread man with one leg?
Limp biskit.

✳ Why did the potato blush?
Because it saw the salad dressing.

✳ Have you heard about the elephant that went on a crash diet?
He wrecked three cars, a bus and two fire engines!

✳ Why do elephants eat raw food?
Because they don't know how to cook!

✳ Two snowmen standing next to each other. One says to the other,
'Can you smell carrots?'

✳ Dijon vu – a feeling you've experienced this mustard before.

✳ Why do bakers work so hard?
Because they need the dough.

✳ Did you hear about the Indian who drank 89 cups of tea?
They found him dead the next morning in his tea-pee.

✳ Why did the little tomato drop out of school?
He could never ketchup.

✳ Of course I enjoy your cooking. Now, do you have a stomach pump?

✳ How do you tease fruit?
Banananananananana!

✳ What's yellow and sniffs?
A banana with the flu.

✳ Everything comes to he who orders hash.

✳ A man walks into a shop and asks for a packet of helicopter flavour
crisps. Guy behind the counter shrugs and says, 'Sorry, we've only
got plain.'

✳ What kind of room has no windows?
A mushroom.

✳ I'm busier than a one-toothed man in a corn-on-the-cob-eating contest.

✳ If a parsley farmer is sued do they garnish his wages?

✳ My wild oats have turned to shredded wheat!

✳ Why did the biscuit go to the hospital?
Because it felt crummy.

✳ What's the difference between mashed potato and pea soup?
Anyone can mash potato.

✳ How does Bob Marley like his doughnuts?
Wi' jammin.
How do his friends like their doughnuts?
We hope they like jammin too.

✳ She always flirts with the butcher. Playing for bigger steaks.

✳ Why do croutons come in airtight packages? Aren't they just stale bread to begin with?

✳ How do you make milk shake?
Give it a good scare!

* A boiled egg is hard to beat.

* What are two things you cannot have for breakfast?
  Lunch and dinner.

* Why did the boy sprinkle sugar on his pillow before he went to sleep?
  So he could have sweet dreams.

* When do you stop at green and go at red?
  When you're eating a watermelon!

* What's the kindest vegetable?
  A sweet potato.

* I bought some Armageddon cheese today, and it said on the packet
  'Best Before End'.

* Every day I try to enjoy something from each of the four food groups:
  the confectionery group, the salty-snack group, the caffeine group,
  and the 'whatever-the-thing-in-the-tinfoil-in-the-back-of-the-fridge-is'
  group.

* Why did the biscuit cry?
  Because his mother was a wafer so long.

Dieting

* He does not eat like a pig; he suffers from reverse bulimia.

✳ 'A quick way to lose weight: subtract your birth weight, because you haven't gained that part.' *Carsten Bang*

✳ I went on the champagne diet – it took off £250.

✳ How is it that 'Fat Chance' and 'Slim Chance' mean the same thing?

✳ My wife more than kept her girlish figure. She doubled it.

✳ 'Now, what are you planning to do about that excess weight you're carrying around?' the doctor asked the patient. 'I just can't seem to lose the weight,' the patient said. 'I must have an overactive thyroid.' 'The tests show your thyroid is perfectly normal,' the doctor said. 'It appears it's your fork that's overactive.'

✳ I'm on a 30-day diet. So far, I have lost fifteen days

✳ 'It's easy to distract fat people. It's a piece of cake.' *Chris Addison*

Waiter, Waiter

✳ Waiter, waiter, do you have frogs' legs?
No, sir, it's just the way I'm standing.

✳ Waiter, waiter, there's a button in my lettuce.
It must have fallen in when the salad was dressing, sir.

✳ Waiter, waiter, the food here is revolting. Let me see the manager.
I can't, sir. He's out to lunch.

✳ Waiter, waiter, how do I get a glass of water in this place?
Set yourself on fire, sir.

✳ Waiter, waiter, this coffee's weak.
What do you expect me to do, give it weight training?

✳ Waiter, waiter, this coffee tastes like tea.
I'm sorry, sir, I've given you tea.

✳ Waiter, waiter, this coffee tastes like mud.
Yes, sir, it's fresh ground.

✳ Waiter, waiter, how do you prepare the chicken?
Nothing special, sir. We just flat out tell 'em they're gonna die…

✳ Waiter, waiter, is this a lamb or pork chop?
Can't you tell the difference?
No, I can't.
Then what does it matter?

✳ Waiter, waiter, a cup of coffee without cream, please.
I'm afraid we are out of cream, sir. Would you like it without milk?

✳ Waiter, waiter, I'll have the steak.
With pleasure, sir.
No, with pepper sauce, please.

✳ Waiter, waiter, how long have you worked here?
One week, sir. Why?
You can't be the one who took my order then.

✳ Waiter, waiter, your tie is in my soup.
Don't worry, sir. It won't shrink.

✳ Waiter, waiter, bring me a glass of milk and a piece of fish.
Fillet?
Yes, right to the top.

✳ Waiter, waiter, there's a dead beetle in my wine.
Well, you did ask for something with a little body, sir.

✳ Waiter, waiter, no mushrooms for me today. I was nearly poisoned
with them last week.
Really, sir? Then I win the bet with chef.

✳ Waiter, waiter, there's a stick in my soup.
Yes, sir. We have branches everywhere.

✳ Waiter, waiter, there's a fly in my soup.
What did you expect at these prices, sir – an elephant?

✳ Waiter, waiter, today I'd like my soup without...
Without what, sir?
Your thumb in it.

✳ Waiter, waiter, what is the meaning of this fly in my teacup?
  I'm a waiter, madam, not a fortune teller.

✳ Waiter, waiter, you're not fit to serve a pig.
  I'm doing my best, sir.

✳ Waiter, waiter, what is this soup?
  Bean soup, sir.
  I don't care what it's been – what is it now?

✳ Waiter, waiter, this soup is disgusting.
  No, sir. Oxtail.

✳ Waiter, waiter, you've got your thumb in my soup.
  Don't worry sir. It's not hot.

✳ Waiter, waiter, there's a fly in my butter.
  Impossible, sir. We only serve margarine.

✳ Waiter, waiter, a dog just ran off with my steak.
  Yes, it is popular, sir.

✳ Waiter, waiter, have you smoked salmon?
  No, sir, although I once tried a pipe.

✳ Waiter, waiter, what do you recommend for my lunch?
  For you, sir, a diet.

✳ Waiter, waiter, do you have pig's trotters?
No, sir. It's these new shoes which make me walk like this.

✳ Waiter, waiter, there's a dead fly in my soup.
Yes, sir. The heat kills them.

✳ Waiter, waiter, do the tablecloths ever get changed here?
I wouldn't know, sir. I've only been here a year.

✳ Waiter, waiter, may I have a table for dinner?
Boiled or roasted, sir?

✳ Waiter, waiter, the crust on my pie was too tough.
You appear to have eaten the plate, sir.

✳ Waiter, waiter, this egg is bad.
I only laid the table, sir.

✳ Waiter, waiter, I can't eat this.
Why not, sir?
You haven't given me a knife and fork.

✳ Waiter, waiter, what's this in my soup?
No idea, sir. All insects look the same to me.

✳ Waiter, waiter, the butter has sand in it.
It's to stop it slipping off the bread, sir.

✳ Waiter, waiter, there's a flea in my soup.
Would you like me to tell him to hop it, sir?

✳ Waiter, waiter, do the band play requests?
They do, sir.
Tell them to play cards until I've finished my dinner.

✳ Waiter, waiter, I think I'll have game today.
Very good, sir. Tiddlywinks or snap?

✳ Waiter, waiter, do you call this a three-course meal?
That's right, sir. Two chips and a pea.

✳ Waiter, waiter, what's this fly doing in my soup?
Trying to get out, sir.

✳ Waiter, waiter, my bill, please.
Very good, sir. How did you find your steak?
Oh, I just moved a potato and there it was.

✳ Waiter, waiter, aren't there any menus in this place?
No, sir.
How do I know what you have, then?
Just look at the tablecloth and guess.

✳ Waiter, waiter, what do you call this?
Cottage pie, sir.
In that case, I think I've just bitten some of the brickwork.

✳ Waiter, waiter, there's a dead beetle in my soup.
Yes, sir. They're terrible swimmers.

✳ Waiter, waiter, do you serve crabs?
We serve anyone. Sit down, sir.

✳ Waiter, waiter, if this is cod then I'm an idiot.
You're right, sir – it is cod.

🐺 FRiENDS

✳ I have friends who swear they dream in colour; I say it's just a pigment of their imagination.

✳ Everyone should have at least two friends. One to talk to and one to talk about.

✳ My mate's so humourless … the last time he cracked a gag was when he was kidnapped!

✳ Why was the guy looking for the food on his friend? Because his friend said it's on me.

✳ Friends help you move. Real friends help you move bodies.

✳ Alzheimer's advantage: New friends every day.

✴ A friend not in need is a friend indeed.

✴ When you find yourself getting irritated with someone, try to remember that all men are brothers … and just give them a Chinese burn.

🐸 FROGS

✴ Where do frogs sit?
On toadstools.

✴ What do you say if you meet a toad?
Wart's new?

✴ What do you call a frog who wants to be a cowboy?
Hoppalong Cassidy!

✴ What did the frog order at McDonald's?
French flies and a Diet Croak.

✴ A boy frog telephones the Psychic Hotline and his personal psychic adviser tells him: 'You are going to meet a beautiful young girl who will want to know everything about you.' The frog is thrilled. 'This is great! Will I meet her at a party?' 'No,' says his adviser, 'in her biology class.'

✳ Did you hear about the illegally parked frog?
He had to be toad away.

✳ Why did the tadpole feel lonely?
Because he was newt to the area!

✳ What do you call a girl with a frog in her hair?
Lily.

✳ Where do frogs fly flags?
Tadpoles.

✳ What did the policeman say to the naughty frog?
'Go on, hop it.'

✳ What's white on the outside and green on the inside and hops?
A frog sandwich.

✳ What's red and green and red and green and red and green?
A frog in a blender.

✳ Where do tadpoles change?
In a croakroom!

✳ What do you get if you cross a dog with a frog?
A dog that can lick you from the other side of the road!

✳ How do frogs die?
They kermit suicide!

✳ What do you get if you cross a frog with some mist?
Kermit the Fog!

🐸 FURNITURE

✳ A young chap strolled into his living room one afternoon with a chair under each arm and a settee on his back. Shocked, his father asked, 'Where in the hell did you get that?!'
'Off an old man down the park,' replied the boy. Immediately, his father jumped up and walloped him. 'What was that for?' screamed the lad in pain. 'For heaven's sake!' shouted his father. 'What did I tell you about taking suites from strangers?'

✳ What's Irish and hangs out in the back yard?
Patty O'Furniture.

✳ Did you hear about the man who ran through a screen door?
He strained himself!

✳ Did you hear about the man who fell into an upholstery machine?
He is fully recovered.

✳ What has four legs but can't walk?
A table!

✳ What does a teddy bear put in his house?
Fur-niture!

✳ I bought a rubbish compactor that takes ten kilos of waste and converts it to ten kilos of waste. I'm getting my money back.

✳ What did the blanket say to the bed?
Don't worry, I've got you covered!

✳ Why should you take a pencil to bed?
To draw the curtains!

✳ What do you get when you roll a hand grenade across a kitchen floor?
Linoleum blownapart!

✳ Bob decided to move into a smaller house for his retirement, so he invited his adult kids over to take a few pieces of furniture he wanted them to have. One item was a beautiful, but very heavy, antique dining-room set. Bob's teenage grandson, Mike, helped wrestle the set into a pick-up. It took the whole day, but finally the table, chairs and china cabinet were sitting in the dining room. 'Just think,' Bob said to his grandson as he rested, 'this set is 100 years old. And one of these days, it will belong to you.' 'Oh, no!' Mike replied with a stricken look on his face. 'You mean I'm going to have to move this thing AGAIN?'

✳ Any closet is a walk-in closet if you try hard enough.

✳ Our furniture goes back to Louis XIV, unless we pay Louis before the 14th.

future

The future will be better tomorrow.

🐾 GAMBLiNG

✳ I bet you I could stop gambling.

✳ Life's a gamble – so when do I get my chips?

✳ Did you hear about the leper playing poker?
He threw his hand in.

✳ It's amazing the poker hands I get when I play bridge.

✳ Gambling away the mortgage money is a moving experience.

✳ Casino: A place where people stand around waiting for their chips to come in.

✳ What do you call a girl who is always in the bookies?
Betty!

✳ I lost £20 playing poker with my mobile phone. By mistake, I called myself.

✳ An archaeologist was digging in the Negev Desert in Israel and came upon a casket containing a mummy. After examining it, he called the curator of a prestigious natural history museum. 'I've just discovered a 3,000-year-old mummy of a man who died of heart failure!' the excited scientist exclaimed. To which the curator replied, 'Bring him in. We'll check it out.' A week later, the amazed curator called the archaeologist. 'You were right about the mummy's age and cause of death. How in the world did you know?' 'Easy. There was a piece of paper in his hand that said "10,000 shekels on Goliath".'

🐾 GEOGRAPHY

✳ What is the most slippery country in the world?
Greece.

✳ What is the smelliest city in America?
Phew York.

✳ Who is the most famous married woman in the USA?
Mrs Sippi.

✳ Those who jump off a Paris bridge are in Seine.

✳ What town in England makes terrible sandwiches?
Oldham.

✳ What has four eyes but no face?
Mississippi!

✳ Cities: Where a large community of people are lonely together.

✳ If Ireland sank into the sea, what county wouldn't sink?
Cork!

✳ How do we know that the earth won't come to an end?
Because it's round!

✳ What is the best thing to take into the desert?
A thirst aid kit!

✳ What is Cheddar Gorge?
A large cheese sandwich!

✳ An American and his wife were driving in Canada and got lost. Finally they came into some city. They saw a gentleman on the sidewalk, so the lady let down her window and asked, 'Excuse me, sir. Where are we?' The gentleman on the street replied, 'Saskatoon, Saskatchewan.' The lady rolled up the window, turned to her husband and said, 'We really are lost. They don't even speak English here!'

✳ What language do they speak in Cuba?
Cubic!

✳ What city cheats at exams?
Peking!

✳ What makes the leaning Tower of Pisa lean?
It doesn't eat much.

✳ Why is Alabama the smartest state in the USA?
Because it has 4 As and one B.

✳ What might you eat in Paris?
The trifle tower!

✳ Why doesn't the sea spill over the earth?
Because it's tied!

GHOSTS

✳ What streets do ghosts haunt?
Dead ends!

✳ Which ghost was president of France?
Charles de Ghoul.

✳ This woman wanted to marry a ghost. I don't know what possessed her.

✳ What kind of spirits like to listen to the accordion?
Polka-geists.

✳ What's a ghost's favourite food?
I-scream!

✸ What do little ghosts drink?
Evaporated milk.

✸ When do ghosts usually appear?
Just before someone screams.

✸ What should you say when you meet a ghost?
'How do you boo?'

✸ Two ghosts are talking. One says to the other, 'I don't seem to have any effect on people any more.' 'I know,' replies the other ghost, 'we might as well be dead for all they care.'

✸ Where do ghosts go at Christmas?
To the phantomime.

✸ What is a ghost's favourite ride?
A rollerghoster.

✸ What do you get when you cross a cocker spaniel, a poodle and a ghost?
Cockapoodleboo!

✸ What do you call a ghostly doctor?
A surgical spirit.

✸ Where do spirits stay on holiday?
At a ghost house.

✸ Did you hear about the ghost who gave up haunting?
He couldn't put any life into it.

✳ How do ghosts lie flat when they sleep?
They use a spirit level.

✳ What happened when Dracula broke up with his girlfriend?
They remained just good fiends.

giraffes

Why do giraffes have such long necks?
To join their heads to their bodies.

Why do giraffes eat their breakfast very early?
So the food will reach their tummies by lunchtime.

Why does a giraffe eat so little?
Because a little goes a long way!

Why is a giraffe's neck so long?
Its feet smell.

🐺 GOING OUT

✳ What did one candle say to the other?
'Going out tonight?'

✳ What did one puppet say to the other puppet?
'I can't go out – I'm tied up.'

🦁 GOOD MANNERS

✳ He is so polite he always takes his own hat off when he mentions his own name.

✳ Every day I give up my seat on the bus to somebody. I walk to work.

✳ Tact: You make your guests feel at home even when you wish they were.

✳ Why is perfume obedient?
Because it is scent wherever it goes!

gorillas

What did the gorilla say when he heard his sister had just had a baby?
Well, I'll be a monkey's uncle.

What's the difference between a gorilla and a banana?
Have you ever tried peeling a gorilla?

What should you do if you find a gorilla sleeping in your bed?
Sleep somewhere else.

gossip

She doesn't like to repeat gossip, but what else can you do with it?

GUNS

- Five doctors went duck shooting one day. Included in the group were a GP, an ear specialist, a psychiatrist, a surgeon and a pathologist. Soon, a bird came winging overhead. The first to react was the GP, who raised his shotgun but then hesitated. 'I'm not quite sure it's a duck,' he said. 'I need to get a second opinion from a specialist.' By that time, the bird was long gone. Another bird appeared in the sky. This time the ear specialist drew a bead on it. He, too, however, was unsure if it was really a duck in his sights – its call didn't sound right. 'I'll have to do some more investigations,' he muttered, as the creature made good its escape. Next to spy a bird flying was the sharp-eyed psychiatrist. Shotgun shouldered, he was more certain of his intended prey's identity. 'Now, I know it's a duck, but does it know it's a duck?' The fortunate bird disappeared while the fellow wrestled with this dilemma. Finally a fourth fowl sped past and this time the surgeon's weapon pointed skyward. BOOM! The surgeon lowered his smoking gun and turned nonchalantly to the pathologist beside him. 'Go see if that was a duck, will you?'

* To be sure of hitting the target, shoot first and call whatever you hit the target.

* A Smith & Wesson beats four aces.

* Gun control: Use both hands.

* If a man with no arms has a gun, is he armed?

* 'The right to bear arms is slightly less ludicrous than the right to arm bears.' *Chris Addison*

* Warning: Trespassers will be shot. Warning: Survivors will be shot again.

* How many guns do the US need to combat an enemy?
  Two: one to shoot and one to tell him to shoot back.

* If at first you don't succeed … go back and reload the gun.

* Some people are only alive because it is illegal to shoot them.

* Guns don't kill people, postal workers do.

* An armed society is a polite society.

* Magnum: The original point and click interface.

* When in doubt empty the magazine.

✴ An IT geek is drafted into the army and sent to the firing range for target practice. He's given a rifle and some bullets, and told to fire at the target. After loosing off a few shots, the report comes back that he has failed to get any on target. He looks at the rifle, then looks at the target. Then he puts one finger into the end of the rifle, and with his other hand squeezes the trigger. His finger is completely blown off. The geek yells towards the target area, 'It's leaving here just fine. The problem must be at your end.'

HAIRDRESSERS/HAIRCUTS

✳ He has such a long face the barber charges him twice for shaving.

✳ My husband gave me a permanent wave, and now he's gone.

✳ When a hairdresser goes for a haircut, who does the talking?

✳ What kind of hair do oceans have?
Wavy!

✳ He's a graduate of the Uncle Fester & Keith Moon School of hair styling.

✳ A barber gave a haircut to a priest one day. When the priest tried to pay for the haircut, the barber refused, saying, 'You do God's work.' The next morning the barber found a dozen Bibles at the door to his shop. A policeman came to the barber for a haircut, and again the barber refused to accept his money. 'You protect the public,' he said. The next morning the barber found a dozen doughnuts at the door to his shop. A lawyer came to the barber for a haircut, and again the barber refused payment, saying, 'You serve justice.' The next morning, the barber found a dozen lawyers standing in line, waiting for a free haircut.

✳ **Barber**: Have you been here before? I don't remember your face.
Man: I have, but it's healed up now.

✳ Bald guys never have a bad hair day.

✳ She has such beautiful hair, every time we go out I insist she wears it.

✳ A little boy took the chair at the barber's. 'How would you like your hair cut today, son?' asked the barber.
'Oh, do it like you do Daddy's, with the big hole at the back.'

✳ Why did the barber win the race?
Because he took a short cut.

✳ What did the bald man say when he was given a comb?
'I'll never part with it.'

happiness (and misery)

No sense being pessimistic. It wouldn't work anyway.

Laugh at your problems; everybody else does.

Happiness is merely the absence of pain.

I'm on the crest of a slump.

HEALTH AND DOCTORS

✹ Did Roman paramedics refer to IVs as '4s'?

✹ What's white and runs through the desert with a bedpan?
Florence of Arabia.

✹ I came from a town so small that the dentist and the proctologist
were the same guy. It was all right, as long as you set up your dental
appointment before noon.

✹ What do you call a surgeon with eight arms?
A doctopus!

✹ Just as a surgeon is finishing up an operation, the patient wakes up,
sits up and demands to know what is going on. 'I'm about to close,'
the surgeon says. The patient grabs his hand and says, 'Oh, no
you're not! I'll close my own incision.' The doctor hands him the
needle and says, 'Suture self.'

✹ While making rounds, a doctor points out an X-ray to a group of
medical students.
  'As you can see,' she says, 'the patient limps because his left
fibula and tibia are radically arched. Mr Jones, what would you do in
a case like this?' 'Well,' ponders the student, 'I suppose I'd limp too.'

✹ A man needing a heart transplant is told by his doctor that the only
heart available is that of a sheep. The man finally agrees and the

doctor transplants the sheep heart into the man. A few days after the operation, the man comes in for a check-up. The doctor asks him, 'How are you feeling?' The man replies, 'Not BAAAAD!'

✳ Isn't it scary that doctors call what they do 'practice'?

✳ **Doctor**: I think the pains in your right leg are caused by old age.
Patient: But, Doctor, my left leg is just as old and it doesn't hurt at all.

✳ A man walked into a doctor's office and the receptionist asked him what he had. He replied, 'I got shingles.' She said, 'Fill out this form and supply your name, address, medical insurance number. When you're done, please take a seat.' Fifteen minutes later a nurse's aide came out and asked him what he had. He said, 'I got shingles.' So she took down his height, weight, and complete medical history, then said, 'Change into this gown and wait in the examining room.' A half hour later a nurse came in and asked him what he had. He said, 'I got shingles.' So she gave him a blood test, a blood pressure test, an electrocardiogram and told him to wait for the doctor. An hour later the doctor came in and asked him what he had. He said, 'Shingles.' The doctor gave him a full examination, and then said, 'I just checked you out thoroughly, and I can't find shingles anywhere.'

The man replied, 'They're outside in the truck. Where do you want them?'

✳ **Man**: Doctor, I keep thinking I'm a dog.
Doctor: OK, lie down on the couch.
Man: I'm not allowed on the couch.

✳ 'Nurse, this patient doesn't seem to be doing very well with this new drip.'
'No, I think he'd be better off with his old doctor.'

✳ He talks so much that when he visited the doctor he gave him a preamble to his constitution.

✳ 'Doctor, I'm worried about my husband. He thinks he's a lorry.'
'I see. You'd better send him to see me straight away.'
'I can't. He's gone to Hull to deliver some ten-ton steel girders.'

✳ Did you hear about the lactose-intolerant man who entered an eating contest?
He won by a narrow margarine.

✳ As soon as the doctor felt his wallet, he admitted there was nothing more he could do.

✳ Kids! I sacrificed everything I had so my son could become a doctor, and now he tells me I've got to stop smoking.

✳ An ageing playboy goes to visit the doctor. 'Well,' says the doctor, 'have you managed to give up wine, women and song?'
   'Oh yes, Doctor,' replies the playboy. 'I've tapered off to beer, one girl and a little light humming instead.'

✳ A young woman wasn't feeling well and asked her friend to recommend a private doctor. 'I know a great one in the city, but he is very expensive. £500 for the first visit and £100 for each one after that.' The woman went to the doctor's and, trying to save a little money, cheerily announced, 'I'm back!' Not fooled for a second, the doctor quickly examined her and said, 'Very good, just continue the treatment I prescribed on your last visit.'

✳ The doctors X-rayed her head. They found nothing.

✳ Man goes to the doctor's with a frog growing out of his neck. Doctor says, 'What's happened there?' The frog says, 'Well, it all started with a boil on my bum.'

✳ **Doctor**: Sorry, John, your condition is pretty bad. My guess is that you have only about three minutes left.
Patient: Oh no! Three minutes! Doctor, please, there isn't anything you can do for me?
Doctor: In three minutes? Well, I can make you a Pot Noodle…

✳ You should consult my doctor. You won't live to regret it.

✳ **Man**: Doctor, I had the worst dream of my life last night. I dreamed I was with twelve of the most beautiful chorus girls in the world. Blondes, brunettes, redheads, all dancing in a row.
Doctor: That doesn't sound so terrible.
Man: Oh yeah? I was the third girl from the end.

✳ 'Doctor, I need something to stimulate me, to put me in fighting trim.'
'You'll find that right in your bill.'

✳ A patient visits his eye doctor: 'I'm very worried about the outcome of this operation, doctor. What are the chances?'
'Don't worry, you won't be able to see the difference.'

✳ A flight attendant runs to the seat where a doctor is seated and exclaims, 'Doctor, there's a man in economy that needs attention right away!' The doctor goes and finds a man clutching his chest and turning blue. He proceeds to take the man's trousers off. The attendant says, 'What are you doing? This man is having a heart attack!' The doctor responds, 'I'm a proctologist – this is the only procedure I know!'

Doctor, doctor

✳ Doctor, doctor, I only drink to calm my nerves.
No one's nerves are that noisy!

✳ Doctor, doctor, is there anything you can do for me?
I don't know. Let me feel your purse.

✳ Doctor, doctor, how long can a man live without a brain for?
I don't know. How old are you?

✳ Doctor, doctor, I swallowed a bone.
Are you choking?
No, I really did!

✳ Doctor, doctor, these pills you gave me for BO…
What's wrong with them?
They keep slipping out from under my arms!

✳ Doctor, doctor, I'm on a diet and it's making me irritable. Yesterday I bit someone's ear off.
Oh dear, that's a lot of calories!

米 Doctor, doctor, I keep thinking I'm God.
When did this start?
Well, first I created the sun, then the earth…

米 Doctor, doctor, I feel like an apple.
We must get to the core of this!

米 Doctor, doctor, I keep painting myself gold.
Don't worry, it's just a gilt complex!

米 Doctor, doctor, I've broke my arm in two places.
Well, don't go back there again then!

米 Doctor, doctor, I think I'm turning into a frog.
You're just playing too much croquet!

米 Doctor, doctor, I've had tummy ache since I ate three crabs yesterday.
Did they smell bad when you took them out of their shells?
What do you mean, 'Took them out of their shells'?

米 Doctor, doctor, my husband smells like fish.
Poor sole!

米 Doctor, doctor, my right ear is warmer than my left one!
You need to adjust your toupee.

米 Doctor, doctor, my mind keeps wandering!
Don't worry, it's too weak to get far.

* Doctor, doctor, my brother thinks he's a chicken.
  We'd better send him to hospital.
  No, don't do that. We need the eggs.

* Doctor, doctor, I'm frightened of lapels.
  I think you've got cholera.

* Doctor, doctor, I think I'm a racehorse.
  Nonsense. Just take one of these pills every four furlongs.

* Doctor, doctor, I keep seeing double.
  Please take a seat in that chair.
  Which one?

* Doctor, doctor, what are you writing on my toes?
  A footnote.

* Doctor, doctor, I feel like a needle.
  Yes, I can see your point.

* Doctor, doctor, I think I'm a bell.
  Take these and if it doesn't help give me a ring.

* Doctor, doctor, I think there's something wrong with my stomach.
  Keep your coat on and no one will notice.

* Doctor, doctor, every bone in my body aches.
  Be glad you're not a herring.

✳ Doctor, doctor, I feel at death's door.
Don't worry, I'll pull you through.

✳ Doctor, doctor, I feel like a yo-yo.
Sit down, sit down, sit down.

✳ Doctor, doctor, I think I'm a thief.
What have you taken for it?

✳ Doctor, doctor, I feel like a snooker ball.
Go to the back of the queue.

✳ Doctor, doctor, I feel like a sock.
Well, I'll be darned.

✳ Doctor, doctor, I feel like a cricket bat.
How's that?

✳ Doctor, doctor, I'm worried about my figure.
You'll have to diet.
What colour?

✳ Doctor, doctor, my hair's falling out. Can you give me something to keep it in?
Certainly, here's a plastic bag.

✳ Doctor, doctor, I've swallowed a spoon.
Lie down and don't stir.

✳ Doctor, doctor, I feel like a window.
Do you have a pain?

✳ Doctor, doctor, I swallowed a clock about a year ago.
Why didn't you come to see me sooner?
I didn't want to alarm anybody.

✳ Doctor, doctor, I think I'm made of bread.
You need to stop loafing around.

✳ Doctor, doctor, can you tell what's wrong with me?
I'm not sure, but it might be the drink.
OK, I'll come back when you're sober.

✳ Doctor, doctor, can you treat water on the brain?
Yes – with a tap on the head.

✳ Doctor, doctor, everyone thinks I'm mad because I like hard-boiled
eggs.
What's wrong with that? I like hard-boiled eggs too.
Do you? Would you like to come round and see my collection? I've
got 6,000.

✳ Doctor, doctor, can you cure my measles?
I never make rash promises.

✳ Doctor, doctor, is there no hope for my husband?
That depends what you're hoping for.

Hospitals

✳ A man visiting a friend in the hospital couldn't help noticing that the nurses wore a badge with an apple on it. He asked one of the nurses what the badge meant. 'Nothing,' she said with a smile. 'It's just to keep the doctors away.'

✳ 'Who are the most decent people in the hospital?'
'The ultrasound people.' *David O'Doherty*

✳ Tony Blair, electioneering, visits an Edinburgh hospital and enters a ward full of patients with no obvious sign of injury or illness. He greets the first patient and the patient replies: 'Fair fa your honest sonsie face, great Chieftain o' the puddin race, aboon them a you take your place, painch, tripe or thairm, as langs my arm.' Tony is confused and moves on to greet the next patient who responds: 'Some hae meat and canna eat, and some wad eat that want it, but we hae meat and can eat, so let the Lord be thankit.'

Even more confused, Tony moves on to yet another patient who begins to chant: 'Wee sleekit, timrous cowrin' beasty, though needna start awa sae hastie, wi bickerin brattle.'

Very alarmed, Tony now turns to the doctor and asks, 'What kind of facility is this? Is it a mental ward?' 'No', replies the doctor, 'this is the Serious Burns Unit.'

✳ Hospital: Where the run down wind up.

✳ Why do surgeons wear masks?
If somebody makes a mistake nobody will know who did it.

✳ Were you long in the hospital?
No, I was the same size that I am now!

✳ I asked the nurse for a bedpan, but she wouldn't give it to me. She said she was the head nurse.

Illness

✳ Gargling is a good way to see if your throat leaks.

✳ An aged woman went to her doctor to see what could be done about her constipation. 'It's terrible,' she said. 'I haven't moved my bowels in a week.' 'I see. Have you done anything about it?' 'Naturally,' she replied. 'I sit in the bathroom for a half-hour in the morning and again at night.' 'No,' the doctor said. 'I mean do you take anything?' 'Naturally,' she answered. 'I take a book.'

✳ Someone I know took so many iron pills that they started to go rusty.

✳ Why was the germ mad at his wife?
She was a flu-zy.

✳ What medicine would you give an ill ant?
Antibiotics!

✳ A man goes to the doctor with terrible constipation. The doctor asks him about his diet, and the man admits that the only vegetable he ever eats is peas. 'That's your problem,' says the doctor. 'All those peas are clogging your system up. You'll have to give them up for ever.' A few years later, and the man is drinking with a colleague who's quite drunk. 'I'd love a cigarette,' says his colleague. 'I gave up years ago but I still miss 'em.' 'Yeah,' says the barman. 'I gave up golf a while back to save my marriage. But I'd still love to play.' 'That's nothing,' says the man. 'I haven't had a pea in four years.' The barman jumps up, screaming, 'OK, everyone who can't swim grab a table...'

* Always keep several get well cards on the mantel. If unexpected guests arrive, they'll think you've been sick and unable to clean.

* Why are haemorrhoids called 'haemorrhoids' instead of 'asteroids'?

* 'I saw a woman wearing a sweatshirt with "Guess" on it. I said, "Thyroid problem?"' *Jimmy Carr*

* I had low blood pressure. My doc sent me a bill. I'm fine now.

* What is hairy and coughs?
  A coconut with a cold!

* How do you cure a headache?
  Put your head through a window and the pane will just disappear.

* How do you stop a cold getting to your chest?
  Tie a knot in your neck!

* An apple every eight hours will keep three doctors away.

✳ Why did the clock get sick?
It was run down!

✳ How do you prevent a summer cold?
Catch it in the winter!

✳ **Patient**: Doctor, I don't feel well.
Doctor: I see. Have you ever been troubled by diphtheria?
Patient: Only when I try to spell it.

Medical definitions

Anally – occurring yearly

Artery – study of paintings

Bacteria – back door of cafeteria

Barium – what doctors do when treatment fails

Bowel – letter like A.E.I.O.U.

Caesarean section – district in Rome

CAT scan – searching for kitty

Cauterize – made eye contact with her

Colic – sheep dog

Coma – a punctuation mark

Congenital – friendly

D&C – where Washington is in America

Diarrhoea – journal of daily events

Dilate – to live long

Enema – not a friend

Fester – quicker

Fibula – a small lie

Genital – non-Jewish

Grippe – suitcase

Hangnail – coathook

Impotent – distinguished, well known

Intense pain – torture in a teepee

Labour pain – got hurt at work

Medical staff – doctor's cane

Morbid – higher offer

Nitrate – cheaper than day rate

Node – was aware of

Outpatient – person who had fainted

Pap smear – fatherhood test

Pelvis – cousin of Elvis

Post-operative – letter carrier

Protein – favouring young people

Rectum – damn near killed 'em

Recovery room – place to do upholstery

Rheumatic – amorous

Scar – rolled tobacco leaf

Secretion – hiding anything

Seizure – Roman emperor

Serology – study of knighthood

Tablet – small table

Terminal illness – sickness at airport

Tibia – country in North Africa

Tumour – an extra pair

Urine – opposite of you're out

Varicose – located nearby

Vein – conceited

Mental illness

✳ Schizophrenia beats being alone.

✳ A woman entered the visitors' lounge at the mental hospital and was confronted by a man who was entirely naked except for a top hat. 'My good man,' she exclaimed, 'why are you walking around in the visitors' lounge without any clothes on?' 'Nobody ever comes to see me,' he said sadly. 'But then, why are you wearing that top hat?' 'Somebody MIGHT come!'

✳ I finally got my head together and my body fell apart.

✳ I have CDO. It's like OCD, but the letters are in alphabetical order as they should be.

✳ My mind not only wanders, sometimes it leaves completely.

✳ Many great minds should be closed for repair.

✳ A visitor at an asylum asks the director what the criteria are for defining whether or not a patient should be institutionalized. 'Well,' says the director, 'we fill up a bathtub; then we offer a teaspoon, a teacup and a bucket to the patient and ask him or her to empty the bathtub.' 'Oh, I understand,' says the visitor. 'A normal person would use the bucket as it's bigger than the spoon or the teacup.' 'No,' says the director. 'A normal person would pull the plug. Do you want a bed by the wall or near the window?'

✳ If you don't change your mind – at least repair it.

✳ Recorded phone ladder at a mental health clinic: 'If you suffer from obsessive-compulsive complex, press 1 repeatedly.' 'If you have multiple-personality disorder, press 2,3, and 4.' 'If you are delusional, press 5 and your call will be beamed directly to the Mother Ship.' 'If you have short-term memory loss, press 6. If you have short-term memory loss, press 6. If you have...'

✳ Jim and Mary were both patients in a psychiatric hospital. One day, while they were walking past the hospital swimming pool, Jim suddenly jumped into the deep end. He sank like a stone to the bottom and stayed there. Mary promptly jumped in to save him. She swam to the bottom and pulled Jim out. The medical director became aware of Mary's heroic act and he immediately ordered her to be discharged from the hospital, as he now considered her to be mentally stable. When he went to tell her the news, he said, 'Mary, I have good news and bad news. The good news is you're being discharged because you were able to jump in and save the life of another patient, so I believe you've regained your senses. The bad news is that Jim, the patient you saved, hung himself in the bathroom with the belt of his robe. I am so sorry, but he's dead.' Mary replied, 'He didn't hang himself, I put him there to dry.'

* Everyone thinks I'm psychotic, except for my friends deep inside the earth.

* I plead contemporary insanity.

What you don't want to hear during your operation

Better save that. We'll need it for the autopsy.

What's THIS doing here?

Someone call maintenance – we're going to need a mop and bucket.

Wait a minute, if this is his spleen, what's that?

Hand me that … uh … that, uh … thingie.

OOPS! By the way, has anyone ever survived 500ml of that stuff before?

Hell, there goes the power again.

Come back with that right now! Bad dog, bad dog!

You know, there's big money in kidneys. There's two here…

Nobody move – I just lost one of my contacts.

Could you stop that thing from beating? It's distracting me, big time.

I hate it when I can't find what I'm looking for!

Nurse, this patient did sign an organ donor card, didn't he?

That's so cool! Now, can you make his leg twitch?

Well, folks, there's always a first time for everything!

Sterile, schmerile, the floor is pretty clean, right?

This patient already has some kids though?

Not to worry, I know it's sharp enough.

Damn! Page 47 of this procedure seems to be missing!

Where's my wedding ring?

hedgehogs

What do you get if you cross a hedgehog with a giraffe?
A very long hairbrush.

What did the porcupine say to the cactus?
'Is that you, Mummy?'

What do you get if you cross a hedgehog with an electrical fuse?
Barbed wire.

🐺 HERMITS

✳ Three hermits move into a cave together and for the first seven years they don't speak to each other. Then one morning a horse runs by the mouth of the cave. Seven years later the first hermit says, 'That was a pretty white horse that ran by.' Seven more years go by and the second hermit says, 'That horse wasn't white, he was black.' Yet another seven years go by and the third hermit starts packing his bags. The other two look at him and he says, 'If all you two are going to do is argue, then I'm leaving.'

✳ A guy joins a monastery and takes a vow of silence: he's allowed to say two words every seven years. After the first seven years, the elders bring him in and ask for his two words. 'Cold floors,' he says. They nod and send him away. Seven more years pass. They bring him back in and ask for his two words. He clears his throats and says, 'Bad food.' They nod and send him away. Seven more years pass. They bring him in for his two words. 'I quit,' he says. 'That's not surprising,' the elders say. 'You've done nothing but complain since you got here.'

✳ Did you hear about the hermit who was arrested for speeding? He was charged with recluse driving!

hiccups

What colour is a hiccup?
Burple.

Did you hear about the portrait painter who became a modern artist by accident?
His model had hiccups.

What is a volcano?
A mountain with hiccups!

hippies

What weights two tonnes and has flowers in its hair?
A hippie-potamus.

What's orange and looks good on a hippy?
Fire.

🐊 HiSTORy

✳ The Dark Ages was caused by the Y1K problem.

* Why did the Roman Coliseum have to close?
  The lions had eaten up all the prophets!

* If history is doomed to repeat itself, bring on the beheadings!

* How do we know Moses wore a wig?
  Because sometimes he was seen with Aaron and sometimes without.

* Why did the historians get together?
  To talk over old times.

* Where was the Declaration of Independence signed?
  At the bottom!

* The Spanish explorers went round the world in a galleon. How many galleons did they get to the mile?

* What cake wanted to rule the world?
  Attila the Bun!

* Did the Native Americans hunt bear?
  Not in the winter!

* Why did Julius Caesar buy crayons?
  He wanted to Mark Antony!

* What was the greatest accomplishment of the early Romans?
  Speaking Latin!

✳ What did they wear at the Boston Tea Party?
  T-shirts!

✳ Why did the Romans build straight roads?
  So their soldiers didn't go around the bend!

✳ What famous chiropodist ruled England?
  William the Corn-cutter!

✳ Which Elizabethan sailor could stop bikes?
  Sir Francis Brake!

✳ One thing you can say about Nelson, he didn't miss the boat.

✳ Where did Columbus stand when he first saw America?
  On his feet.

✳ How do we know that Joan of Arc was French?
  She was maid in France!

✳ Why did Henry VIII have so many wives?
  He liked to chop and change!

✳ What was the first thing Queen Elizabeth did on ascending to the throne?
  Sat down!

✳ What is the fruitiest lesson?
  History, because it's full of dates!

✳ How was the Roman Empire cut in half?
With a pair of Caesars!

✳ What did Noah do while spending time on the ark?
Fished, but he didn't catch much. He only had two worms!

✳ What did Caesar say to Cleopatra?
Toga-ether we can rule the world!

🐵 HOLES

✳ There were two men working for the council. One would dig a hole and the other would come behind him and fill the hole. These two men worked furiously; one digging a hole, the other filling it up again. A man was watching from the pavement and couldn't believe how hard these men were working, but couldn't understand what they were doing. Finally he had to ask them. He said to the hole digger, 'I appreciate how hard you work, but what are you doing? You dig a hole and your partner comes behind you and fills it up again!' The hole digger replied, 'Oh yeah, must look funny, but the guy who plants the trees is sick today.'

✳ What gets bigger and bigger as you take more away from it?
A hole!

✳ Who invented underground tunnels?
A mole!

✳ Did I tell you about the three holes in my backyard?
No? Well, well, well…

✺ HOLiDAYS

✳ Last time I went on holiday, I flew with BA. It was terrible. He kept shouting, 'You crazy fool, I ain't getting on no plane!'

✳ What is the best day to go to the beach?
Sunday, of course!

✳ Business is so bad at that hotel, they're stealing towels from the guests.

✳ The hotel was so dull I sent down for another Bible.

✳ **Innkeeper**: The room is £150 a night. It's £5 if you make your own bed.
Guest: I'll make my own bed.
Innkeeper: Good. I'll get you some nails and wood.

✳ What did the Scotsman say to the Michelin man?
Nice tan.

✳ They asked me if I had reservations. I said, 'What am I, an Indian?'

✳ We stayed at the Biltmore Hotel. It was built more like a stable.

✳ I've never taken a hotel towel, and I've got the silverware to prove it.

✳ A man and his wife check into a hotel. 'Carry your bag, sir?' asks the bellhop. 'No. Let her walk,' replies the man.

✳ A rich and spoiled young man walked into a travel agency. He asked the agent, 'How about suggestions on places to go?' The agent responded, 'How about Hawaii?' 'Nah, I go there a lot.' 'How about the Virgin Islands?' 'No, too hot this time of year.' 'Paris?' 'Nope, went there last year.' 'London?' she suggested, by now a little irritated. 'Nope, don't like the rain here, so why would I want to go there?' Finally, in exasperation, she spun a globe on her desk and said, 'You pick a spot and I'll get you there!' Looking over the spinning globe, the fellow finally said, 'Is this all you've got?'

✳ What washes up on very small beaches?
Microwaves!

✳ Summer holiday was over and the teacher asked Little Rodney about his family trip. 'We visited my grandmother in Llandudno in Wales.' The teacher asked, 'Good, can you tell the class how you spell that?' Little Rodney replied, 'My mistake. Actually, she lives in Bath.'

honeymoons

I went alone on our honeymoon. My wife had already seen the Niagara Falls.

I would have liked to have taken my wife along on our honeymoon, but she couldn't get the time off work.

HORSES/HORSE RIDING

* How do you hire a horse?
  Stand it on four bricks.

* What is the slowest racehorse in the world?
  A clotheshorse!

* Why didn't the Horses' Parliament ever pass any legislation?
  Because no matter what was proposed, they always voted 'neigh'.

* A champion jockey is about to enter an important race on a new horse. The horse's trainer meets him before the race and says, 'All you have to remember with this horse is that every time you approach a jump, you have to shout, "ALLLLEEE OOOP!" really loudly in the horse's ear. Providing you do that, you'll be fine.' The jockey thinks the trainer is mad but promises to shout the

command. The race begins and they approach the first hurdle. The jockey ignores the trainer's ridiculous advice and the horse crashes straight through the centre of the jump. They carry on and approach the second hurdle. The jockey, somewhat embarrassed, whispers 'Aleeee ooop' in the horse's ear. The same thing happens: the horse crashes straight through the centre of the jump. At the third hurdle, the jockey thinks, It's no good, I'll have to do it, and yells, 'ALLLEEE OOOP!' really loudly. Sure enough, the horse sails over the jump with no problems. This continues for the rest of the race, but due to the earlier problems the horse only finishes third. The trainer is fuming and asks the jockey what went wrong. The jockey replies, 'Nothing is wrong with me, it's this stupid horse. What is he, deaf or something?' The trainer replies, 'Deaf? DEAF? He's not deaf, he's BLIND!'

✸ I bet on a horse that did a mile in two minutes. But he didn't do so well out of the truck.

✸ The horse I bet on came in so late, he had to tiptoe into the barn not to wake the other horses.

✸ What did the horse say when it got to the end of its nosebag?
That's the last straw.

✸ Why couldn't the pony talk?
He was a little horse.

✸ 'More hay, Trigger?'
'No, thanks, Roy, I'm stuffed!'

✳ What kind of horse can swim underwater without coming up for air? A seahorse!

🐺 HOTELS

✳ A businessman had a tiring day on the road. He checked into a hotel and, because he was concerned that the dining room might close soon, left his luggage at the front desk and went immediately to eat. After a leisurely dinner, he reclaimed his luggage and realized that he had forgotten his room number. He went back to the desk and told the bellhop on duty, 'My name is Bob Smith. Could you please tell me what room I'm in?' 'Certainly,' said the clerk. 'You're in the lobby.'

✳ A man e-mailed a seaside hotel to ask its location. 'It's only a stone's throw away from the beach,' he was told. 'But how will I recognize it?' asked the man. Back came the reply: 'It's the one with all the broken windows.'

✳ A travelling salesman finds himself stranded in the tiniest town in the Australian outback. He knocks on the door of a little hotel. 'Sorry, we don't have a spare room,' says the manager, 'but you're welcome to share with a little red-headed schoolteacher, if that's OK.' 'Oh, that'll be great,' says the salesman, grinning from ear to ear. 'And don't worry, I'll be a real gentleman.' 'Just as well,' says the manager. 'So will the little red-headed schoolteacher.'

HOUSES AND HOUSE BUYING

* House buying hint: Don't get too big a garden if your wife tires easily. When selecting a lawnmower, buy one that will last your wife several years.

* Did you hear about the man who changed his address? It was a moving story.

* My cellar is so damp that when I put out a mousetrap I caught a herring.

* What did one wall say to the other wall? I'll meet you at the corner.

* 'I bought my parents a house. Unfortunately it was worse than the one they had before.' *Todd Barry*

* At our wedding we looked like a new house. She was freshly painted and I was plastered.

* Our new house is so far in the country that out postman posts us our mail.

* I live on a one-way dead-end street.

* 'Get out of here. This isn't your house!' 'That's OK, I'm not feeling myself tonight.'

✳ My next house will have no kitchen – just vending machines and a large trash can.

✳ What's the best way to kill a houseplant?
Hang it.

hunting

'Have you ever hunted bear?'
'No, but I've gone fishing in my shorts.'

He likes to hunt mules. He gets a big kick out of it.

How does a hunter like his eggs?
Poached.

iMPONDERABLES

* I have not yet begun to procrastinate.

* I got a fortune cookie once that said, 'You like Chinese food.'

* Before they invented drawing boards, what did they go back to?

* How can you tell when sour cream goes bad?

* If work is so terrific, how come they have to pay you to do it?

* If you steal a clean slate, does it go on your record?

* If matches are made in heaven, why do they cost 25p a box?

* If homosexuality is a disease, can I call into work 'gay'?

* If ignorance is bliss, why aren't more people happy?

* Even at a Mensa convention someone is the dumbest person in the room.

✳ If today is the first day of the rest of our lives, what was yesterday?

✳ I don't have a solution, but I do admire the problem.

✳ A day for firm decisions! Or is it?

✳ If you live in a crevice, have you found your niche in life?

✳ Is a sports fan an athletic supporter?

✳ Why does everything you sit on feel like underwear?

✳ What if there were no hypothetical questions?

✳ If someone says, 'I never forget a face,' how would he know?

✳ Do we make bombs better or worse?

✳ If a person told you they were a pathological liar, would you believe them?

🐾 iNFORMATiON TECHNOLOGy

✳ Computers are like air conditioners. They work fine until you start opening windows.

✳ Which way did the programmer go?
He went data way!

＊ What did the computer do at lunchtime?
Had a byte!

＊ HR manager to job candidate: 'I see you've had no computer training. Although that qualifies you for upper management, it means you're under-qualified for our entry level positions.'

＊ What do you get if you cross a computer with a herb?
A thyme machine.

＊ What do you get if you cross a computer and a policeman?
PC Plod.

＊ Why was the IT support worker bad-tempered?
Because he had a chip on his shoulder.

＊ Why did the boy mouse like the girl mouse?
They just seemed to click.

＊ I walked into the computer repair place with my broken Macintosh computer. I looked at the stack of them on the rack and said, 'What's that, Broke Mac Mountain?'

＊ C program run. C program crash. C programmer quit.

＊ Double your drive space. Delete Windows!

＊ What do computers do when they get hungry?
They eat chips!

* Pentiums melt in your PC, not in your hand.

* F u cn rd ths, u cn gt a gd jb n cmptr prgrmmng.

* Error, no keyboard. Press F1 to continue.

* Hit any user to continue.

* Bad command or file name. Bad, bad command! Sit! Stay! Staaaay!

* What is a cursor?
  Someone having computer problems.

* There are only two kinds of computer. The latest model, and the obsolete.

* Software isn't released, it's allowed to escape.

* Smash forehead on keyboard to continue...

* Enter any 11-digit prime number to continue...

* ASCII stupid question, get a stupid ANSI!

* When you get to the point where you really understand your computer, it's probably obsolete.

* Do files get embarrassed when they're unzipped?

✷ A man and his girlfriend encountered several problems while assembling a new computer system, so the man called the Help Desk. The man on the phone started to talk to him in computer jargon, which confused him even more. 'Sir,' the man politely said, 'please explain what I should do as if I were a four-year-old.' 'OK,' the computer technician replied. 'Son, could you please put your mummy on the phone?'

✷ A mechanical, electrical and a software engineer from Microsoft were driving through the desert when the car broke down. The mechanical engineer said, 'It seems to be a problem with the fuel injection system, why don't we pop the hood and I'll take a look at it.' To which the electrical engineer replied, 'No I think it's just a loose ground wire. I'll get out and take a look.' Then, the Microsoft engineer jumps in. 'No, no, no. If we just close up all the windows, get out, wait a few minutes, get back in, and then reopen the windows everything will work fine.'

✷ A printer consists of three main parts: the case, the jammed paper tray and the blinking red light.

✷ Daddy, why doesn't this magnet pick up this floppy disk?

✷ Earth is 98% full. Please delete anyone you can.

The internet

✷ A rather fat young girl had an accident and her mother accompanied her to the hospital. The nurse asked for her height and weight: 'Five foot eight, eight stone two pounds.' While the nurse pondered this information, her mother leaned over. 'Sweetheart,' she gently chided, 'this is not the internet.'

✳ How do insects communicate?
By bee mail.

✳ This website may not be idiot proof, but at least it's dimwit resistant.

✳ The web isn't better than sex, but sliced bread is in serious trouble.

✳ A life? Cool... Where can I download one of those?

✳ A man and wife were both in an internet business, but it was the husband who truly lived, ate and breathed computers. His wife finally realized how bad it was when one day she was scratching his back, and he said, 'No, not there. Scroll down a little.'

✳ What kind of doctor fixes broken websites?
A URLologist.

✳ Why did the Irishman give up internet shopping?
The trolley kept falling off the computer.

✳ Why did the lumberjack get nowhere with the internet?
He kept logging on and off.

✳ What goes 'choo choo choo' while online?
Thomas the search engine.

✳ What did the spider do on the computer?
Made a website!

✳ A child was watching his mother sift through and delete a long list of junk e-mails on the computer screen. 'This reminds me of the Lord's Prayer,' the child said. 'What do you mean?' the mother asked. 'You know. That part about "deliver us from e-mail".'

✳ A man's kids loved surfing the web, and they kept track of their passwords by writing them on Post-it notes. He noticed their main password was 'MickeyMinnieGoofyPluto,' and so he asked why it was so long. 'Because,' his son explained, 'they say it has to have at least four characters.'

Viruses

✳ Prozac Virus: Messes up your RAM but your processor doesn't care.

✳ Viagra Virus: Expands your hard drive, while putting too much pressure on your zip drive.

✳ Airline Virus: You're in London, but your data is in Singapore.

✳ Private Health Care Virus: Tests your system for a day, finds nothing wrong, and sends you a bill for £4,500.

✳ Disney Virus: Everything in the computer goes Goofy.

✳ Ellen Degeneres Virus: Your IBM suddenly claims it's a MAC.

Computer haiku

* *Your file was so big.*
  It might be very useful.
  But now it is gone.

* *The website you seek*
  Cannot be located, but
  Countless more exist.

* *Chaos reigns within.*
  Reflect, repent, and restart.
  Order shall return.

* *With searching comes loss*
  And the presence of absence:
  'My Novel' not found.

* *A crash reduces*
  Your expensive computer
  To a simple stone.

* *Having been erased,*
  The document you're seeking
  Must now be retyped.

* *You step in the stream,*
  But the water has moved on.
  This page is not here.

Ways to tell if a yokel has been working on your computer

✳ The monitor is up on blocks.

✳ Outgoing e-mails have tobacco stains on them.

✳ The six front keys have rotted out.

✳ The extra RAM slots have tractor parts stored in them.

✳ The numeric keypad only goes up to six.

✳ The password is 'Jethro'.

✳ There's a turnip mounted on the CPU.

✳ There's a cider can in the CD-ROM drive.

✳ The keyboard is painted in camouflage.

✳ The mouse is referred to as a 'little bugger'.

insurance

An insurance salesman was trying to persuade a housewife that she should take out life insurance. 'Suppose your husband were to die,' he said. 'What would you get?' The housewife thought for a while, and then said, 'Oh, a parrot, I think. Then the house wouldn't seem so quiet.'

🦟 iNSULTS

※ 'You remind me of the sea.'
'Why, because I'm wild and romantic?'
'No, you make me sick.'

※ It's been lovely, but I have to scream now.

※ Thank you for not annoying me more than you do.

※ Support your local Search and Rescue unit. Get lost.

※ How do you keep an idiot in suspense?
I'll tell you later.

※ I don't know what your problem is, but I bet it's hard to pronounce.

※ It's OK to let your mind go blank; but please turn off the sound.

※ She has a soft heart, and a head to match.

※ Have you been to the zoo? As a visitor, I mean.

※ Don't be humble; you're not that great.

※ Is that your face or are you breaking it in for a baboon?

※ She was as pretty as a picture, but the frame was a mess.

* The last time I saw a face like yours, I threw it a fish.

* Whenever it rains I think of him. Drip… Drip… Drip…

* I like the way you dress. Who wears your clean clothes?

* Most people aren't as deep as my toilet bowl.

* When she told me I was average, she was just being mean.

* He was hairier than Chewbacca dipped in Regaine.

* The problem with the gene pool is that there is no lifeguard.

* The gene pool could use a little chlorine.

* If I want your opinion, I'll ask you to fill out the necessary forms.

* The last thing I want to do is insult you. But it IS on the list.

* If you can't be kind, at least have the decency to be vague.

* Those of you who think you know everything are very annoying to those of us who do.

* You may pretend to dislike me, but deep down, you know you hate me.

* Wait… I'm trying to imagine you with a personality.

✳ I'm sorry, do I resemble your therapist?

✳ If brains were dynamite you wouldn't have enough to blow your nose.

✳ When all else fails, admit I'm right and kiss my ass.

✳ She's so ugly, she fell out of the ugly tree and hit every branch on the way down.

✳ 100,000 sperm and you were the fastest?

✳ She's so wrinkled, her mother was a Shar Pei.

✳ Does your face hurt, because it's killing me!

✳ He's so dumb, he sits on the TV and watches the sofa.

✳ You're so ugly, when you go into the bank they turn off the surveillance cameras.

✳ Those people are so dumb, one of 'em was killed in a pie-eating contest when the cow sat on him.

✳ Never miss a good chance to shut up.

✳ In a battle of wits, she's unarmed.

✳ The oven's on, but nothing's cooking.

✳ He's a little too tall for his blood supply.

✳ When I think of all the people I respect the most, you're right there, serving them drinks.

✳ I haven't been ignoring you; I've been prioritizing you.

✳ Since my last report, he has reached rock bottom and has started to dig.

✳ I'm not saying she was dirty, but I thought she was wearing black gloves until she washed her hands.

✳ No, those trousers don't make you look fatter. I mean, how could they?

✳ He's a few clowns short of a circus.

✳ She's a few fries short of a Happy Meal.

✳ The wheel's spinning, but his hamster's dead.

✳ Give a jackass an education and you get a smartass.

✳ He's all foam and no beer.

✳ He couldn't pour water out of a boot with instructions on the heel.

✳ He has an intellect rivalled only by garden tools.

✳ She's as clever as bait.

✳ He doesn't have all his dogs on one leash.

✳ He forgot to pay his brain bill.

✳ Never worry about being a little behind; worry about being a big one.

✳ She's proof that evolution CAN go in reverse.

✳ This employee is really not so much of a has-been, but more of a definite won't be.

✳ She sets low personal standards and then consistently fails to achieve them.

✳ This employee should go far – and the sooner he starts, the better.

✳ I love you more today than tomorrow.

✳ She's got a photographic memory but with the lens cover glued on.

✳ He's as bright as Alaska in December.

✳ Single-celled organisms outscore him in IQ tests.

✳ He donated his brain to science before he was done using it.

✳ He fell out of the family tree.

* Some drink from the fountain of knowledge; he only gargled.

* Takes him one and a half hours to watch 60 minutes.

* He's been working with glue too much.

* He brings a lot of joy whenever he leaves the room.

* When his IQ reaches 50, he should sell.

* If you see two people talking and one looks bored, he's the other one.

* He's an experiment in Artificial Stupidity.

* He was born during low tide in the gene pool.

* He can't find his ass with two hands and a periscope.

* She's deaf, dumb and blonde.

* His deck has no picture cards.

* He doesn't have his belt through all the loops.

* His jogging trail doesn't go all the way around the lake.

* Bureaucrats cut red tape. Lengthways.

✳ There's only one problem with her face. It shows.

✳ Some girls have dishpan hands. She has a dishpan face.

✳ If his face is his fortune, he'll never have to pay tax.

✳ The only way she can get colour in her face is to stick her tongue out.

✳ Is that your real face, or are you wearing a gas mask?

✳ She has a good head on her shoulders, although it would look better on her neck.

✳ She has a heart of gold; hard and yellow.

✳ She's so stupid she can't spell Anna backwards.

✳ What's the difference between a hedgehog and a Range Rover? The pricks are on the inside in a Range Rover.

✳ A baby-sitter is a teenager acting like an adult while the adults are out acting like teenagers.

✳ When I want your opinion, I'll remove the duct tape.

✳ I'm not saying they're ugly; the pictures in their family album are fine. It's just that they forgot to put the jokes under them.

✳ She swears she's never been kissed. You can't blame her for swearing.

✳ She was so stupid she'd look for a wishbone in a boiled egg.

🐵 iNVENTiONS

Invented by a blonde

1) The water-proof towel

2) Solar-powered flashlight

3) Submarine screen door

4) A book on how to read

5) Inflatable dart board

6) A dictionary index

7) Ejector seat in a helicopter

8) Powdered water

9) Pedal-powered wheelchair

10) Waterproof tea bag

11) Glow-in-the-dark sunglasses

12) Wooden soap

✳ What happened when the wheel was invented?
It caused a revolution!

✳ Humans were invented by water, for transporting it uphill.

✳ What did the little light bulb say to its mum?
'I wuv you watts and watts.'

✳ What happens if you plug an electric blanket into a toaster?
You keep popping up all night.

🐵 JOKES

✳ Old jokes never die. They just sound that way.

✳ The world's oldest joke: When Eve asked Adam, 'Do you love me?' and he replied, 'Who else?'

✳ He who laughs last probably planned to tell the same joke himself a bit later.

✳ Did you hear the joke about the roof?
Never mind, it's over your head!

✳ I'm thankful for laughter, except when milk comes out my nose.

✳ What's a sick joke?
Something you shouldn't bring up in private conversation.

✳ Going to comedian school was easy. All the lessons were a joke.

✳ Want to hear two short jokes and a long joke?
Joke. Joke. Joooooooooooooooooooooookkkkkkkkkkkkkkkkke.

🐨 KANGAROOS

⁂ Did you hear about the exhausted kangaroo?
He was out of bounds.

⁂ What do you get if you cross a sheep and a kangaroo?
A woolly jumper!

⁂ A kangaroo kept getting out of his enclosure at the zoo. After recapturing the kangaroo, the zookeeper put up a ten-foot fence. Again the kangaroo was out the next morning, roaming around the zoo. So the fence was extended to twenty feet. But again the kangaroo was out the next morning. Frustrated zoo officials built a fence forty feet high.

A camel in the next enclosure asked the kangaroo, 'How much higher do you think they'll go?' The kangaroo said, 'About a thousand feet, I guess – unless somebody starts locking the gate!'

⁂ Why didn't the kangaroo mother want her baby to watch too much TV?
Because she didn't want her to become a pouch potato.

kites

What is the best material for kites?
Fly paper.

KNiGHTS

✴ Why did the knight run about shouting for a tin opener?
He had a bee in his suit of armour!

✴ What was Camelot?
A place where people parked their camels!

✴ What was Camelot famous for?
Its knight life!

✴ What was King Arthur's favourite game?
Knights and crosses!

✴ Why did King Arthur have a round table?
So no one could corner him!

✴ Who invented King Arthur's round table?
Sir Cumference!

✳ Where did knights learn to kill dragons?
At knight school!

✳ Which knight drools a lot?
Sir Liver.

✳ Which knight makes pottery?
Sir Amic.

✳ When a knight in armour was killed in battle, what sign did they put on his grave?
Rust in peace!

✳ What English king invented the fireplace?
Alfred the Grate!

✳ When were King Arthur's army too tired to fight?
When they had lots of sleepless knights!

✳ Have you heard about the cowardly dragon that didn't observe the Sabbath?
He only preyed on weak knights.

🐶 KNOCK, KNOCK

✳ Who's there? A little old lady. A little old lady who? I didn't know you could yodel.

✳ Who's there? Woo. Woo hoo? No need to get carried away, it's just a joke.

✳ Who's there? Euripides. Euripides who? Euripides dese trousers, you pay for dese trousers.

✳ Who's there? Dwayne. Dwayne who? Dwayne de bath, I'm dwowning.

✳ Who's there? Wendy. Wendy who? Wendy wed wed wobin comes bob bob bobbin' along...

✳ Who's there? Graham Elliot. Graham Elliot who? How soon we forget!

✳ Who's there? The Gestapo. The Gestapo who? Ve ask ze questions, schwein.

🦁 KNOCK, KNOCK... IT'S CHRISTMAS

✳ Who's there? Wenceslas. Wenceslas who? Wenceslas train home?

✳ Who's there? Snow. Snow who? Snow business like show business!

✳ Who's there? Wayne. Wayne who? Wayne in a manger.

✳ Who's there? Doughnut. Doughnut who? Doughnut open till Christmas!

✳ Who's there? Oakham. Oakham who? Oakham all ye faithful...

✳ Who's there? Avery. Avery who? Avery merry Christmas!

✳ Who's there? Holly. Holly who? Holly-days are here again!

✳ Who's there? Rudolph. Rudolph who? Money is the Rudolph of all evil!

✳ Who's there? Igloo. Igloo who? Igloo knew Suzie like I knew Suzie...

✳ Who's there? Mary. Mary who? Mary Christmas!

🗣 LANGUAGE

✴ Silence is evidence of superb language skills.

✴ A woman goes into labour and yells, 'Shouldn't! Wouldn't! Couldn't! Can't!' She was having contractions.

✴ Man invented language to satisfy his deep need to complain.

✴ This sentence contradicts itself – no, actually it doesn't.

✴ Why is it against the law to whisper?
Because it isn't aloud.

✴ I speak eight languages. Unfortunately, all at the same time.

✴ What did the linguist wear to the beach?
A dipthong.

✴ A Swiss guy visiting Sydney, Australia, pulls up at a bus stop where two locals are waiting. '*Entschuldigung, koennen Sie Deutsch sprechen?'* he asks. The two Aussies just stare at him. *''Excusez-moi, parlez vous Francais?'* he tries. The two continue to stare. *'Parlare Italiano?'* No response. *'Hablan ustedes Espanol?'* Still nothing. The Swiss guy drives off, disgusted. The first Aussie turns to the second and says, 'Y'know, maybe we should learn a foreign language.' 'Why?' says the other. 'That guy knew four languages, and it didn't do him any good.'

🐺 LAWYERS

✳ Out of courtesy, sharks never attack lawyers.

✳ A man rings up his lawyer and says, 'How much would you charge to answer three questions?' The lawyer thinks for a moment, and says, 'Two thousand pounds, plus VAT.'

  'TWO THOUSAND!' cries the man. 'That's a bit expensive, isn't it?'

  'Yes, I suppose it is,' says the lawyer, after thinking for a moment longer. 'What's your third question?'

✳ What's the difference between a lawyer and a mosquito?
A mosquito drops off you when you die!

✳ Two small boys met during their first day at school. 'My name is Billy. What's yours?' asked the first boy. 'Tommy,' replied the second. 'My daddy's an accountant. What does your daddy do for a living?' asked Billy. Tommy replied, 'My daddy's a lawyer.' 'Honest?' asked Billy. 'No, just the normal kind,' replied Tommy.

✳ What do you get when you cross a godfather with a lawyer?
An offer you can't understand.

✳ A jury consists of twelve people chosen to decide who has the best lawyer.

✳ A lawyer is standing in a long line at the post office. Suddenly, he feels a pair of hands kneading his shoulders, back, and neck. The lawyer turns around. 'What the hell do you think you're doing?' 'I'm a chiropractor,' says the man. 'I'm just keeping in practice while I'm waiting in line.' 'Well, I'm a lawyer, but you don't see me pickpocketing the guy in front of me.'

✳ When you ask a housewife, accountant, and lawyer what two plus two is, what do they give you? The housewife says, 'Four.' The accountant says, 'It's either three or four, let me run it through my spreadsheet again.' The lawyer closes the shutters, turns down the lights, and whispers, 'What do you want it to be?'

✳ What do lawyers wear to court?
Lawsuits!

✳ Someone mistakenly leaves the cages open in the reptile house at the local zoo. Visitors are ushered out and the zoo is closed as snakes slither all over the place. Frantically, the keeper tries everything, but no matter what he tries, he can't get them back in their cages. Finally he turns to his aide and says, 'I had hoped it would not come to this, but desperate times call for desperate measures. Run to the office and call a lawyer!' 'A lawyer? Why?' 'We need someone who speaks their language!'

✳ A man was chosen for jury service but he very much wanted to avoid it. He tried every excuse he could think of but none of them worked. On the day of the trial he decided to give it one more shot. As the trial was about to begin he asked if he could approach the bench. 'Your Honour,' he said, 'I must be excused from this trial because I am prejudiced against the defendant. I took one look at the man in the blue suit with those beady eyes and that dishonest face and I said, "He's a crook! He's guilty, guilty, guilty." So, Your Honour, I could not possibly stay on this jury!' The judge replied, 'Get back in the jury box. You are just the kind of juror we are looking for – a good judge of character. That man is his lawyer.'

✳ A big-city lawyer was representing the railroad in a lawsuit filed by an old rancher. The rancher's prize bull was missing from the section through which the railroad passed. The rancher only wanted to be paid the fair value of the bull. The case was scheduled to be tried before the justice of the peace in the back room of the general store. The attorney for the railroad immediately cornered the rancher and tried to get him to settle out of court. The lawyer did his best selling job, and finally the rancher agreed to take half of what he was asking. After the rancher had signed the release and took the check, the young lawyer couldn't resist gloating a little over his success, telling the rancher, 'You know, I hate to tell you this, old man, but I put one over on you in there. I couldn't have won the case. The engineer was asleep and the fireman was in the caboose when the train went through your ranch that morning. I didn't have one witness to put on the stand. I bluffed you!' The old rancher replied, 'Well, I'll tell you, young feller, I was a little worried about winning that case myself, because that bull came home this morning.'

✴ Why do bankruptcy lawyers expect to be paid?

✴ A teacher stood before his class and posed the following problem: 'A wealthy man dies leaving an estate worth ten million pounds. One-third is to go to his wife, one-fifth is to go to his son, one-sixth to his butler, one-eighth to his secretary, and the rest to charity. 'Now, what does each get?' After a very long silence in the classroom, a hand was raised.

The teacher called on the student. 'A good lawyer?'

✴ A snotty Ivy League New York lawyer always felt it his duty to correct the language of those around him. In line at an airline counter in Texas, an unintelligible rush of language, dialect and other jargon confronted him. Thoroughly confused, he didn't know where to start the inevitable criticism. Finally, in exasperation, he observed, 'I do wish you Southerners would speak English.' 'We do,' replied the young woman behind the counter. 'Well, it's not the King's English,' he protested. 'Sure it is,' the woman responded. 'Elvis was a Southerner.'

laziness

Just for today, I will not sit in my living room all day watching TV. Instead I will move my TV into the bedroom.

Why are tall people more lazy?
Because they lie longer in bed.

Why did the lazy man want a job in a bakery?
So he could loaf around!

My dog is so lazy that he waits for another dog to bark then opens his mouth.

LETTERS

* How many letters are in the alphabet? Only 24, since ET went home.

* What one word has the most letters in it?
  Alphabet.

* Today, I wrote three letters: A, H, and X.

* A nursery teacher asks a boy to recite the alphabet. The boy replies: 'A B C D E F G H I J K L M N O Q R S T U V W X Y and Z.' The teacher asks: 'Where's the P?' The boy says: 'Running down my leg.'

* Have you ever seen a duchess?
  Yes, it's the same as an English 'S'!

* Why is the letter 'G' scary?
  It turns a host into a ghost.

✳ I met the bloke who invented crosswords today. I can't remember his name, it's P something T something R.

✳ How did the Vikings send secret messages?
By norse code!

libraries

What building has the most stories?
The library.

LiFE

✳ Life is an open door. It can be closed at any time, so don't complain about the draught.

✳ Life's a bitch, and then you're reincarnated.

✳ You WILL be a winner today. Pick a fight with a four-year-old.

✳ If I had my whole life to live over again, I don't think I'd have the strength.

✳ If life hands you lemons, break out the tequila!

✳ Life is a car wash … and I'm on a bicycle.

🦁 LiGHT BULBS

✳ How many feminists does it take to change a light bulb?
That's not funny.

✳ How many Zen Buddhists does it take to change a light bulb?
Three – one to change it, one to not change it, and one to neither change nor not change the light bulb.

✳ How many mystery writers does it take to change a light bulb?
Two – one to screw it in, and one to give it a good twist at the end.

✳ How many druids does it take to change a light bulb?
Sixteen. One to change the light bulb, and fifteen to realign the stones.

✳ How many Amish does it take to change a light bulb?
What is a light bulb?

✳ How many computer programmers does it take to change a light bulb?
Please… Replacing low-cost units designed primarily to emit photons in the visible electromagnetic spectrum is easy.

✳ How many drummers does it take to change a light bulb?
One, as long as a roadie puts up a ladder, climbs it and puts the light in the socket first.

✳ How many sociologists does it take to change a light bulb?
None, but it takes fifteen to write a paper entitled 'Coping with Darkness'.

✳ How many cockroaches does it take to screw on a light bulb?
Can't tell. As soon as the light comes on, they scatter!

✳ How many psychiatrists does it take to change a light bulb?
How long have you been having this 'light bulb' fantasy?

✳ How many psychoanalysts does it take to change a light bulb?
How many do you think it takes?

✳ How many male chauvinists does it take to change a light bulb?
None, she can cook in the dark.

✳ How many roadies does it take to change a light bulb?
One. One two. One two. Two.

✳ I have to admit it, Smith had offered a brilliant proposal to resolve our troublesome problem. He suggested we form three committees, one to study the problem directly, one to study how other companies had resolved similar problems, and a third to oversee the first two and coordinate their efforts into a workable solution. The plan worked flawlessly and we assigned the janitor to change the light bulb.

✸ How many folk musicians does it take to change a light bulb?
Four. One to change it, and three to complain it's gone electric.

✸ How many mathematicians does it take to screw in a light bulb?
Approximately 1.000000000000000000000000.

✸ How many health and safety officers does it take to screw in a light bulb?
Four. Two to hold the ladder, one to screw in the bulb, and one to observe correct procedure is being followed.

✸ How many visitors to a gallery does it take to change a light bulb?
Two. One to do it, and the other one to say, 'My four-year-old could gave done that.'

✸ How many pimps does it take to change a light bulb?
Two. One to hold the bulb, and the other to drive the pink Cadillac round in circles.

✸ How many science-fiction writers does it take to change a light bulb?
Two, but it's actually the same person doing it. He went back in time and met himself in a doorway then sat on his own shoulders so he could reach it.

✸ How many televangelists does it take to change a light bulb?
One. But for the message of light to continue to shine, send in your donation today.

✳ How many ADD kids does it take to change a light bulb?
Let's throw stones at that dog.

✳ How many actors does it take to change a light bulb?
Ten. One to change the light bulb and nine to say it should be me up there.

✳ 'How many members of U2 does it take to change a light bulb?
Just Bono… He holds it and the world revolves around him.'
Al Pitcher

✳ Two men working in a factory were talking. 'I know how to get some time off,' said one. 'How are you going to do that?' 'Watch,' he said, and climbed up onto a rafter. When the foreman arrived and asked what he was doing up there, the man replied, 'I'm a light bulb.' 'I think you need some time off,' the foreman said, and the first man walked out of the factory. After a moment, the second man followed him. 'Where do you think you're going?' the foreman shouted. 'Well, I sure can't work in the dark!' he replied.

🐶 LIMERICKS

✳ *There was an old man of Darjeeling*
Who boarded a bus bound for Ealing
It said on the door
'Don't spit on the floor'
So he stood up and spat on the ceiling

✳ On the breast of a barmaid named Gail,
   Were tattooed the prices of ale
   And on her behind
   For the sake of the blind
   Was the same, but written in Braille

✳ There once was a man from Nantucket
   Who kept all of his cash in a bucket
   But his daughter, named Nan
   Ran away with a man
   And as for the bucket, Nantucket

✳ There was a young man who said, 'Why
   Can't I look in my ear with my eye?
   I think that I might
   If I stretch very tight
   You never can tell 'til you try!

✳ A fellow who lived in New Guinea
   Was known as a silly young ninny
   He utterly lacked
   Good judgement and tact
   For he told a plump girl she was skinny

✳ There was a young woman named Bright
   Whose speed was much faster than light
   She set out one day
   In a relative way
   And returned on the previous night

✳ An epicure dining at Crewe
   Found a very large bug in his stew
   Said the waiter, 'Don't shout
   And wave it about
   Or the rest will be wanting one too'

✳ There once was a lady, Irene
   Who lived on distilled kerosene
   But she started absorbin'
   A new hydrocarbon
   And since then she's never benzene

✳ There was a young lady one fall
   Who wore a newspaper dress to a ball
   The dress caught fire
   And burned her entire
   Front page, sporting section and all

✳ There was a young lady from Niger
   Who smiled as she rode on a tiger
   After the ride
   She was inside
   And the smile was on the face of the tiger

✳ There once was a poet named Dan
   Whose poetry never would scan
   When told this was so
   He said, 'Yes, I know,
   It's because I try to put every possible syllable into the very last line
     that I can!

✳ *There was an old lady from Clyde*
Who ate forty apples and died
The apples fermented
Inside the lamented
And made cider inside her insides

✳ *There once was a lady named Lynn*
Who was so uncommonly thin
That when she assayed
To drink lemonade
She slipped through the straw and fell in!

✳ *A wonderful bird is the pelican*
His beak can hold more than his belly can
He can hold in his beak
Enough food for a week
But I'll be darned if I know how the hellican

✳ *There once was a fellow named Jim*
Who took his girl out for a spin
The speedometer rose
The gas pedal froze
They found parts of her but not him

✳ *There was a young man from the Clyde*
Who fell down a sewer and died
Along came his brother
Who fell down another
And now they're interred side by side

✳ *I met a man once named Job*
Who made an earring from a glob
Now, isn't that queer?
A glob on his ear?
He now has a twenty-foot lob

✳ *There once was a man named Clegm*
Who had a great deal of phlegm
Ahegm, ahegm,
Ahegm, ahegm,
Ahegm, ahegm, ahegm

✳ *There once was a lady from Spain*
Who was sick as she rode on a train
Not once, but again
and again and again
and again and again and again

✳ *There was a young fellow of Leeds*
Who swallowed six packets of seeds
In a month, silly ass
He was covered with grass
And he couldn't sit down for the weeds

✳ *There once was a woman from Crete*
Who was so exceedingly neat
When she got out of bed
She stood on her head
To keep from soiling her feet

✳ *There was a young man who said God*
Must think it exceedingly odd
If he finds that this tree
Continues to be
When there's no one about in the Quad

✳ *Dear Sir*
Your astonishment's odd:
I am always about in the Quad
And that's why the tree
Will continue to be
Since observed by
Yours Faithfully
GOD

✳ *A senora who strolled on the Corso*
Displayed quite a lot of her torso
A crowd soon collected
And no one objected
Though some were in favour of more so

✳ *A flatulent actor named Barton*
Led a life exceedingly spartan
Til a playwright one day
Wrote a well-received play
With a part for Barton to fart in

✳ *There once was an old man of Esser*
Whose knowledge grew lesser and lesser
It at last grew so small
He knew nothing at all
And now he's a college professor

✳ *There was a young man from Marseilles*
Who lived on fruit juice and snails
When he couldn't afford these
He lived on the cheese
He scraped from his toes with his nails

✳ *There once was a lady from Devizes*
Who had breasts of two different sizes
One was rather small
And round like a ball
And the other was big and won prizes

✳ *There once was a man from Calcutta*
Who coated his tonsils with buttah
Reducing his snore
From a thunderous roar
To a soft, oleaginous muttah

✳ *I knew an old lady, Miss Tripp*
Whose nose had a permanent drip
One day I watched her at length
While a drip gathered strength
And fell, plop, on her fat bottom lip

✳ A psychiatrist fellow from Rye
Went to visit another close by
Who said, with a grin
As he welcomed him in
'Hello, Smith! You're all right! How am I?'

✳ There was a teacher from Calcutta
Who had a severe type of stutta
When he tried to give a talk
People attending would baulk
So he delivered his speech in a mutta

✳ A limerick packs laughs anatomical
Into space that is quite economical
The good ones I've seen
So seldom are clean
And the clean ones so seldom are comical

✳ There once was a girl from Great Britain
Who carelessly sat on her kitten
Imagine her surprise
And the look in her eyes
When on the behind she was bitten

✳ There was a young curate from Kew
Who kept a tom cat in a pew
And taught it to speak
Alphabetical Greek
But it never got further than 'μ'

✴ *There was an old man from Peru*
Who dreamed he was eating his shoe
He awoke through the night
With a terrible fright
And found it was perfectly true

✴ *There once was a man from the sticks*
Who liked to compose limericks
But he gave up the sport
Cos he wrote 'em too short

🐱 LiONS/FEROCiOUS CATS

✴ Who went into the lion's den and came out alive?
The lion.

✴ What flies around your light at night and can bite off your head?
A tiger moth!

✴ What is Tarzan's favourite Johnny Cash song?
I Walk The Lion.

✴ A man went to work for a zoo vet. 'Look in the lion's mouth,' the vet told him. 'How do I do that?' he asked. 'Carefully,' replied the vet.

✳ What does a lion brush his mane with?
A catacomb!

✳ What do you get if you cross a dog and a cheetah?
A dog that chases cars and catches them!

✳ A small puppy named August got into a fight with a lion. The next day was the first of September. Why?
Because that was the last of August.

✳ What's the difference between a lion and a thunderstorm and a lion with toothache?
One pours with rain, the other roars with pain.

✳ The lions were so fierce that when the tamer went in the cage with a chair he didn't get a chance to sit down.

✳ In the park this morning I was surrounded by lions! Lions? In the park? Well, dandelions!

✳ What happened when the slave put his head into a lion's mouth to count how many teeth he had?
The lion closed its mouth to see how many heads the slave had!

✳ What is a lion's favourite food?
Baked beings!

love

It was love at first sight. Then I had a second look.

He loved her so much he worshipped the ground her father struck oil on.

In the dark I hold your hand, because in the light you look like a man.

If love is blind, how can we believe in love at first sight?

She was only a bootlegger's daughter, but I loved her still!

When two egotists meet, it's an I for an I.

LUCK

✳ He was so unlucky, his swimming pool burned down.

✳ Bad luck: Being shipwrecked on a desert island with your own wife.

✳ His troubles were down to three things: women, money and both.

✳ Any time things appear to be going better, you have overlooked something.

✳ Anybody can win, unless there happens to be a second entry.

✳ Anything you lose automatically doubles in value.

✳ The chance of a piece of bread falling the buttered side down is directly proportional to the cost of the carpet.

✳ If Fortune had a daughter, what would her name be? Misfortune.

It's a bad day when...

✳ You've been at work three hours before you notice that your fly is open.

✳ Your twin forgets your birthday.

✳ Your blind date turns out to be your ex-wife.

✳ It costs more to fill up your car than it did to buy it.

✳ The bird singing outside your window is a vulture.

✳ Your mother approves of the girl you are dating.

✳ That interesting new person you are chatting with online turns out to be your ex.

✱ Nothing you own is actually paid for.

✱ Everyone loves your driver's licence picture.

✱ You invite the peeping Tom in ... and he says no.

MADNESS

✷ A guy's walking past an asylum, and can hear all the inmates inside screaming at the top of their lungs. 'Thirteen! Thirteen! Thirteen!' He peeks through a hole in the fence to see what all the commotion is about, and a finger suddenly pops out and jabs him in the eye. He yells in pain, and the inmates all start gleefully shouting, 'Fourteen! Fourteen! Fourteen!'

✷ A wild-looking man dressed in a Napoleonic costume and holding his hand inside his coat entered the psychiatrist's office and nervously announced, 'Doctor, I need your help right away.' 'I can see that,' replied the doctor. 'Please lie down on the couch and tell me your problem.' 'I don't have any problem,' the man snapped. 'In fact, I am the Emperor of France. I have everything I could possibly want. But I'm afraid my wife, Josephine, is in deep mental trouble.' 'I see,' said the psychiatrist, humouring the man. 'And what seems to be her problem?' 'For some strange reason she thinks she's Mrs Smith.'

✷ I sometimes go to my own little world, but that's OK, they know me there.

✳ Don't give up. Moses was once a basket case.

✳ I used to be indecisive; now I'm not so sure.

✳ I've got a mind like a … a … what's that thing called?

✳ Did you hear about the guy who was diagnosed as psychoceramic?
He was a real crackpot.

✳ How do crazy people go through the forest?
They take the psycho path.

✳ Of course I'm out of my mind! It's dark and scary there!

✳ One by one, the penguins steal my sanity.

✳ Last night I was having dinner with Charles Manson, and in the middle
of dinner he turned to me and said, 'Is it hot in here, or am I crazy?'

✳ Did you hear about the man who worked in the lunatic asylum?
People were crazy about him.

✳ I'm not crazy, I've just been in a very bad mood for 30 years.

✳ Allow me to introduce my selves.

✳ Honesty is the best policy, but insanity is a better defence.

✳ In some cultures what I do would be considered normal.

✳ When is your mind like a used bed?
When it isn't made up.

✳ Never get into an argument with a schizophrenic and say 'Who do you think you are?'

✳ The voices in my head may not be real, but they have some good ideas!

✳ What steps would you take if a madman came rushing at you with a knife?
Great big ones!

✳ 'This morning my dad gave me soap flakes instead of corn flakes for breakfast.' 'I bet you were mad.' 'Mad? I was foaming at the mouth!'

✳ I can't remember if I'm the good twin or the evil one.

✳ When I say I'm telekinetic somehow everyone moves away.

✳ There isn't enough insanity to spread to my other half.

✳ I may be schizophrenic but at least I have each other.

✳ Sanity is a state of mind ... but the prices were so high I had to move away.

✳ Some people are on the edge. Some people are over it. I'm hang-gliding.

✳ Don't trust reality. After all, it's only a collective hunch.

✳ A man goes to his doctor. 'If I see someone riding a bike when I'm walking down the street, I get this terrible urge to throw myself under the wheels. Have you ever heard of such a thing?' The doctor thinks for a moment, then says, 'Yes, I have heard of one other case. You are what we call a cycle path.'

✳ Of all the things I've lost, I miss my mind the most.

✳ I hope I can settle my internal conflicts without bloodshed.

✳ I'm not myself today. Maybe I'm you.

✳ I'm trying to find myself. If I should return before I get back, please ask me to wait.

🐶 MAIL

✳ What letters are not in the alphabet?
The ones in the post, of course!

✳ The two most beautiful words in the English language are 'cheque enclosed'.

✳ What starts with a P, ends with an E, and has a million letters in it?
Post Office!

✳ What did the stamp say to the envelope?
Stick with me and we'll go places!

✳ What does an envelope say when you lick it?
Nothing. It just shuts up.

✳ Did you hear that Fed Ex and UPS are going to merge? They're going to call it FED UP!

✳ After trying a new soup for the first time, a man wrote an enthusiastic letter of approval to the manufacturer. Several weeks later he came home from work to a large box in the middle of the floor. Inside were free samples of the many products the company produced: biscuits, drinks, snacks and fancy foods. 'Well, what do you think?' his wife asked, smiling. 'Next time,' he replied, 'I'm writing to Ford!'

✳ When is an envelope like a snooty person?
When it's stuck up.

✿ MARRIAGE

✳ Six stages of married life:
  1: Tri-weekly.
  2: Try weekly.
  3: Try weakly.
  4: Try oysters.
  5: Try anything.
  6: Try to remember.

✳ Marriage is very much like a violin; after the sweet music is over, the strings are attached.

✳ A marriage certificate is just another word for a work permit.

✳ They say when a man holds a woman's hand before marriage, it is love; after marriage, it is self-defence.

✳ There was this lover who said that he would go through hell for her. They got married, and now he is going through hell.

✳ A spouse is someone who'll stand by you through all the trouble you wouldn't have had if you'd stayed single.

✳ I love being married. It's so great to find that one special person you want to annoy for the rest of your life.

✳ Real men wear pink. Why? Because their wives make them.

✳ Did you know my wife went to a self-help group for compulsive talkers? It's called On and On Anon.

✳ In the first year of marriage, the man speaks and the woman listens. In the second year, the woman speaks and the man listens. In the third year, they both speak and the neighbours listen.

✳ Shotgun wedding: A case of wife or death.

✷ Upset over a newly-wed squabble with her husband, a girl went to her mother to complain. Trying to console her, her father said that men are not all like this all the time. 'Nonsense,' she said. 'Men are good for only one thing!' 'Yes,' her mother interjected, 'but how often do you have to parallel park?'

✷ A man seeks a doctor's advice because the 'thrill' was gone from his marriage. The doctor tells him that exercise will build up his stamina and suggests that he jog ten miles a day for 30 days. The man does this, calls the doctor, thanks him for the advice, noting that he feels great. The doctor asks how his love life is. The man replies: 'How the heck would I know? I'm 300 miles from home.'

✷ Newly-weds were talking on the morning after their wedding night. 'Be honest, now, baby. How am I as a lover?' the husband coyly asked. She replied, 'I would definitely say that you're warm.' 'Really?' he said excitedly. 'Yes, in fact I would say that you're the dictionary definition of the word "warm".' On their return home two weeks later he went straight to his dictionary and flicked through to 'W'. 'WARM: Not so hot.'

✷ A husband and wife were with some friends when the subject of marriage counselling came up. 'Oh, we'll never need that. My husband and I have a great relationship,' the wife explained. 'It's all about education,' she continued. 'He did a communications course in college and I studied drama. He communicates very well and I act like I'm listening.'

✷ Three weeks after her wedding day, Daphne called her mother. 'Mum,' she wailed, 'John and I had a dreadful fight!' 'Calm down,' said her mum, 'it's not half as bad as you think. Every marriage has to have its first fight!' 'I know, I know!' said Daphne. 'But what am I going to do with the BODY?'

✷ A henpecked husband was advised by a psychiatrist to assert himself. 'You don't have to let your wife bully you,' he said. 'Go home and show her you're the boss.' The husband decided to take the doctor's advice. He went home, slammed the door, shook his fist in his wife's face, and growled, 'From now on you're taking orders from me. I want my supper right now, and when you get it on the table, go upstairs and lay out my clothes. Tonight I am going out with the boys. You are going to stay at home where you belong. Another thing, you know who is going to tie my bow tie?' 'I certainly do,' said his wife calmly. 'The undertaker.'

✷ A husband is someone who after taking the rubbish out, gives the impression he just cleaned the whole house.

✷ Marriage is popular because it combines maximum temptation with maximum opportunity.

✷ Matrimony is the high sea for which no compass has been invented.

✷ A man's wife had just bought a new line of expensive cosmetics guaranteed to make her look years younger. She sat in front of the mirror for what had to be hours, applying the 'miracle' products. Finally, when she was done, she turned to her husband and said,

'Darling, honestly now, what age would you say I am?' He nodded his head in assessment, and carefully said, 'Well, judging from your skin, twenty. Your hair, eighteen. Your figure, twenty-five.' 'Oh, you're so sweet!' gushed the wife. 'Well, hang on,' he replied, 'I'm not finished adding it up yet.'

★ Marriage. An expensive way of getting your laundry done for free.

★ Married men live longer than single men, but they're a lot more willing to die.

★ An enormously wealthy 65-year-old man falls in love with a young woman in her twenties and is contemplating proposing. 'Do you think she'd marry me if I tell her I'm 45?' he asked a friend. 'Your chances are better,' said the friend, 'if you tell her you're 90.'

★ Every girl should learn to cook and clean the house, in case she doesn't get married.

★ 90% of men kiss their wife goodbye when they leave the house. The rest kiss their house goodbye when they leave the wife.

★ Adam and Eve had an ideal marriage. He didn't have to hear about all the men she could have married, and she didn't have to hear about the way his mother cooked.

★ How did the telephone get married?
In a double ring ceremony.

✳ A man is driving in America, when he picks up a Navajo man hitchhiking. They are making small talk when the Navajo notices a brown paper bag with something in it. The driver notices his glance and explains, 'That's a bottle of wine. I got it for my wife.' The Navajo man nods solemnly, 'Good trade.'

✳ A husband got in big trouble after forgetting his wedding anniversary. His wife gave him an ultimatum: 'Tomorrow there better be something in the driveway for me that goes from zero to 200 in two seconds flat.' The next morning the man woke his wife, and urged her to look out of the window at the drive. She did, and let out a scream when she saw he had bought her... A set of bathroom scales.

✳ All the time I was in the navy my wife sent me nagging letters. I couldn't even enjoy the war in peace.

✳ Last winter I was laid up at home with the flu. My fiancée called and volunteered to come over and fix dinner and play nursemaid to me. I declined, not wanting to pass on the flu to her. 'OK, honey,' she told me. 'We'll wait till after we get married. Then we can spend the rest of our lives making each other sick!'

✳ Although married people fax often, there are many single people who fax complete strangers every day.

✳ Love means telling you why you're sorry.

✳ Marriage means commitment. Of course, so does insanity.

✳ She's taken so many trips to the altar the last one was blindfold.

✳ A couple had been married for 50 years and decided they wanted to renew their vows. They were discussing the details of their second wedding with their friends. She wasn't going to wear a traditional bridal gown, and she started describing the dress she was planning to wear. One of her friends asked what colour shoes she had to go with the dress. She replied, 'Silver.' At that point, her husband chimed in, 'Yep, silver ... to match her hair.' Shooting a glaring look at his bald spot, her friend shot back, 'So, I guess you're going barefoot.'

✳ What's the best way to get coffee in the morning?
Wake up your wife.

✳ He bought his wife an electric typewriter. Now he's looking for a chair to match.

✳ Marriage is wonderful. To be able to sit at home, relax, drink beer and watch all your wife's favourite programmes.

✳ What's the quickest way to acquire a big vocabulary?
Get married.

✳ We're equal partners in our marriage. I'm the silent one.

✳ Their marriage got off to a bad start. They weren't married by a Justice of the Peace, but by the Minister of Defence.

✳ A man is on his deathbed, his wife by his side. 'Darling, you've always been by my side,' he says. 'When I broke my leg at 25, you were by my side. When I had my first heart attack at 45, you were by my side. When I had my second heart attack at 65, you were by my side. When I broke my hip at 75, you were by my side. And now when I'm dying, you are at my side … You're a bleeding jinx!'

✳ Marriage is like crossing the road. First you stop, then you look, and then you listen.

✳ I never knew what real happiness was until I got married; then it was too late.

✳ Love and marriage go together like a horse and carnage.

✳ A woman's work that is never done is the stuff she asks her husband to do.

✳ Losing a husband can be hard: in my case it was almost impossible.

✳ Have you heard about the man who has been married for 25 years and he spends every evening at home? His doctor says it's paralysis.

✳ Don't get married. Find a woman you hate and buy her a house. It's a lot easier on you.

✳ A little honey is good for your health – unless your wife finds out.

🐛 MEDICINE

✳ What did one virus say to another?
Stay away, I think I've got penicillin!

✳ Granddad comes home from his doctor and, though usually quite active with his grandchildren, seems to make every effort to avoid them this day. His son notices his dad avoiding the kids and asks him why this is so. Immediately the old man whisks his medicine prescription out of his pocket and hands it to his son. 'Read that label. That's why!' The son takes the bottle and reads, 'Take two pills a day. KEEP AWAY FROM CHILDREN.'

✳ I'm so depressed … my doctor refused to write me a prescription for Viagra. He said it would be like putting a new flagpole on a condemned building.

✳ Have you heard about the wine which cures incontinence? It's made from a new grape variety – Pinot More.

✳ Did you hear about the pharmaceutical company developing a suppository made from the leaves of palm trees? Their marketing slogan is 'With Fronds Like These, Who Needs Enemas?'

🐛 MEMORY

✳ If you tell the truth you don't have to remember anything.

* Improve your memory: lend money.

* My memory is excellent. There are only three things I have trouble with. I can't remember names and I can't remember faces and now I've forgotten the other thing.

* He's a mental tourist. His mind wanders.

* Old age: You keep chasing after women, but you can't remember why.

* For those of you with short-term memory loss: 'Knock.'

* Drugs cause amnesia and other things I can't remember.

* Memory is the thing we forget with.

middles

What can you find in the middle of nowhere?
The letter H.

Why is an island like the letter T?
It's in the middle of water.

What is the centre of gravity?
The letter V!

midgets

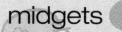

Elevators smell different to midgets.

🦗 MILITARY AND NAVY

✳ Where did Saddam Hussein keep his CDs?
In Iraq.

✳ Never underestimate the power of a small tactical nuclear weapon.

✳ Why do all Iraqi soldiers carry a piece of sandpaper?
They need a map.

✳ A private was brought up before the unit CO for some offence. 'You can take your choice, Private – one month's restriction or twenty days' pay,' said the officer. 'All right, sir,' said the bright soldier, 'I'll take the money.'

✳ Friendly fire ... isn't.

✳ What soldiers smell of salt and pepper?
Seasoned troops!

✳ He was such an egotist that he joined the navy so the world could see him.

✳ Which month do soldiers hate most?
March!

✳ A soldier stationed abroad received a 'Dear John' letter from his girlfriend back home. It read: 'Dear Dave, I can no longer continue our relationship. The distance between us is just too great. I must admit that I have cheated on you twice, since you've been gone, and it's not fair to either of us. I'm sorry. Please return the picture of me that I sent to you. Love, Kim.' The soldier, with hurt feelings, asked his fellow squaddies for any snapshots they could spare of their girlfriends, sisters, ex-girlfriends, aunts, cousins, etc. In addition to the picture of Kim, Ricky included all the other pictures of the pretty girls he had collected from his buddies. There were 57 photos in that envelope, along with this note: 'Dear Kim, I'm so sorry but I can't quite remember who you are. Please take your picture from the pile, and send the rest back to me. Take care, Dave.'

✳ (*This is the transcription of an actual radio conversation between the British and the Irish off the coast of Kerry, October 1998. Radio conversation released by the Chief of Naval Operations.*)
IRISH: Please divert your course 15 degrees to the south to avoid a collision.
BRITISH: Recommend you divert your course 15 degrees to the north to avoid a collision.
IRISH: Negative. You will have to divert your course 15 degrees to the south to avoid a collision.
BRITISH: This is the captain of a British navy ship. I say again, divert YOUR course.

IRISH: Negative. I say again, you will have to divert YOUR course.

BRITISH: THIS IS THE AIRCRAFT CARRIER HMS *BRITIANNIA*! THE SECOND LARGEST SHIP IN THE BRITISH ATLANTIC FLEET. WE ARE ACCOMPANIED BY THREE DESTROYERS, THREE CRUISERS AND NUMEROUS SUPPORT VESSELS. I DEMAND YOU CHANGE YOUR COURSE 15 DEGREES NORTH. I SAY AGAIN, THAT IS 15 DEGREES NORTH OR COUNTER-MEASURES WILL BE UNDERTAKEN TO ENSURE THE SAFETY OF THIS SHIP.

IRISH: We're a lighthouse. Your call.

* 'What were you in civilian life, soldier?'
  'Happy, sir.'

* Old soldiers never die. Young ones do.

* The beatings will continue until morale improves.

mistakes

A little inaccuracy sometimes saves a ton of explanation.

A long-forgotten loved one will appear soon. Buy the negatives at any price.

She's so clumsy that if she fell down she'd probably miss the floor.

🍩 MONEY

* What's a doughnut?
  Someone who is crazy about money.

* 'My grandfather always said, "Don't watch your money; watch your health." So one day while I was watching my health, someone stole my money. It was my grandfather.' *Jackie Mason*

* A crusty-looking old man walks into a bank and says to the woman at the window, 'I want to open a damn account.' To which the astonished woman replies, 'I beg your pardon, sir? I must have misunderstood you. What did you say?' 'Listen up, damn it. I said I want to open a damn account right now!' 'I'm very sorry, sir, but we do not tolerate that kind of language in this bank.' With that the woman leaves the window and goes over to the bank manager to tell him about her situation. They both return and the manager asks the old geezer, 'What seems to be the problem here?' 'There's no damn problem,' the man says. 'I just won 50 million bucks in the damn lottery and I want to open a damn account in this damn bank!' 'I see,' says the manager, 'and this bitch is giving you a hard time?'

* All most people want is a chance to prove money can't make them happy.

* Why did the man put his money in the freezer?
  He wanted cold hard cash!

* A lot of money is tainted: 'Taint yours, and 'taint mine.

* Two can live as cheaply as one, for half as long.

* If Asda is lowering prices every day, why isn't anything in the shop free yet?

* A fool and his money can throw one hell of a party.

* When someone asks you, 'A penny for your thoughts,' and you put your two cents in, what happens to the other penny?

* Money is the root of all evil, and man needs roots.

* Money should be utilized as a tool. You just gotta know which nuts to screw.

* A man went to his lawyer and told him, 'My neighbour owes me £500 and he won't pay up. What should I do?' 'Do you have any proof he owes you the money?' asked the lawyer. 'Nope,' replied the man. 'OK, then write him a letter asking him for the £1,000 he owed you,' said the lawyer. 'But it's only £500,' replied the man. 'Precisely. That's what he will reply and then you'll have your proof!'

* Money isn't everything but it sure keeps the kids in touch.

* Inland Revenue: We've got what it takes to take what you've got.

* OK, who put a stop payment on my reality check?

✳ Despite the cost of living, have you noticed how popular it remains? If you think nobody cares, try missing a couple of payments.

✳ **Teacher**: If you had one pound, and you asked your mother for one pound, how many pounds would you have?
Pupil: I'd have one pound.
Teacher: You don't know much about maths!
Pupil: You don't know much about my mother!

✳ My wife and I have a joint account. I deposit money and she withdraws it.

✳ My bank is so big, they even have a special window for hold-ups.

✳ A government subsidy is just getting some of your money back.

✳ Every man has his price. Mine is £3.95.

✳ Everyone has a scheme for getting rich quick that will not work.

✳ If we really did profit from our mistakes, I'd be extremely rich by now.

✳ The cost of living is the difference between your net income and your gross habits!

✳ Hang in there. Retirement is only twenty years away!

✳ Animals are friends but they can't lend you money.

✹ Budgeting: When you work out that the money you owe is exactly the same as the money you spent.

✹ I wish the buck stopped here; I sure could use a few.

✹ It's not hard to meet expenses – they're everywhere.

✹ Anybody with money to burn will easily find someone to tend the fire.

✹ All I ask for is the opportunity to prove that money doesn't buy happiness.

✹ My bank called. It's official. My yearnings exceed my earnings.

✹ **Mortal**: What is a million years like to you?
God: Like one second.
Mortal: What is a million pounds like to you?
God: Like one penny.
Mortal: Can I have a penny?
God: Just a second…

✹ Using a credit card is a convenient way to spend money you wish you had.

✹ A fool and his money are soon partying.

✹ Why do banks leave both doors open, yet they chain pens to the countertops?

✳ A bargain: Something you cannot use at a price you cannot resist.

✳ If money grew on trees, there wouldn't be much shade.

✳ Eat, drink and be merry, for tomorrow they take away your credit card.

✳ Did you hear about the cover-all insurance policy? If you bump your head, they pay you a lump sum.

✳ What did the one American penny say to the other penny?
We make perfect cents.

✳ What did the American say after he learned how to count money?
'It all makes cents now!'

✳ They say about money that you can't take it with you. I can't even afford to go.

✳ I'm saving my money. One day it might be worth something.

✳ Money talks, but it doesn't say when it's coming back.

✳ Two elderly gin-soaked colonels are sitting at the bar of their club. 'Lend me a tenner for a month, old boy,' says one. 'What does a month-old boy want a tenner for?' asks the other.

✳ What is the best way to keep your bills down?
Use a paperweight!

✳ A will is a dead giveaway.

✳ Our body cells renew while asleep. If only our wallets could do the same.

✳ A teacher was giving her pupils a lesson in logic. 'Here is the situation,' she said. 'A man is standing up in a boat in the middle of a river, fishing. He loses his balance, falls in, and begins splashing and yelling for help. His wife hears the commotion, knows he can't swim, and runs down to the bank. Why do you think she ran to the bank?' A girl raised her hand and asked, 'To draw out all his savings?'

✳ Earn cash in your spare time. Blackmail your friends.

✳ Nothing will dispel enthusiasm like a small admission fee.

🐵 MONKEYS

✳ When is a monkey like a flower?
When it's a chimp-pansy.

✳ How do monkeys keep rumours circulating?
On the apevine.

✳ Contrary to popular belief, a barrel full of monkeys isn't fun at all, and is in fact quite horrifying.

✳ How do monkeys make toast?
Put it under the g'rilla.

✳ What's a monkey's favourite month?
Ape-ril.

✳ What kind of key opens a banana?
A monkey!

✳ One day the zookeeper noticed that the orang-utan was reading two books – the Bible and Darwin's *Origin of Species*. In surprise he asked the ape, 'Why are you reading both those books?' 'Well,' said the orang-utan, 'I just wanted to know if I was my brother's keeper or my keeper's brother.'

✳ 'So I was in the jungle and there was this monkey with a tin opener. I said, "You don't need a tin opener to peel a banana." He said, "No, this is for the custard."' *Tommy Cooper*

🐉 MONSTERS

✳ Why did it take the monster ten months to finish a book?
Because he wasn't very hungry.

✳ What do you get if you cross a Scottish legend and a bad egg?
The Loch Ness Pongster!

✳ What did the depressed zombie say to his friend?
'Mind if I pick your brain for a bit?'

✳ Do zombies like being dead?
Of corpse.

✳ What happens when monsters hold a beauty contest?
Nobody wins.

✳ What is big and green and sits in the corner all day?
The incredible sulk.

✳ What's a monster's favourite soup?
Scream of tomato.

✳ I used to be a werewolf, but I'm all right noooooooooooooooooow.

✳ What do you call a brave and hairy Tibetan?
Yak the giant killer.

✳ How does Frankenstein eat his dinner?
He bolts it down.

✳ What sort of jewels do monsters wear?
Tomb stones.

moon

What is heavier, a full moon or a half moon?
A half moon. A full moon is lighter!

morals

I have a strong will but a weak won't.

Never let your sense of morals prevent you from doing what is right.

Never tell a lie unless it is absolutely convenient.

🦟 MOSQUITOES

🔥 What is the most religious insect?
A mosque-ito!

🔥 What has six legs, bites and talks in code?
A morse-quito!

🔥 What is the difference between a mosquito and a fly?
Try sewing buttons on a mosquito!

☀ What do you call it when a mosquito commits suicide?
Insecticide.

☀ What has antlers and sucks blood?
A moose-quito!

☀ Why are mosquitoes religious?
They prey on you!

🐾 MOTHERS

☀ Mother told me to be good, but she's been wrong before.

Your mother's so fat...

☀ ...her driver's licence picture is an aerial photograph.

☀ ...when she walked into traffic a car swerved to miss her and ran out of gas.

☀ ...she puts mayonnaise on aspirin.

☀ ...when she wears heels, they're flats by the afternoon.

☀ ...when she goes to a restaurant, she looks at the menu and says, 'OK.'

✳ …when she went to Seaworld, people paid to see her.

✳ …when she wore the Malcom X T-shirt, helicopters tried to land on her.

✳ …when she wears a yellow raincoat, people yell 'Taxi!'

✳ …she has her own gravity.

✳ …when she steps on a weighing machine, the display reads 'To be continued…'

✳ A young man excitedly tells his mother he's fallen in love and is going to get married. He says, 'Just for fun, Mum, I'm going to bring over three women and you try and guess which one I'm going to marry.' The mother agrees. The next day, he brings three beautiful women into the house and sits them down on the couch and they chat for a while. He then says, 'OK, guess which one I'm going to marry.' She immediately replies, 'The one in the middle.' 'That's amazing, Mum. You're right. How did you know?' 'I don't like her.'

✳ What does 'maximum' mean?
A very big mother!

✳ What does 'minimum' mean?
A very small mother!

✳ Recently a large seminar was held for vicars in training. Among the guests were many well-known motivational speakers. One trainee boldly approached the pulpit and, gathering the entire crowd's attention, said, 'The best years of my life were spent in the arms of a woman that wasn't my wife!' The crowd was shocked. He followed up by saying, 'And that woman was my mother!' The crowd burst into laughter and he gave his speech, which went well. About a week later one of the clergy who had attended the seminar decided to use that joke in his sermon. As he shyly approached the pulpit one sunny Sunday, he tried to rehearse the joke in his head. It seemed a bit foggy to him this morning. Getting to the microphone he said loudly, 'The greatest years of my life were spent in the arms of another woman that was not my wife!' His congregation sat shocked. After standing there for almost ten seconds trying to recall the second half of the joke, the pastor finally blurted out, '…and I can't remember who she was!'

* A professor was giving a lecture on company slogans in a university advertising and marketing class. 'John,' he asked, 'which company has the slogan, "Come fly the friendly skies"?' 'United,' Joe answered. 'Brenda, can you tell me which company has the slogan, "Don't leave home without it"?' Brenda answered with the correct credit card company with no difficulty. 'Now, Paul, tell me who uses the slogan, "Just do it".' Paul was quiet for a moment before answering, 'Mum?'

* If evolution is fact, why do mothers only have two hands?

* He asked his mother to sit on the front step. He always wanted a stepmother.

🐾 MOThERS-iN-LAW

✳ A young enthusiastic vicar was taking up a new post. This chap had a particular passion for animal rights. So you can imagine his utter disgust when one day he witnessed one of his parishioners walking down the street in the longest fur coat you've ever seen. Storming over to her, he shouted, 'And what poor creature had to die so you could wear that fur coat?' The lady parishioner was stunned but managed to stammer, 'M-m-m-my mother-in-law.'

✳ 'Honolulu – it's got everything. Sand for the children, sun for the wife, sharks for the wife's mother.' *Ken Dodd*

✳ They say every woman has her price. I've got a mother-in-law you can have cheap.

✳ Did you hear about the weatherman's mother-in-law?
She was fair to meddling

✳ I've just got back from a pleasure trip. Took my mother-in-law to the station.

✳ We've had some upsetting news. Last week my mother-in-law was dangerously ill. Now I hear that she's dangerously well again.

✳ Two friends meet each other on the street. 'Hello! Where are you coming from?' asked Bill. 'Oh, don't ask me! I'm coming from the cemetery. I just buried my mother-in-law,' replied Sid. 'I'm so sorry!'

said Bill. 'But why is your face scratched all over?' 'It wasn't so easy,' said Sid. 'She put up a hell of a fight!'

✳ It was a particularly horrific crime, and the judge could not refrain from saying so to the defendant. As the defendant was brought before him for sentencing, the judge said, 'You are charged with throwing your mother-in-law out of your fourth-storey window.' The defendant responded, 'I did it without thinking, Your Honour.' The judge scolded, 'That's no excuse! What if someone had been passing underneath at the time?'

🐺 MOUNTAiNS

✳ What did the little mountain say to the big mountain?
Hi Cliff!

✳ Why don't mountains get cold in the winter?
They wear snow caps.

✳ Why are mountain climbers curious?
They always want to take another peak.

✳ A plateau is a high form of flattery.

✳ Hans and Fritz went mountain climbing with their mother. She slipped and fell a thousand feet and Fritz hollered, 'Look, Hans! No ma!'

✳ A search and rescue team was assembled and sent on a mission to find an aeroplane that had crashed on top of a mountain. It was their duty to rescue any survivors. After finally reaching the top of the mountain, they came upon the crash site. At the site, one lone survivor sat with his back against a tree, chewing on a bone. As he tossed the bone onto a huge pile of bones, he noticed the rescue team. 'Thank you, God!' he cried out in relief. 'I am saved!' The rescue team did not move, as they were in shock, seeing the pile of human bones beside this lone survivor. Obviously he had eaten his comrades. The survivor saw the horror in their faces and hung his own head in shame. 'You can't judge me for this,' he insisted. 'I had to survive. Is it so wrong to want to live?' The leader of the rescue team stepped forward, shaking his head in disbelief. 'I won't judge you for doing what was necessary to survive but, my God, man, your plane only went down yesterday!'

mules

Who has the most fun when you tickle a mule?
He may enjoy it but you'll get a bigger kick out of it.

🐦 MURDER

✳ It's better to be wanted for murder that not to be wanted at all.

✳ The dumber people think you are, the more surprised they're going to be when you kill them.

✳ Three may keep a secret, if you kill two of them.

✳ A little old man was escorted into the witness box. He was sworn in and asked by the lawyer to explain what happened. After a lengthy discussion of the events leading up to the incident he finally got around to the meat of the case: 'And then she hit me with a maple leaf.' 'A maple leaf? Surely that couldn't have caused you any serious injury,' said the lawyer. 'Are you kidding?' exclaimed the old man. 'It was the leaf from the centre of our dining room table.'

🐾 MUSIC AND MUSICIANS

✳ What pet makes the loudest noise?
A trum-pet!

✳ What do you call the girl on a trombone player's arm?
A tattoo.

✳ Why can't a gorilla play trumpet?
He's too sensitive.

✳ What would a violin player do if he won a million pounds?
Keep playing gigs until the money ran out.

✳ How do you improve the aerodynamics of a drummer's car?
Take the Domino's Pizza sign off the roof.

✳ How do you make a drummer leave your front door?
Pay him for the pizza.

✳ An anthropologist decides to investigate the natives of a far-flung tropical island. He flies there, and finds a guide with a canoe to take him up the river to the remote site. About noon on the second day of travel up the river they begin to hear drums. Being a city boy by nature, the anthropologist is disturbed by this. He asks the guide, 'What are those drums?' The guide turns to him and says, 'Drums OK, but VERY BAD when they stop.' Then, after some hours, the drums suddenly stop. This hits the anthropologist like a ton of bricks, and he yells at the guide: 'The drums have stopped, what happens now?' The guide crouches down, covers his head with his hands and says, 'Bass solo.'

✳ A couple were having marital difficulties and consulted a marriage counsellor. After meeting with them, the counsellor told them that their problems could all be traced to a lack of communication. 'You two need to talk,' he said. 'So, I recommend that you go to a jazz club. Just wait until it's time for the bass player to solo. Then you'll be talking just like everyone else.'

✳ What's the definition of an optimist?
A folk musician with a mortgage.

✺ Why is crossing the road like playing the piano?
C sharp or B flat.

✺ If you drop an accordion and a set of bagpipes out of a tenth-floor window, which hits the ground first?
Who cares?

✺ My brother practised the violin for 20 years. Unfortunately, it took him 19 years to realize you didn't blow it.

✺ Show me a piano falling down a mine shaft and I'll show you A-flat miner.

✺ Two dogs go into Wigmore Hall and one wants to buy tickets to a concert. The ticket seller says, 'But you're dogs! What could you possibly know about classical music?' The first dog replies, 'Are you kidding? He Bach and I Offenbach!'

✺ Why can't Cab Callaway's wife water the lawn?
Because he 'hide-dee-hide-dee-hose'.

✺ What's the difference between a musician and a savings bond?
One of them eventually matures and earns money.

✺ Why doesn't the piano work?
Because it only knows how to play.

✺ I sing for charity. I have to, nobody will pay me.

✳ Do you sing Faust? Yes, and I can sing slow as well.

✳ What's the definition of a gentleman?
Someone that can play the bagpipes, but doesn't.

✳ Did you hear about the cow that drank a bottle of ink and then mood indigo?

✳ **Musician**: Did you hear my last recital?
Friend: I hope so.

✳ 'Do you love music?'
'Yes, but never mind, you may continue playing.'

✳ Why couldn't the maestro find the composer?
Because he was Haydn.

✳ What does a guitar player do when he locks his keys in the car?
He breaks the window to get the bass player out.

✳ Music sung by two people at the same time is called a duel.

✳ **Wolfgang**: Did you hear the one about the classical string quartet that could not sell tickets to their concerts?
Johannes: No, I didn't. What happened to them?
Wolfgang: They went baroque.

✳ A management consultant gave his report on Schubert's Unfinished Symphony: 'All twelve violins played the same notes. This is unnecessary duplication. Their number should be cut. For a considerable period oboe players had nothing to do. Their number should be reduced and their work spread evenly among other staff. No useful purpose is served by repeating with horns the passage that was already handled by the strings. If such redundancies were eliminated, the concert could be cut by twenty minutes. The symphony has two movements. Mr Schubert should have been able to achieve his musical goals in one. Conclusion: If Mr Schubert had paid attention to these matters, he would have had time to finish the symphony.'

✳ Modern music isn't always as bad as it sounds.

✳ He broke into song because he couldn't find the key.

✳ What has loads of keys but can't open doors?
A piano.

✳ What's green, lives in your refrigerator and sings?
Elvis Parsley.

✳ What do you call an ant who can't play the piano?
Discordant!

✳ A guy goes into a bar with his pet monkey and says, 'I bet £50 that no one here has a musical instrument that this monkey can't play – and play well.' The people in the bar look around and someone fetches an old guitar. The monkey has a look, picks it up, tunes up the strings and starts playing a complicated classical piece. The monkey's owner pockets the £50. The next guy comes up with a trumpet. The monkey takes the horn, loosens up the keys, licks its lips and starts playing a moving jazz solo. The guy hands over another £50 to the monkey's owner. The barman has been watching all this and disappears out the back, coming back a few moments later with a set of bagpipes under his arm. He puts them on the bar and says to the guy, 'Now if your monkey can play that, I'll give you £100.' The two men both place their bets on the bar. The monkey looks at the bagpipes, takes them in his arms and begins to play. The barman immediately reaches for the £200 but the monkey's owner stops him. 'Hey! What are you doing? He plays the bagpipes very well!' 'Oh yeah?' responds the barman as he puts the money in his pocket. 'Prove it!'

✳ Two men are in a bar. 'I decided to give up the saxophone,' says one. 'Really? Was it too hard to master?' replies his friend. 'No, I saw my neighbours coming home with a gun.'

✳ Stevie Wonder is playing his first gig in Tokyo and the place is absolutely packed to the rafters. In a bid to break the ice with his new audience he asks if anyone would like him to play a request. A little old Japanese man jumps out of his seat in the first row and shouts at the top of his voice, 'Play a jazz chord! Play a jazz chord!' Amazed that this guy knows about the jazz influences in Stevie's varied career, the blind impresario starts to play an E minor scale and then goes into a difficult jazz melody for about ten minutes. When he finishes the whole place goes wild. The little old man jumps up again and shouts, 'No, no, play a jazz chord! Play a jazz chord!' A bit cheesed off by this, Stevie, being the professional that he is, dives straight into a jazz improvisation with his band around the B flat minor chord and really tears the place apart. The crowd goes wild with this impromptu show of his technical expertise. The little old man jumps up again. 'No, no. Play a jazz chord! Play a jazz chord!' Well and truly cheesed off that the little man doesn't appreciate his playing ability, Stevie says to him from the stage, 'OK, smart guy. You get up here and do it!' The little old man climbs up onto the stage, takes hold of the mike and starts to sing. 'A jazz chord to say I love you...'

✳ How do you make a bandstand?
Pull their chairs away!

✳ What weighs eight pounds and won't be plucked next Christmas?
John Denver's guitar.

✳ What was the gangster's last words?
Who put that violin in my violin case!

✳ When I am sad, I sing, and then the world is sad with me.

✳ What did the boy say when it was time for his violin lesson?
Oh, fiddle!

✳ Why do people take an instant dislike to banjo players?
It saves time in the long run.

✳ What do you get when you cross a stereo with a fridge?
The coolest music in town.

✳ What's Beethoven's favourite fruit?
(To the tune of the 5th Symphony) Ba-na-na-NAAH.

✳ What do you call a bee in a rock band?
The lead stinger.

✳ They all laughed when I walked over to the piano, but they were right. I couldn't lift it.

✳ Why did the pianist hit his head on the keyboard?
He was playing by ear.

✳ Frank Sinatra, 'Old Blue Eyes', has died... Frank will now be known as 'Old Closed Eyes'.

✳ Bono is at a U2 concert in Ireland when he asks the audience for some quiet. Then in the silence, he starts to slowly clap his hands. Holding the audience in total silence, he says into the microphone, 'Every time I clap my hands, a child in Africa dies.' A voice from near the front of the audience pierces the silence: 'Stop doing it then!'

✳ What did the drummer get on his music exam?
Dribble.

✳ What do you get if you cross a grizzly bear and a harp?
A bear-faced lyre!

✳ What's the best or fastest way to tune a banjo?
With wirecutters.

✳ Why is a person who plays the piano called a pianist but a person who drives a racecar is not called a racist?

✳ What's the definition of perfect pitch?
Throwing a piano in a skip without it touching the sides.

✳ Three musicians come out from taking an IQ test. 'Well, my IQ is 220,' says the first one. 'That's amazing. You're so clever, you must be a synth programmer,' says the second one. 'That's right, I am,' he replies. 'I scored 175,' says the second musician. 'That's pretty good,' says the third guy, 'you must be a lead guitarist. My IQ was only 15.' 'Really?' says the lead guitarist. 'What sticks do you use?'

✳ What's the difference between God and Bono?
God doesn't wander around Dublin thinking he's Bono.

🐺 MY WiFE

✳ A man walks to Piccadilly Circus in London during a downpour and somehow manages to get a taxi straight away. He gets into the taxi, and the cabbie says: 'Perfect timing. You're just like Paul.' 'Who?' says the man. 'Paul Jones. He was a man who got everything right. Like my taxi being free during a rainstorm. It would have happened for Paul.' 'Surely no one is perfect. There are always a few clouds over everybody,' the man replies. 'Not Paul,' says the cabbie. 'He was a great athlete. He could have turned professional at football or tennis and he danced like Fred Astaire. He was handsome and sophisticated, more than George Clooney. He had a better body than Brad Pitt in his prime. He was something! Somehow Paul just knew exactly how to make women happy. He had a memory like a computer. Could remember everybody's birthday. He could fix anything. Not like me. I change a fuse and the whole house blacks out.' 'No wonder you remember him!' says the man. 'I never actually met Paul,' admits the cabbie. 'Then how do you know so much about him?' asks the man. 'After he died I married his wife.'

* A man was up in court for breaking into a ladies' outfitters. 'It says here you have broken into the dress shop four times,' said the judge. 'Is this correct?' 'Yes,' answered the suspect. 'Yet you stole only one dress?' 'One dress, Your Honour,' replied the subject. 'One dress?' echoed the judge. 'But you admit breaking in four times!' 'Yes, Your Honour,' sighed the suspect. 'The first three times, my wife didn't like the colour.'

* My wife was so ugly, she had calves only a cow could love.

* 'My wife has lots of personality.'
  'Mine is ugly, too.'

* My wife's so ugly when she wears a mini-skirt men turn to look the other way.

* My wife has terrible sinus trouble: 'Sinus a cheque for this, sinus a cheque for that.'

* My wife's so ugly, when she goes to the beauty parlour she gets an estimate.

✳ My wife brings more bills into the house than an MP.

✳ My wife does bird impressions. She watches me like a hawk.

✳ My wife gave me the best years of her life. Now here come the worst years.

✳ My wife skin looks like a million dollars – wrinkled and green.

✳ My wife dresses to kill, and cooks the same way.

✳ My wife always wears a dress with a square neck – to match her head.

✳ 'My wife's gone to the West Indies!' 'Jamaica?' 'No. She went of her own accord.'

✳ I'm not saying my wife is a bad cook, but my doctor advised me to eat out more regularly.

✳ Love is a matter of chemistry. That is why my wife treats me like toxic waste.

✳ Any man who thinks he is more intelligent than his wife is married to a very smart woman.

✳ My wife gives me breakfast in bed – if I sleep in the kitchen.

NAGGiNG

✺ Her husband was so henpecked, he had to wash and iron his own apron.

✺ Adult: One old enough to know better.

✺ You haven't nagged me all evening, darling. Is there someone else?

✺ A henpecked man and his wife went on holiday to Jerusalem. While they were there, the wife passed away. The local undertaker told the husband, 'You can have her shipped home for £5,000, or you can bury her here in the Holy Land, for £150.' The man thought about it and told him he would just as soon have her shipped home. The undertaker was surprised. 'Why would you spend £5,000 to ship your wife home, when it would be wonderful to be buried here and only cost you £150?' The man replied, 'Long ago a man died here, was buried here, and three days later he rose from the dead. I just can't take that chance.'

✳ I told my wife that a man is like a fine wine, he gets better with age. The next day, she locked me in the wine cellar.

🐺 NAMES

✳ How can you get your name in lights the world over?
Change your name to Emergency Exit!

✳ What do you call a woman with legs the same length?
Nolene.

✳ What do you call a man with a shovel in his head?
Doug.

✳ What do you call a man without a shovel in his head?
Douglas.

✳ What do you call a man with a wooden head?
Edward.

✳ What do you call a lady with a toothpick in her head?
Olive.

✳ What do you call a man with his legs chopped off at the knees?
Neil.

✳ What do you call a man being electrocuted?
Buzz.

✳ What do you call a man who sits by your front door?
Matt.

✳ What do you call a man between two buildings?
Ali.

✳ What is Mary short for?
She's just got little legs.

✳ If John's mum has five sons and their names are Ja, Je, Ji, and Jo, who is the last one? John.

✳ What are good names for identical twin boys?
Pete and Repeat.

✳ Did you hear about the little boy that they named after his father?
They called him Dad!

✳ What is Kentucky's wife's name?
Barbie Tucky.

✳ What do you call an Italian guy with a rubber toe?
Roberto!

✳ 'Here's your package. The address is right but the name is smudged.'
'Then it can't be mine, my name is Smith.'

nature

Rainbows are just to look at, not to really understand.

NEiGHBOURS

* What do you call a man who lends his tools to a neighbour?
  A saw loser.

* My neighbour is a nightmare. He keeps borrowing back everything I take from him.

* Let he who takes the plunge remember to return it.

* Save water – take a bath with your neighbour's daughter.

* I'm not saying my neighbours are nosy, but they asked me to wash my windows because they were getting eye strain.

nightmares

Why did the woman take a loaf of bread to bed with her?
To feed her nightmare!

🐺 NUDISM

* 'It's true that the clothes make the man; naked people have little or no influence in society.' *Mark Twain*

* Most nudists are people you don't want to see naked.

* Being in a nudist colony probably takes all the fun out of Halloween.

* Is a shell-less turtle homeless or just naked?

* Did you hear about the strict nudist? Wouldn't even put dressing on his salad.

* 'Honey, it's just too hot to wear clothes today,' Jack said to his wife as he stepped out of the shower. 'What do you think the neighbours would think if I mowed the lawn like this?' 'They'd probably think I married you for your money,' she replied.

* What fur did Adam and Eve wear?
Bareskins.

numbers

What did zero say to eight?

'Nice belt!'

I wouldn't touch the metric system with a 3.048m pole!

OCTOPUS AND SQUID

✳ How does an octopus go to war?
Well armed!

✳ Where do you find a down-and-out octopus?
On squid row!

✳ What did the boy octopus say to the girl octopus?
'I wanna hold you hand, hand, hand, hand, hand, hand, hand, hand!'

✳ Who has eight guns and terrorizes the ocean?
Billy the Squid!

✳ Who held the baby octopus to ransom?
Squidnappers!

✳ A restaurant kitchen in London is busy every lunchtime and the head
chef, Yufas, has a fearsome reputation among his staff. This particular

morning the restaurant takes delivery of their seafood from Billingsgate, and as Yufas is checking the order he realizes that one of the squid is acting very peculiarly. The squid in question is not pink, like squids should be, but is in fact green, and seems to be sporting a moustache. To top it all off, the squid is saying 'Hi' to everyone it sees and trying to strike up conversations. Yufas is aghast, and his normally stern approach visibly weakens as the squid asks him whether he's had a nice day so far. Yufas knows the squid is fated to be dropped into boiling water, and shouldn't be having conversations with the staff, but just can't bring himself to drop the little fella in the pot. Wanting to deputize the responsibility, he looks around the kitchen and spots the new guy, Hans, who is busy with cleaning all the pots and pans. 'Hans,' says the chef, 'come over here and prepare this squid. I've got more important things to be doing.' Hans, thinking he is finally getting recognized for his work, comes over to prepare the squid. On seeing the little guy, and being complimented by the squid on his good taste in shoes, Hans just can't bring himself to kill the squid either. What is the moral here? Hans that does dishes is as soft as Yufas, with the mild, green, hairy-lipped squid.

🦑 OLD AGE

✳ Three sisters, ages 92, 94, and 96, live in a house together. One night the 96-year-old draws a bath. She puts her foot in and pauses. She yells down the stairs, 'Was I getting in or out of the bath?' The 94-year-old yells back, 'I don't know. I'll come up and see.' She starts up the stairs and pauses. 'Was I going up the stairs or down?' The

92-year-old is sitting at the kitchen table having tea listening to her sisters. She shakes her head and says, 'I sure hope I never get that forgetful.' She knocks on wood for good measure. She then yells, 'I'll come up and help both of you as soon as I see who's at the door.'

* A reporter was interviewing an 104-year-old woman: 'And what do you think is the best thing about being 104?'
She simply replied, 'No peer pressure.'

* At the shops a man noticed a lady eyeing his two adopted children curiously. The boy was blond, while the girl was black. The lady continued staring. Finally, she asked, 'Those your kids?' 'Yes, they are!' he answered proudly. 'They adopted?' she asked. 'Yes,' he replied. 'I thought so,' she concluded. 'I figured you're too old to have kids that small.'

* Here is a little secret for building your arm and shoulder muscles. You might want to adopt the regimen for yourself – but be careful to take it gradually. Three days a week works well. Begin by standing straight, with a 5 lb potato sack in each hand. Extend your arms straight out from your sides and hold them there as long as you can. Eventually try to reach a full minute. Relax. After a few weeks, move up to 10 lb potato sacks, and then 50 lb potato sacks, and eventually try to get to where you can lift a 100 lb potato sack in each hand and hold your arms straight out for more than a full minute. After you feel confident at that level, start putting a couple of potatoes in each sack, but be careful not to overdo it.

* When she saw her first strands of grey hair, she thought she'd dye.

✳ A woman is looking at herself naked in the mirror. She says to her husband, 'Darling, I'm old and fat. Cheer me up. Pay me a compliment.' 'Well,' he replies, 'your eyesight is still good!'

✳ Age doesn't always bring wisdom. In your case it came alone.

✳ I don't know how I got over the hill without making it to the top.

✳ The census taker knocked on old Miss Barker's door. She answered all his questions except one. She refused to tell him her age. 'But everyone tells their age to the census taker,' he said. 'Did Miss Maisy Hill and Miss Daisy Hill tell you their ages?' she asked. 'Certainly,' he replied 'Well, I'm the same age as they are,' she snapped. 'As old as the Hills,' he wrote on his form.

✳ Three deaf old ladies are walking down the street. One: 'Whew, it's windy today!' Two: 'No. Today's Thursday!' Three: 'So am I! Let's get a drink!

✳ The best contraceptive for old people is nudity.

✳ There were four 80-year-old men playing golf. One complained the hills were too high. The second complained the bunkers were too deep. The third said the holes were too wide. The fourth one said, 'Shut up! At least we're still on the right side of the grass!'

✳ George, Bob and Jeff are sat talking in the old folks' home.
George: 'This getting old is no fun. I wake at six o'clock every morning, by ten past I need a pee. But for the life of me, I just can't manage it. It is so uncomfortable.'

Bob: 'That's nothing, mate. I wake at six o'clock and by twenty past I need a dump. But for the life of me, I just can't manage it. It is so uncomfortable.'

Jeff: 'That is nothing, gents. I go for a wee at ten past six, and a dump at twenty past six every morning without fail.'

Bob: 'What is so bad about that?'

Jeff: 'I don't wake up until seven.'

✱ Two old gents and their nurse were sitting on the lawn of the nursing home enjoying the afternoon, when a little bird flew over and dropped a load on the bald head of one of the old men. The nurse got all flustered and said, 'Don't you go anywhere, I'll run in and get some toilet paper,' and off she goes. The two looked at each other and one of them said, 'Are we crazy or is she crazy? By the time she gets back with the toilet paper, that bird will be a half a mile away.'

✱ 'How old is your granddad?'
'I don't know but we've had him a long time!'

✱ Three dead bodies turn up at the mortuary, all with very big smiles on their faces. The coroner calls in the police to tell them what has happened. 'First body: Frenchman, 60, died of heart failure while drinking vintage champagne and eating foie gras. Hence the enormous smile, Inspector,' says the coroner. 'Second body: Scotsman, 25, won £1,000 on the lottery, spent it all on whisky. Died of alcohol poisoning, hence the smile.' The inspector asks, 'What of the third body?' 'Ah,' says the coroner. 'This is the most unusual one: Big Seamus Quinn from Donegal, 30, struck by lightning.' 'Why is he smiling then?' enquires the inspector. 'He thought he was having his photo taken.'

✳ My father lived to be 100, which he put down to tomatoes. He never touched them.

✳ He was so old his toupee went grey.

✳ Things improve with age. I'm approaching magnificent.

✳ A tour bus driver is driving with a bus load of OAPs when he is tapped on his shoulder by a little old lady. She offers him a handful of peanuts, which he gratefully munches up. After about fifteen minutes, she taps him on his shoulder again and she hands him another handful of peanuts. When she is about to hand him another batch he asks her: 'Why don't you eat the peanuts yourself?' 'We can't chew them because we've no teeth,' she replies. 'We just love the chocolate around them.'

✳ A man in his late 70s is at the pub with a mate of his, discussing their respective wives. 'Mine still thinks she's a young woman.' 'If you want to know how young she is, you could try this little trick. When you get home, ask her what's for dinner from several distances. Start at 30 feet, then 25 feet, then 20, and so on. The sooner she hears you, the younger she is.' So, an hour later, the man arrives home and shouts, at a distance of about 30 feet from his wife: 'Honey, what's for dinner?' No answer. He goes a bit closer. 'Honey, what's for dinner?' Still no answer. He goes closer, asks it again, no response... When he's finally standing in the doorway of the kitchen, about five feet away from his wife, he yells, 'Honey, what's for dinner?!' His wife turns around briskly and says, sounding irritated: 'I've already told you three times now: chicken and mushrooms!'

✳ At the urging of his doctor, an elderly man moved to the deepest countryside. After settling in, he met a neighbour who was also an older man. 'Say, is this really a healthy place?' 'It sure is,' the man replied. 'When I first arrived here I couldn't say one word. I had hardly any hair on my head. I didn't have the strength to walk across a room, and I had to be lifted out of bed.' 'That's wonderful!' said the newcomer. 'How long have you been here?' 'I was born here.'

✳ I knew her 30 years ago, and she looked just like she looks today. Haggard.

✳ As a child I was very young.

Old is when...

✳ ...your wife says, 'Let's go upstairs and make love,' and you answer, 'Honey, I can't do both!'

✳ ...your friends compliment you on your new alligator shoes and you're barefoot.

✳ ...a sexy babe catches your fancy and your pacemaker opens the garage door nearest your car.

✳ ...you remember when the Dead Sea was only sick.

✳ ...going bra-less pulls all the wrinkles out of your face.

* ...you don't care where your spouse goes, just as long as you don't have to go along.

* ...when it takes longer to rest than to get tired.

* ...when you are cautioned to slow down by the doctor instead of by the police.

* ... 'getting a little action' means you don't need to take any fibre today.

* ... 'getting lucky' means you find your car in the parking lot.

* ... an 'all nighter' means not getting up to pee.

* ...your idea of a night out is sitting on the patio.

* ...happy hour is a nap.

* ...you're on holiday and your energy runs out before your money.

* ...in a hostage situation you're likely to be released first.

* ...it's harder and harder for sexual harassment charges to stick.

* ...kidnappers are not very interested in you.

* ...no one expects you to run into a burning building.

✻ ...people call at 9 p.m. and ask, 'Did I wake you?'

✻ ...people no longer view you as a hypochondriac.

✻ ...there's nothing left to learn the hard way.

✻ ...things you buy now won't wear out.

✻ ...you can eat dinner at four o'clock.

✻ Statistics show that at the age of seventy, there are five women to every man. Isn't that an ironic time for a man to get those odds?

✻ His forehead's so wrinkled he can screw on his hat.

✻ The older someone is, the further they walked to school as children.

✻ Middle age is when you know your way around but don't feel like going.

✻ Age is what the onlooker sees, not what the looked upon feels.

✻ Hannah and Gavin were having dinner with a couple they'd lost touch with when they moved to another city many years ago. Over the meal, the couples took turns catching up. 'And soon after we were married,' Hannah began, 'we were blessed with a marvellous, chubby creature with cute bow legs and no teeth.' 'Oh, you had a baby!' said the other husband. 'Nope,' Gavin broke in, 'Hannah's mother came to live with us.'

opera

I'm a regular at the opera, whether I need the sleep or not.

Opera in English is a great idea. It helps you understand what's boring you.

opportunity

Opportunity knocked on my door today, but I didn't answer. I waited for it to knock twice.

Opportunity knocks only once, but temptation bangs at the door for years.

OUTER SPACE AND THE UNIVERSE

✳ What is an astronaut's favourite place on a computer?
  The space bar!

✳ What do they call *Star Trek* in Japan?
  Sulu, Master Navigator.

✳ What do you call a man in a black helmet, wearing a black cape, breathing heavily, standing in two feet of water?
Darth Wader.

✳ In what form does a message from a parallel universe come in?
A parallelo-gram.

✳ Why did the astronomer hit his head with a hammer when he got up in the morning?
He wanted to see stars in the day.

✳ How does the moon cut his hair?
Eclipse it!

✳ If athletes get athletes foot, what do astronauts get?
Missletoe.

✳ What do you call an ant in space?
Cosmonants & Astronants!

✳ Two American astronomers were visiting a French observatory. One asks the other, 'Comet Halley view?'

✳ Why did Captain Kirk pee on the ceiling?
He wanted to go where no man had ever gone before.

✳ Very funny, Scotty, now beam down my clothes.

✳ The universe is a figment of its own imagination.

* Reality is for people who can't stand *Star Trek*.

* The man in the moon isn't as interesting as the girl in the *Sun*.

* What do you call a foreign body in a chip pan?
  An Unidentified Frying Object!

* There were three astronauts, an American, a Russian, and an Irishman, who were discussing who had the best space programme. The Russian says, 'We have the best space programme. We were the first country to put a satellite into orbit.' The American replies, 'That's nothing, we put the first man on the moon.' Then the Irishman says, 'No, we are the best, we're going to put the first man on the sun.' The Russian and the American laugh. 'That's not possible – you'd burn up.' 'No, no, we have it all planned out. See, we will go at night!'

* What sort of star is dangerous?
  A shooting star!

* What illness did everyone on the *Enterprise* catch?
  Chicken Spocks!

* What does one star say to another star when they meet?
  Glad to meteor!

* Why are astronauts successful people?
  Because they always go up in the world!

✳ When do astronauts eat?
At launch time!

owls

What do you get if you cross an owl with a skunk?
Something that smells but doesn't give a hoot

What is an owl's favourite dance?
The Hoo-la.

🐺 PARACHUTES

✳ A man always wanted to parachute jump but was finding it difficult to pluck up the courage. He goes to an airport and enquires about what is involved in doing a jump. The manager explained the procedure to him: 'We are expert chute packers and have never had a failure. We take you up in that plane and tell you when to jump out. You pull the main chute ripcord. It always works but if it doesn't, you pull the auxiliary chute ripcord. You float softly to the ground and we will meet you in that truck over there.' The man decides to go for it. The plane takes off and circles the airfield. He jumps out and the main chute fails. He pulls the second ripcord and that fails. He looks down and says, 'I'll bet that damned truck is not there either.'

✳ You do not need a parachute to skydive. You only need a parachute to skydive twice.

paranoia

It IS as bad as you think, and they ARE out to get you.

Only a lack of imagination saves me from immobilizing myself with imaginary fears.

They're only trying to make me LOOK paranoid!

I have this nagging fear that everyone is out to make me paranoid.

Only the paranoid survive.

Paranoid Schizophrenic: Are you staring at us?

PARROTS

✳ How do you get a parrot to talk properly?
   Send him to polytechnic!

✳ A man went into a pet shop to buy a parrot. He found one that he liked and went up to the counter to buy it. The shopkeeper saw which parrot he had picked out and said, 'That parrot repeats everything he hears.' 'That's all right,' the man replied, 'I'll take it.' As he was walking down the street, he saw a cop chasing a robber. The

cop shouted to his partner, 'Shoot him down, shoot him down!' Then
the parrot said, 'Shoot him down, shoot him down!' They kept
walking and found a man who was trying to prise his car off the
ground with a crowbar because his wheels had been stolen. The man
said, 'Pop it up, pop it up!' The parrot said, 'Pop it up, pop it up!'
They kept on walking to a carnival. A man at a game stand yelled,
'Hit a big one, win a prize!' The parrot said, 'Hit a big one, win a
prize!' Then they walked into a church and sat down. The minister
was in the middle of the sermon. He said, 'The Lord is above us.'
The parrot said, 'Shoot him down, shoot him down!' The minister
said, 'The devil is below us.' The parrot said, 'Pop it up, pop it up.'
Then the minister got angry and threw a Bible at the parrot. The
parrot ducked and the Bible hit a fat lady behind him. The parrot said,
'Hit a big one, win a prize!'

* Why did the parrot wear a raincoat?
  He wanted to be a polyunsaturated!

* What's orange and sounds like a parrot?
  A carrot.

* What do parrots eat?
  Polyfiller.

* What do you get if you cross a parrot with a woodpecker?
  A bird that talks in morse code!

* What do you call a Scottish parrot?
  A Macaw.

✳ What do you get if you cross a parrot with an elephant?
An animal that tells you everything that it remembers!

✳ A guy has a parrot that can sing and speak beautifully. He takes it to the church on Palm Sunday and makes a wager that the bird can conduct the service better than the bishop. When the big moment comes, though, the parrot is silent. The guy is outraged. He takes the bird home and is about to kill it when the bird finally speaks: 'Wait! Think of the odds we'll get at Christmas.'

✳ Polynesia: Memory loss in parrots.

✳ What flies through the jungle singing opera?
The parrots of Penzance!

✳ Whose parrot sits on his shoulder squawking, 'Pieces of four! Pieces of four!'?
Short John Silver's.

✳ A sailor was picked up after drifting alone in a lifeboat for weeks. 'How did you survive?' asked his rescuers. 'Oh,' said the sailor, 'I ate my pet parrot to keep me alive.' 'What was it like?' they asked. 'Chicken, duck, turkey,' he replied. 'You name it, that bird could imitate anything.'

🐵 PARTiES

※ I went to a fancy dress party last week dressed as sodium chloride. The minute I got in the door, this bloke threw sulphuric acid over me. It was terrible. I didn't know how to react.

※ A weekend wasted isn't a wasted weekend.

※ When I was younger, I hated going to weddings. It seemed that all of my aunts and the grandmotherly types used to come up to me, poking me in the ribs and cackling, telling me, 'You're next. You're next.' They stopped that stuff after I started doing the same thing to them at funerals.

※ How do you know when you're at a bulimic stag party? The cake jumps out of the girl.

※ I won't rise to the occasion, but I'll slide over to it.

※ The reception had ended and the newly-weds had just sneaked off to the honeymoon resort. After supper and champagne, the groom retired to the bedroom. But the bride pulled a chair up to the balcony doors and sat there, gazing at the stars. 'Dear,' asked the somewhat impatient husband, 'aren't you coming to bed?' 'No,' she announced. 'My mother told me this was going to be the most beautiful night of my life, and I don't want to miss a single minute of it.'

✳ Did you hear about the Irish party?
The water flowed like champagne.

✳ Did you hear about the woman with varicose veins who went to the fancy dress party?
She went as a road map.

✳ I went to a surprise party. I was surprised when they let me in.

✳ On New Year's Day two neighbours meet in the hall of their block of flats. 'That was some party last night,' says one blearily. 'Yes,' replies the other, annoyed. 'And didn't you hear me banging on the ceiling last night?' 'No,' says the first man, 'we were making far too much noise.'

🐶 PENS AND PENCILS

✳ **Teacher:** This homework appears to be in your father's handwriting.
Pupil: Yes – I used his pen.

✳ If number 2 pencils are the most popular, are they still number 2?

✳ 2B or not 2B? I think it's a grade of pencil.

✳ What did the pencil sharpener say to the pencil?
Stop going in circles and get to the point!

✳ What is the best hand to write with?
Neither – it's best to write with a pen!

✳ I'd tell you another joke about a pencil. But it doesn't have any point!

penguins

What kind of bird can write?
A PENguin.

What kind of biscuit would you find at the South Pole?
A Penguin.

Why don't polar bears eat penguins?
They can't get the wrappers off.

What's black and white and black and white and black and white?
A penguin rolling downhill.

🐸 PERSONALITY TRAITS

✳ Under my gruff exterior lies an even gruffer interior.

✳ I'd like to have more self-esteem, but I don't deserve it.

✳ I demand compromise! If that's something you can live with.

✳ As I said before, I never repeat myself.

✳ Genius does what it must, talent does what it can, and you had best do what you're told.

✳ Oh Lord, give me patience, and GIVE IT TO ME NOW!

✳ Pride is what we have. Vanity is what others have.

🐾 PHiLOSOPHY

✳ Can we ever really know when our philosophy essay is due?

✳ Don't believe everything you think!

✳ I thought I was wrong once, but it turns out I was mistaken.

✳ 'I was thrown out of college for cheating in my metaphysics exam. I looked into the soul of the person next to me.' *Woody Allen*

✳ Why should you take riding classes before studying philosophy? You can't put Descartes before the horse.

✳ I used to have a handle on life, and then it broke.

✳ I don't think, therefore I am not.

✳ I'm a nobody, nobody is perfect, therefore I'm perfect.

✳ I've got to sit down to work out where I stand.

✳ It's not reality that's important, but how you perceive things.

✳ Life: The brief interlude between nothing and eternity.

✳ What is a free gift? Aren't all gifts free?

✳ I doubt, therefore I might be.

✳ You can only live once, but if you do it right, once is enough.

✳ What the hell. Go ahead. Put all your eggs in one basket.

✳ I made the mistake of taking my car to a quantum mechanic. He told me my car was and wasn't running. So I asked if he had bothered to look under the bonnet. He answered, 'No. The act of observing the engine will alter its reality dimension.'

🐵 PHOTOGRAPHY

✳ Everyone has a photographic memory; some just don't have film.

✳ What's taken before you get it?
Your picture.

✳ What did Cinderella say while she was waiting for her photos?
Some day my prints will come.

✳ When cheese gets its picture taken, what does it say?

✳ What do you get if you cross an athlete with a camera?
Film that develops itself at the gym.

✳ What do you get if you cross a dentist with a camera?
A man with a film on his teeth.

✳ I used to be twins. My mother has a picture of me when I was two.

✳ If you really look like your passport photo, chances are you're too unwell to travel.

✳ A man and a woman are looking at a picture of themselves taken at their wedding. 'I don't like this picture – it doesn't do me justice,' says the woman. 'Justice!' says the man 'It's not justice you need, it's mercy.'

pigeons

Two pigeons were sitting chatting on the roof of a house, wondering what to do next. 'You know that new car showroom on the high street?' asked one. 'Yes,' said the other. 'Let's fly over there and put a deposit on a Rolls-Royce.'

PIGS

* What is a pig's favourite karate move?
  A pork chop.

* What do you call a pig with three eyes?
  A piiig.

* 'I'm letting my pet pig sleep on my bed.'
  'What about the smell?'
  'He'll just have to get used to it!'

* What do you get if you cross a teddy bear with a pig?
  A teddy boar!

* What do you call a pig that took a plane?
  Swine flu!

* What do you get if you cross a pig with a billy goat?
  A crashing boar.

* Why do pigs never recover from illness?
  Because you have to kill them before you cure them!

* What do you call a pig who's been arrested for dangerous driving?
  A road hog!

* What did one pig say to the other pig?
  Let's be pen friends.

✴ Why did the pig run away from the pig-sty?
He thought that the other pigs were taking him for grunted.

✴ What do you call a pig with no clothes on?
Streaky bacon!

✴ Why did the farmer feed his pigs sugar and vinegar?
He wanted sweet and sour pork.

✴ What do you call high-rise flats for pigs?
Sty-scrapers.

✴ Where does a woodsman keep his pigs?
In a hog cabin!

🐗 PiRATES

✴ How do you know if you're a pirate?
You just arrrrrggghh.

✴ Where does a pirate go for vacation?
Aaarrrgentina.

✴ Where does a pirate find his family?
Arrrkansas.

✴ What does a pirate do with his wife?
Aaarrrgue.

✳ Where does a pirate use to flavour his fish?
Taarrrtarrrr sauce.

✳ Why does a pirate's phone go beep beep beep beep beep?
Because he left it off the hook!

✳ What's a pirate's second choice job?
An arrrrrchitect.

✳ Why couldn't the pirate play cards?
Because he was sitting on the deck!

✳ How much do pirates pay for their earrings?
Buccaneer.

✳ You hear about that new pirate movie?
It's rated ARRR.

✳ What kind of socks do pirates wear?
Aaaarrrrrgyle.

plastic surgery

Keep your nose to the grindstone and your shoulder to the wheel...
It's cheaper than plastic surgery.

Did you hear about the stupid plastic surgeon?
He stood in front of the fire and melted!

pms

They call it PMS because Mad Cow Disease was already taken.

🐵 POLICING

* How do you join the police?
  Handcuff them together.

* Did you hear about the policeman who found a stolen car on Acacia Street?
  He pushed it onto Park Street – he couldn't spell Acacia.

* You have the right to remain silent. Anything you say will be misquoted, then used against you.

* 'If you're being chased by a police dog, try not to go through a tunnel, then on to a little seesaw, then jump through a hoop of fire. They're trained for that.' *Milton Jones*

* One night, a lady with a black eye stumbled into the police station. She told the desk sergeant that she had heard a noise in her back yard and gone to investigate. The next thing she knew, she was hit in the face and knocked out cold. An officer was sent to her house to

investigate, and he returned a few minutes later, also with a black eye. 'Did you get hit by the same attacker?' his captain asked. 'No, sir,' he replied. 'I stepped on the same rake.'

※ A rabbi and a priest crash into each other at a four-way junction. They both get out of their cars and look at the wreck. They both thank God they are OK, and the priest says, 'This must be a sign that God wanted us to meet.' The rabbi says, 'Yes, indeed, let's drink.' So the rabbi gets out some wine. They toast each other and the priest drinks his glass. But the rabbi doesn't take a taste of his drink. Priest: 'Why aren't you drinking?' Rabbi: 'I'm waiting for the police.'

※ The cop said, 'Pull over!' I said, 'No, cardigan, but thanks for noticing!'

※ Why did the policeman carry a pencil and a piece of very thin paper? He wanted to trace someone.

※ What do you call a dog in jeans and a sweater?
A plain clothes police dog!

※ In a job interview for the police, the applicants are shown a profile picture of a man, and the interviewer says, 'The job that you're applying for requires powers of observation. Make one observation about this man.' The first applicant enters and says, 'This man has just one ear.' 'Get out!' screams the interviewer. The second applicant enters and says, 'This man has one ear.' 'Get out!' screams the interviewer again. Then the third applicant gets up to go in for his interview. The first two guys are out there and they tell him, 'The guy that's giving the interview doesn't like to hear that the man in the picture has one ear.' 'Thanks for the tip,' says the third applicant. So the third applicant enters, stares at the picture for a while and finally he says, 'This man wears contact lenses.' The interviewer is impressed and says, 'Excellent observation. Tell me, how could you tell?' So the guy says, 'Well, this man has just one ear. How could he wear glasses?'

✳ The local police force was looking for recruits, so Jim went in to try out for the job. 'OK,' the sergeant asked, 'Jim, what is one and one?' 'Eleven,' he replied. The sergeant thought to himself, that's not what I meant, but he's right. 'What two days of the week start with the letter T?' 'Today and tomorrow.' The sergeant was again surprised that Jim supplied a correct answer that he had never thought of himself. 'Now, Jim, listen carefully. Who killed President Kennedy?' Jim looked a little surprised himself, then thought really hard for a minute and finally admitted, 'I don't know.' 'Well, why don't you go home and work on that one for a while?' So Jim wandered over to the pub where his pals were waiting to hear the results of the interview. Jim was exultant. 'It went great! First day on the job and I'm already working on a murder case!'

🦁 POLITICS

✳ A policeman was coming home from work one day. He noticed that there was a lot more traffic than normal. As he got further up the road all of the traffic had come to a halt. He saw a colleague coming towards his car, so he asked what was wrong. The cop said, 'We are in a crisis situation. Tony Blair is in the road very upset. He does not have the £15 million that he owes his lawyers, and his family hates him. He is threatening to douse himself in gasoline and start a fire.' The policeman asked exactly what he was doing there. His colleague said, 'I feel sorry for the prime minister so I am going car to car asking for donations.' 'How much do you have so far?' asked the policeman. 'Well, as of right now only 33 gallons, but many people are still siphoning as we speak!'

※ Heard about the new German-Chinese restaurant? The food is great, but an hour later, you're hungry for power.

※ Newscaster announcing an election special: More on candidates at 10 p.m.

※ Little boy to his father: I didn't know they could call them 'morons' on TV!

※ A dejected Communist Party candidate trudges home after the polls close. 'So, Vladimir, how many votes did you get?' asks his wife. 'Two,' he responds. She slaps him hard across the face. 'What was that for?' 'You have a mistress now, do you?!'

※ A Conservative is a person who lives in a past that never existed.

✳ At a meeting for peace negotiations, Bill Clinton and Saddam Hussein were in Baghdad, and when Bill sat down in the conference room he noticed Saddam with three buttons on the arm of his chair. After a few minutes Saddam pressed the first button and a boxing glove sprung up and hit Bill square in the jaw. In the spirit of peace Bill decided to ignore this and continued talking until Saddam pressed the second button and a wooden bat swung out and hill Bill in the chin. Saddam started laughing. But again Bill ignored this and continued. A minute later Bill saw Saddam press the third button and he jumped in the air. A big boot sprung out and hit him in the butt. Bill decided he had had enough of this and went back home. Three weeks later the peace negotiations were rescheduled in Washington and as Saddam sat down in Bill's conference room, he noticed Bill had three buttons on the arm of his chair. A little while after they started talking, Bill pressed the first button but nothing happened. Bill started giggling. They continued to talk then Bill pressed the second button. Saddam moved but again nothing happened. Saddam was getting a little jumpy and Bill was laughing even harder. A few minutes later Bill pressed the third button and started pissing himself but again nothing happened. Saddam had had enough of this, so stood up and said, 'That's it! I'm going back to Baghdad!' To which Bill replied, 'What Baghdad?'

✳ A politician was once asked about his attitude towards whisky. 'If you mean the demon drink that poisons the mind, pollutes the body, desecrates family life, and inflames sinners, then I'm against it. But if you mean the elixir of Christmas cheer, the shield against winter chill, the taxable potion that puts needed funds into public coffers to comfort little crippled children, then I'm for it. This is my position, and I will not compromise!'

- Marx's tomb is a communist plot.

- Freedom of speech is wonderful – right up there with the freedom not to listen.

- What's the difference between feudalism and democracy? In a democracy your vote counts. In feudalism, your count votes.

- Have you heard about the prime minister doll?
  You wind it up and it does nothing for five years.

- How come we choose from just three people to run for prime minister and 50 for Miss World?

politically correct

Being politically correct means always having to say you're sorry.

🐵 POVERTY

- One afternoon, a man was riding in the back of his limousine when he noticed two men eating grass by the roadside. He ordered his driver to stop and he got out to investigate. 'Why are you eating grass?' he asked one man. 'We don't have any money for food,' the poor man replied. 'Oh, come along with me then,' the man from the limousine said excitedly. 'But, sir, I have a wife with two children!' 'Bring them along! And you, come with us too!' he said to the other man. 'But sir, I have a wife with six children!' the second man answered. 'Bring them as well!' So they all climbed into the car, which was no easy task, even for a vehicle as large as the limousine. One of the poor fellows expressed his gratitude, 'Sir, you are too kind. Thank you for taking all of us with you.' The rich man replied, 'No, thank you... The grass at my place is about three feet tall and I could use the help!'

✳ I taught my dog to beg; today he came back with £2.70.

✳ A lady is throwing a party for her granddaughter, and had pulled out all the stops – a caterer, band, and a hired clown. Just before the party started, two tramps showed up looking for a handout. Feeling sorry for them, the woman told them that she would give them a meal if they would help chop some wood for her. Gratefully, they headed to the rear of the house. The guests arrived, and all was going well, with the children having a wonderful time. But the clown hadn't shown up. After half an hour, the clown finally called to report that he was stuck in traffic, and would probably not make the party at all.

The woman was very disappointed and unsuccessfully tried to entertain the children herself. She happened to look out the window and saw one of the tramps doing cartwheels across the lawn. She watched in awe as he swung from tree branches, did mid-air flips, and leaped high in the air. She spoke to the other tramp and said, 'What your friend is doing is absolutely marvellous. I have never seen such agility. Would your friend consider repeating this performance for the children at the party? I would pay him £50!' The other tramp says, 'Well, I dunno. Let me ask him. "HEY WILLIE! FOR £50, WOULD YOU CHOP OFF ANOTHER TOE?"'

✳ Blessed are the poor. The more things you can afford, the more things you have to dust.

✳ I was too poor to afford plastic surgery, so for a small fee my doctor touched up my X-rays.

✳ You are stuck with your debt if you can't budge it.

✳ We were so poor that my parents couldn't afford shoes for me. They painted my feet black and laced up my toes.

✳ She's too poor to afford make-up. Instead of eye shadow she just sticks her head up the chimney and blinks.

✳ We were so poor that when I got ill I could only afford to have one measle at a time.

✳ We were so poor we had to watch TV by candlelight.

✳ I live in a rough area. I hung up my Christmas stocking and Santa stole it.

✳ We were so poor I was fourteen before I realized people ate three meals a day.

❋ A poor man was poaching lobsters at a beach. A game warden, his first day on the job, saw him and said: 'I'm going to have to arrest you. Poaching is illegal.' 'I'm not poaching lobsters,' the man said. 'These are my pets. I'm exercising them. I throw them into the sea, then whistle, and they come back.' 'Show me,' the warden said in disbelief. The man threw the lobsters into the water and started to walk away. 'Wait!' the warden shouted. 'Don't you have to whistle to call your lobsters back?' The man looked at the warden, paused, and said, 'What lobsters?'

🦁 PRISON

❋ What do prisoners use to call each other?
Cell phones.

❋ A man is in prison and his dad sends him a letter. The letter says: 'Dear son, now that you're in jail, I have no one to weed my garden.' The son writes a letter back, saying: 'Dad, you can't weed the garden. That's where I buried the bodies.' The police intercept the letters and learn that the bodies are hidden in the garden. A team of forensic officers spend two weeks digging it up. They find nothing. A letter arrives some time later from the son: 'Dear Dad. Sorry, that was the best I could do.'

❋ Why did the belt go to jail?
Because it held up a pair of trousers!

* IN PRISON... you spend the majority of your time in an 8 x 10 cell.
AT WORK... you spend the majority of your time in a 6 x 8 cubicle.

* IN PRISON... you get three meals a day.
AT WORK... you only get a break for one meal and you have to pay
for it.

* IN PRISON... you get time off for good behaviour.
AT WORK... you get rewarded for good behaviour with more work.

* IN PRISON... the guard locks and unlocks all the doors for you.
AT WORK... you must carry around a security card and open all the
doors for yourself.

* IN PRISON... you can watch TV and play games.
AT WORK... you get fired for watching TV and playing games.

* IN PRISON... you get your own toilet.
AT WORK... you have to share.

* IN PRISON... they allow your family and friends to visit.
AT WORK... you can't even speak to your family.

* IN PRISON... all expenses are paid by the taxpayers with no work
required.
AT WORK... you get to pay all the expenses to go to work and then
they deduct taxes from your salary to pay for prisoners.

✳ **IN PRISON**… you spend most of your life looking through bars from inside wanting to get out.
AT WORK… you spend most of your time wanting to get out and go inside bars.

✳ **IN PRISON**… there are wardens who are sadistic.
AT WORK… they are called managers.

✳ He's very popular in prison – the lifer of the party.

✳ Prison food is very tasty. I got out ten years ago and I can still taste it.

🐶 PROFESSiONS

✳ A mathematician is a device for turning coffee into theorems.

✳ Bakers trade bread recipes on a knead to know basis.

✳ An accountant is someone who knows the cost of everything and the value of nothing.

✳ An auditor is someone who arrives after the battle and bayonets all the wounded.

✳ An economist is an expert who will know tomorrow why the things he predicted yesterday didn't happen today.

✳ A statistician is someone who is good with numbers, but lacks the personality to be an accountant.

✳ Electrical engineers do it with less resistance.

✳ Why is a shoemaker like a clergyman?
They both try to save souls.

✳ An actuary is someone who brings a fake bomb on a plane because that decreases the chances that there will be another bomb on the plane.

✳ A programmer is someone who solves a problem you didn't know you had in a way you don't understand.

✳ Acupuncture: A jab well done.

✳ A lawyer is a person who writes a 10,000-word document and calls it a 'brief'.

✳ Did you hear about the exhibitionist who was thinking of retiring?
He decided to stick it out for another year.

✳ An archaeologist is a person whose career lies in ruins.

✳ An architect is someone who makes beautiful models, but unaffordable realities.

✳ A chemical engineer is doing for a profit what an organic chemist only does for fun.

✹ A consultant is someone who takes the watch off your wrist and tells you the time.

✹ An editor is a person employed on a newspaper whose business it is to separate the wheat from the chaff, and to see that the chaff is printed.

✹ A journalist is someone who spends 50 per cent of the time not saying what they know and the other 50 per cent of the time talking about things they don't know.

✹ A philosopher is a person who doesn't have a job but at least understands why.

✹ A psychologist is a person whom you pay a lot of money to ask you questions that your spouse asks free of charge.

✹ A schoolteacher is a disillusioned person who used to think they liked children.

✹ A sociologist is someone who, when a beautiful woman enters the room and everybody looks at her, looks at everybody.

✹ A cub reporter for a small town newspaper was sent out on his first assignment. He submitted the following report to his editor. 'Mrs Smith was injured in a car accident today. She is recovering in the local hospital with lacerations on her breasts.' The editor scolded the new reporter. 'This is a family paper. We don't use words like breasts here. Now go back and write something more appropriate!' The young reporter thought long and hard. Finally he handed the editor the following report: 'Mrs Smith was injured in a car accident today. She is recovering in hospital with lacerations on her (.)(.)'

✳ The repairman will never have seen a model quite like yours before.

✳ A young man reported for his first day of work at a supermarket. The manager greeted him with a warm handshake and a smile, gave him a broom and said, 'Your first job will be to sweep out the warehouse.' 'But I'm a graduate,' the young man replied indignantly. 'Oh, I'm sorry. I didn't know that,' said the manager. 'Here, give me the broom – I'll show you how.'

✳ The school of road sweeping's head of admissions was interviewing a prospective student. 'Why have you chosen this career?' he asked. 'I dream of making a million pounds in road sweeping, like my father,' the student replied. 'Your father made a million pounds in road sweeping?' echoed the man, much impressed. 'No,' replied the applicant. 'But he always dreamed of it.'

✳ How do fishermen make nets?
They sew a lot of holes together.

✳ What kind of lice does a journalist get?
Headlice.

promises

Broken promises don't upset me. I just think, Why did they believe me?

🐸 PSYCHICS

✳ Psychic exhibition cancelled due to unforeseen circumstances.

✳ Why do psychics have to ask you for your name?

✳ Prediction is very difficult – especially for the future.

✳ Why aren't psychics rich?

✳ After Mary Poppins was done with her film, she went to California and became an expert at predicting people with bad breath. Her sign read: 'Super California Psychic – expert, halitosis.'

✳ Did you hear about the poor fortune teller?
He's not making much of a prophet.

✳ **Fortune teller**: You will be miserable, depressed and unhappy until your 40th birthday.
Client: Then things will improve?
Fortune teller: No, you'll just get used to it by then.

✳ A ventriloquist sets up a new shop. He has a big sign, but no one comes in. He's in business six months and still not a single customer. A friend gives him a tip: 'There's no money in ventriloquism. Séances are where the money is, not ventriloquism!' So the man changes his entire shop, sign and all. Sign now says: 'Séances – £25-£50-£125.' First day he's open a woman comes in and enquires about a séance to talk to her dead husband. She asks about the different prices. 'What do you get for £25?' 'Well, for £25 you get to talk to your husband.' 'What about £50?' 'Well, for £50 you get to talk to him and he talks back.' 'What do you get for £125?' 'For £125, you talk to him and he talks back to you while I drink a glass of water!'

psychology

One psychologist greets another on the street: 'You're fine, how am I?'

Everybody repeat after me: 'We are all individuals.'

What's the Freudian diagnosis for a plain M&M?
Peanuts envy.

🐾 PSYCHIATRY

✳ A noted psychiatrist was a guest at an academic function, and his hostess naturally broached the subject with which the doctor was most at ease. 'Would you mind telling me, Doctor,' she asked, 'how you detect a mental deficiency in somebody who appears completely normal?' 'Nothing is easier,' he replied. 'You ask a simple question which anyone should answer with no trouble. If the person hesitates, that puts you on the track.' 'What sort of question?' 'Well, you might ask him, "Captain Cook made three trips around the world and died during one of them. Which one?"' The hostess thought a moment, then said with a nervous laugh, 'You wouldn't happen to have another example, would you? I must confess I don't know much about history.'

✳ A man was feeling down and decided to seek the aid of a psychiatrist. He went, laid on the couch, spilled his guts then waited for the profound wisdom of the psychiatrist to make him feel better. The psychiatrist asked a few questions, took some notes then sat thinking in silence for a few minutes with a puzzled look on his face. Suddenly, he looked up with an expression of delight and said, 'Ummmmm, I think your problem is low self-esteem. It is very common among losers.'

✳ Therapy is expensive. Popping plastic bubble wrap is cheap. You'll see.

✳ An Indian chief walks into a psychiatrist's office. The doctor says, 'What seems to be the problem?' The chief excitedly exclaims, 'I'm a wigwam, I'm a teepee, I'm a wigwam, I'm a teepee!' The psychiatrist tells him, 'Relax, Chief, you're just two tents.'

✳ A man says to his psychiatrist, 'Doctor, my brother thinks he's an orange.' The psychiatrist says, 'So when can I see him?' And the man says, 'Hold on, let me just pull him out of my pocket.'

✳ A psychiatrist met with a prospective client one morning and asked the client what he wanted to get out of their sessions. 'Clarity,' the client said very firmly. 'And on what issues are you looking for clarity?' the coach asked. 'Well,' he said in a less confident tone, 'I'm not sure.'

✳ After twelve years of therapy my psychiatrist said something that brought tears to my eyes. He said, '*No habla ingles.*'

✳ Did you hear about the car mechanic who went to the psychiatrist? He lay down under the couch.

✳ Did you hear about the cannibal who went to the psychiatrist because he was fed up with people?

✳ There's nothing wrong with the average person that a good psychiatrist can't exaggerate.

✳ My psychiatrist is great. He's taken all my nagging little worries and lumped them into one great big complex.

✳ How do you spot a psychiatrist in a nudist camp? He's the one listening instead of looking.

✳ My psychiatrist gave me homework. I have to go home straight away and dream.

✳ My psychiatrist really helped me with my phobias. I never used to answer the phone because I was afraid. Now I answer it whether it rings or not.

✳ What did the Freudian analyst say to his patient?
'If it isn't one thing, it's your mother!'

🐵 QUASiMODO

❋ Have you seen Quasimodo? I have a hunch he's back!

❋ Quasimodo is sitting at home with Esmeralda. 'Am I really the ugliest man alive?' he asks her. 'Go upstairs and ask the magic mirror,' Esmeralda tells him. A little while later Quasimodo comes downstairs and sits quietly at the table. After a while he turns to Esmeralda and asks, 'Who is Iain Dowie?'

❋ What's brown and wrinkled and lives in the bell tower?
The lunchbag of Notre Dame.

❋ Where does Quasimodo keep his pet rabbit?
In a hutch, back of Notre Dame.

🐰 RABBiTS

✳ How do you know carrots are good for your eyes?
   Because you never see rabbits wearing glasses!

✳ How do you catch a unique rabbit?
   Unique up on him.

✳ How do you catch a tame rabbit?
   The tame way, unique up on him!

✳ What do you get if you pour boiling water down a rabbit hole?
   Hot cross bunnies.

✳ Which side of a rabbit has the most fur?
   The outside.

✳ When is rabbit soup not good?
   When there's a hare in it!

✳ What did the rabbit want to do when it grew up?
Join the hare force.

✳ What do you get if you cross a rabbit with a flea?
Bugs Bunny.

✳ What do you get if you cross a rabbit with a shallot?
A bunion.

✳ What is invisible and smells like carrots?
Bunny farts!

✳ What do you get when you cross a perm with a rabbit?
Curly hare.

✳ Energizer Bunny Arrested; charged with battery.

✳ What do you call a rabbit with a lot of money?
A millionhare.

✳ The infant teacher asked her class, 'Do you know what sound doggies make?' Everyone in the class said, 'Woof woof.' So the teacher asked, 'Do you know what sound a kitty makes?' 'Meow, meow,' answered the class. 'Do you know what sound sheep make?' The entire class answered, 'Baa, baa.' 'And now for a gold star, do you know what sound a bunny rabbit makes?' There was a long silence and then one little boy stood up and said, 'What's up, Doc?'

✳ What do you call a hundred bunnies standing in a row taking one step backwards?
A receding hare line.

✿ READING

✳ 'Have you read the new book, *The History of Glue*? You can't put it down.' *Tim Vine*

✳ What do you get if you cross a novel with a wheel?
A book that turns its own pages.

✳ My problem is it takes me six weeks to read the book of the month.

✳ I hate books. They only teach us to talk about things we know nothing about.

✳ I have a hundred books, but no bookcase. No one will lend me a bookcase.

✳ I'm reading a very unusual murder mystery. Seems that the victim was shot by a man from another book.

✳ Even if you can't read a girl like a book, it's nice to thumb the pages.

✳ Reading while sunbathing makes you well red.

* Her mind was a closed book, and worse still, it came in a horribly plain jacket.

* A man walks into a book shop and asks the guy behind the counter, 'Do you like Kipling?' The guy says, 'I don't know... I've never Kipled.'

* What's black, white and red all over?
A book.

* How many books can you put in an empty backpack?
One! After that it's not empty!

Batty Books

Living with Apes by Bab Boone

Make Your Own Sweets by Oliver Nutherone

Mother of Five by Berta Quinns

Time for School by R.U. Upjohn

House Repairs by Rufus Quick

Target Shooting by Mr Completely

A Matter of Doubt by Willie Wontie

Banbury Cross by Rhoda Whitehorse

Policing Today by Laura Norda

The Life of a Highwayman by Ann Dover

Sad Women by Paul Aidy

Tug of War by Paul Hard

Hole in my Bucket by Lee King

No Way Out by Isadora Neggsitt

Quick Snacks by T. N. Biskits

The Unemployed Conjuror by Trixie Coulden-Dou

Suburban Living by Bill Tupperea

The Haunted House by Hugo First

The Match on the Grass by Lorna Light

Learn Calypso by Lydia Binn

Off to Market by Tobias A. Pigg

🐸 RELATiONSHiPS

※ **Husband to wife:** I'm feeling so depressed today.
   Wife: Why, darling?
   Husband: It's just that sometimes I feel so alone and useless.
   Wife: Oh, you don't have to feel so alone. A lot of people think you're useless.

※ 'Will you love me when I'm old and ugly?'
   'Darling, of course I do.'

✳ A man needs a mistress to break the monogamy.

✳ Wanted: Meaningful overnight relationship.

✳ I am not single, I'm romantically challenged.

✳ 'You have to remember all the trivia that your girlfriend tells you, because eventually you get tested. She'll go: "What's my favourite flower?" And you murmur to yourself: "Damn, I wasn't listening... Self-raising?"' *Addy Van Der Borgh*

✳ I'm still single because my family-in-law can't have children.

✳ Early to bed, early to rise, and your girlfriend goes out with other guys.

✳ If I ever find the girl of my dreams, what will I tell my wife?

✳ 'I hear your boyfriend is an electrician.'
'Yes. He alternates between me and the girl next door.'

✳ She took after her mother who took after her father who took after the au pair.

✳ I like being single. I'm always there when I need me.

✳ Definition of a bachelor: A man who has missed the opportunity to make some woman miserable.

✳ I still miss my ex. But my aim is getting better.

✳ I think, therefore I'm single.

✳ My girlfriend is good at keeping secrets. We were engaged for four months before I knew about it.

Break-ups

✳ When a man steals your wife, there is no better revenge than to let him keep her.

✳ I've split up with my girlfriend. She was smart, incredibly hot, her sense of humour was excellent. She could have you in stitches with a couple of snappy one-liners in minutes. But like a fool, I have split up with her for a silly, selfish reason. The reason I split up with her was because she was a small pink mouse that lived on the moon. Now I realize I've dropped a clanger!

✳ Sitting at the bar, glum Dave told the barman that he was drinking to forget the heartbreak of his broken engagement. 'Yeah,' said Roger, 'would you marry someone who didn't know the meaning of the word faithful, and who was flip and even vicious when the subject of fidelity came up?' 'No way,' the barman said. 'Well,' said Roger, 'neither would my fiancée.'

✳ My wife ran off with my best friend... I'll really miss him.

✳ I had terrible luck. My best friend ran away without my wife.

✳ A man tells his wife he is leaving her for another woman. 'What has she got that I don't have?' she asks.
'Would you like that alphabetically?'

Dating

✳ A man on a date wonders if he'll get lucky. The woman already knows.

✳ I used to go out with a girl with a wooden leg but I had to break it off.

✳ A woman was very distraught at the fact that she had not had a date in quite some time. She was afraid she might have something wrong with her so she decided to seek the medical expertise of a therapist. Her doctor recommended she see the well-known Chinese therapist, Dr Chang. Upon entering the examination room, Dr Chang said, 'OK, take off all your crose.' The woman did as she was told. 'Now, get down and craw reery, reery fass to odder side of room.' Again, the woman did as she was instructed. Dr Chang then said, 'OK, now craw reery, reery fass back to me.' So she did. Dr Chang shook his head slowly and said, 'Your probrem vely bad. You haf Ed Zachary Disease, worse case I ever see, dat why you not haf any dates.' Worried, the woman asked anxiously, 'Oh no, Dr Chang, what is Ed Zachary Disease?' Dr Chang looked the woman in the eye and replied, 'Unfortunately, your face look Ed Zachary like your bum.'

✳ 'I hate to say this but your girlfriend looks like a monkey.'
'True, but she's the gorilla my dreams.'

✳ A lonely man joined an online dating club. After a few emails he found himself attracted to a particular lady, who wrote to him regularly. He plucked up the courage to suggest they should meet, but decided to be completely truthful. He wrote: 'I'm not very handsome. I am very short and fat, and covered in red boils. My eyes are different colours and one leg is shorter than the other. I am also very hairy. Please meet me at 1pm at the Starbucks on the corner.' Almost immediately he got a reply: 'I am not bothered about your looks, and I'm looking forward to meeting you. Could you carry a copy of *The Times*, so I can recognize you.'

✳ I've been on so many blind dates, I should get a free dog.

✳ What did the mean man do when his girlfriend asked for a fur for Christmas?
He scraped some out of the kettle.

✳ I asked a girl if I could see her home, so she got out a photograph.

✳ Poor old Bob sent his photograph off to a Lonely Hearts Club. They sent it back saying they weren't that lonely.

✳ A man is dining in a fancy restaurant and there is a gorgeous redhead sitting at the next table. He has been checking her out since he sat down, but lacks the nerve to start a conversation. Suddenly she sneezes, and her glass eye comes flying out of its socket towards the man. He reaches out, grabs it out of the air, and hands it back. 'Oh my, I am so sorry,' the woman says as she pops her eye back in place. 'Let me buy your dinner to make it up to you,' she says. They enjoy a wonderful dinner together, and afterwards they go to the theatre, followed by drinks. They talk, they laugh, she shares her deepest dreams and he shares his. She listens. They have a wonderful, wonderful time. The next day they meet, she cooks a gourmet meal with all the trimmings. The guy is amazed! Everything has been SO incredible! 'You know,' he said, 'you are the perfect woman. Are you this nice to every guy you meet?' 'No,' she replies. 'You just happened to catch my eye.'

✳ Two guys are playing golf and one of them shanks his ball over a hill and into the next fairway. He goes to look for it but returns empty-handed. 'Where's your ball?' his friend asks. 'I can't go get my ball. I looked over the hill and there's my wife AND my girlfriend. They're playing golf together. If I go over there, I'll get killed. You have to get my ball.' The friend walks up the hill and comes running back a few minutes later. 'What's the matter?' asks the first golfer. 'Wow, small world,' the second replies.

Divorce

✳ Did you hear about the new 'Divorce Barbie'? It comes with all Ken's stuff.

✳ A man was reading the paper when an ad caught his eye. It announced, 'New Porsche, £50!' The man thought it had to be a joke, but he said to himself, 'Just in case, it's worth a shot.' So he called the number and then went to the home of the lady selling the sports car. She led him into the garage. Sure enough, there was an almost brand new Porsche.

'Wow!' the man said. 'Can I take it for a test drive?' 'Sure,' answered the lady. The man was surprised to learn that the car ran perfectly. When he got back to the lady's house, he asked her, 'Why are you selling me this great Porsche for only £50?' Then the lady replied with a laugh, 'My husband just ran off with his secretary, and he told me, "You can have the house and the furniture, just sell my Porsche and send me the money."'

✳ A man and his wife divorced over religious differences. She worshipped money and he didn't have a penny.

✳ A woman told her husband one day they had to get divorced. He asked why and she said they were imcompatible. He said, '*Incompatible*? How can you say that after eighteen years?' She said, 'You don't have enough income and I'm not pattable.'

✳ A strikingly beautiful young woman boards Concorde for a transatlantic flight. All the passengers notice her beauty, as well as a huge diamond ring on her left hand, as she takes her seat. The guy sitting next to her has to remark on the huge gem. 'Oh, this?' she replies. 'This is a Rivara diamond. And it comes with a curse!' Shocked, the man asks, 'A curse! What's the curse?' 'Mr Rivara,' she replies.

✳ An old lady tottered into a lawyer's office and asked for help in arranging a divorce. 'A divorce?' asked the unbelieving lawyer. 'Tell me, how old are you?' 'I'm eighty-four,' answered the old lady. 'Eighty-four! And how old is your husband?' 'My husband is eighty-seven.' 'My, my,' said the lawyer, 'and how long have you been married?' 'Next September will be sixty-two years.' 'Married sixty-two years?! Why would you want a divorce now?' 'Because,' the woman answered calmly, 'enough is enough.'

✳ 'Mr Clark, I have reviewed this case very carefully,' the divorce court judge said, 'and I've decided to give your wife £500 a week.' 'That's very fair, Your Honour,' the husband said. 'And every now and then I'll try to send her a few bucks myself!'

✳ A Polish man is married to an English woman. They are known for their happy marriage, so a lawyer friend is surprised when the man comes into his office extremely agitated, demanding a divorce. He claims his wife is plotting to kill him. The lawyer demands to see some evidence for this accusation. The man rummages around in his briefcase and brings out a cosmetic bag, from which he takes a small bottle. 'Look here. She buy this bottle, she keep it in bathroom. Look what it say: "Poison: Polish remover!"'

✳ Alimony: Funds which allow a woman who lived unhappily married to live happily unmarried.

✳ Alimony is having an ex-husband you can bank on.

✳ How are a Texas tornado and a Tennessee divorce the same? Either way, somebody's gonna lose a trailer.

rednecks

How can you tell if a redneck is married?

There are tobacco spit stains on BOTH sides of his pickup truck.

RELiGiON

★ A woman walks up to a bishop at an ordination and says, 'Bishop, I love your dress, but your handbag is on fire.'

★ 'I like the Ten Commandments but have a problem with the ninth. It should be: "Thou shalt not covet thy neighbour's ox – except in Scrabble."' *David O'Doherty*

★ A clergyman parked his car on a double yellow line in a large city because he was in a hurry and couldn't find a parking space. He left a note under the windscreen wiper that read: 'I have circled the block 10 times. If I don't park here, I'll miss my appointment. Forgive us our trespasses.' When he returned, he found under the wiper a ticket from a parking warden along with this note: 'I've circled this block for 10 years. If I don't give you a ticket, I'll lose my job. Lead us not into temptation.'

★ A father was in church with his three young children. As was customary, he sat in the very front row so that the children could properly witness the service. During this particular service, the minister was baptizing a tiny infant. The man's five-year-old daughter was particularly enthralled by the procedure of pouring water over the infant's head. With a quizzical look on her face, the little girl turned to her father and whispered, 'Daddy, is he brainwashing that baby?'

✳ After a long, dry sermon, the minister announced that he wished to meet with the church board after the service. The first man to arrive was a stranger. 'You misunderstood my announcement,' said the minister. 'This is a meeting of the board.' 'Well,' said the man. 'If there is anyone here more bored than I am, I'd like to meet him.'

✳ At a Catholic school gathering, Mother Superior stacked a pile of apples on one end of a table with a sign saying, 'Take only one apple, please – God is watching.' On the other end of the table was a pile of biscuits where a student had placed a sign saying, 'Take all the biscuits you want – God is watching the apples.'

✳ 'Ask people about God nowadays and they usually reply, "I'm not religious, but deep down, I'm a very spiritual person.' What this phrase really means is: "I'm afraid of dying, but I can't be bothered going to church."' *Colin Ramone*

✳ As the master said to his confused disciple, 'That was Zen, this is Tao.'

✳ Church: The only society on earth that exists for the benefit of non-members.

* Moses and his flock arrive at the sea, with the Egyptians in hot pursuit. Moses calls a staff meeting. Moses said, 'Well, how are we going to get across the sea? We need a fast solution. The Egyptians are close behind us.' The General of the Armies responded, 'Normally, I'd recommend that we build a pontoon bridge to carry us across. But there's not enough time – the Egyptians are too close.' The Admiral of the Navy said, 'Normally, I'd recommend that we build barges to carry us across. But time is too short.' 'Does anyone have a solution?' Moses asked. Just then, his Public Relations man raises his hand. Moses called on him. 'You! You have a solution?' The PR man said, 'No, but I can promise you this: if you can find a way out of this one, I can get you a lot of coverage in the Old Testament.'

* In the beginning the universe was created. This has made a lot of people very angry and been widely regarded as a bad move.

* Who was the best actor in the Bible?
  Samson – he brought the house down!

* Could God make a curry so hot he couldn't eat it?

* Dear Lord, thus far today you should be proud of me. I haven't gossiped, lost my temper, spoken in anger, been greedy, grumpy, selfish or over-indulgent. No ill feeling has entered my heart, nor have I begrudged another soul. I am very pleased with the way I have performed thus far. However, in a few minutes, Lord, I will be getting out of bed to begin the day, and from that point on I will be in much need of your help and understanding. Thank you for being there for me. Amen.

✳ St Peter was waiting by the Pearly Gates when 40 people from Liverpool showed up. Never having seen anyone from Liverpool at heaven's door, St Peter said he would have to check with God. After hearing the news, God instructed him to admit the ten most virtuous people from the group. A few minutes later, St Peter returned to God, breathless, and said, 'They're gone!' 'What? All of the Liverpudlians are gone?' asked God. 'No!' replied St Peter. 'The Pearly Gates!'

✳ The new priest is nervous about hearing confessions, so he asks an older priest to sit in on his sessions. After the young man hears several confessions, the older priest asks him to step out of the confessional for a few suggestions. The old priest suggests, 'Cross your arms over your chest and rub your chin with one hand.' The new priest tries out the gesture. The old priest suggests, 'Try saying things like, "I see, yes, go on," and "I understand – how did you feel about that?"' The new priest repeats what the older man has said and nods. The old priest says, 'Now, don't you think that's a little better than slapping your knee and saying, "No way! What happened next?"'

✳ How do you make holy water?
Boil the hell out of it.

✳ Sign on a church bulletin board: 'You aren't too bad to come in. You aren't good enough to stay out.'

✳ The flood is over. The ark is parked neatly on the top of Mount Ararat, and Noah is standing alone on its deck, not one animal on board. 'Flipping Animal Liberation League!' exclaims Noah.

✳ An embarrassed woman approached the vicar after a church service. 'I hope you didn't take it personally, Reverend, when my husband walked out during your sermon.' 'I did find it rather disconcerting,' the vicar replied. 'It's not a reflection on you,' insisted the churchgoer. 'He's has been walking in his sleep ever since he was a child.'

✳ One Sunday a vicar told the congregation that the church needed some extra money and asked the people to prayerfully consider giving a little extra in the offering plate. He said that whoever gave the most would be able to pick out three hymns. After the offering plates were passed, the vicar glanced down and noticed that someone had placed a £500 note in the offering. He was so excited that he immediately shared his joy with his congregation and said he'd like to personally thank the person who placed the money in the plate. A very quiet, elderly, saintly lady at the back shyly raised her hand. The vicar asked her to come to the front. Slowly she made her way. He told her how wonderful it was that she gave so much and in thanksgiving asked her to pick out three hymns. Her eyes brightened as she looked over the congregation, pointed to the three most handsome men in the building and said, 'I'll take him and him and him.'

✳ A minister's son had a pet dog that sadly died. Feeling that a proper burial should be performed, they had secured a small box, then dug a hole and made ready for the disposal of the deceased. The minister's son was chosen to say the appropriate prayers and with sonorous dignity intoned his version of what he thought his father always said: 'Glory be unto the Faaather, and unto the Sonnn, and into the hole he gooooes.'

* **2000 BC** – Here, eat this root.
  1000 AD – That root is heathen. Here, say this prayer.
  1850 AD – That prayer is superstition. Here, drink this potion.
  1940 AD – That potion is snake oil. Here, swallow this pill.
  1985 AD – That pill is ineffective. Here, take this antibiotic.
  2000 AD – That antibiotic is artificial. Here, eat this root.

* A man was in church, thanking God for his new-found girlfriend. 'Why did you make her so kind-hearted?' 'So you could love her, my son.' 'God, why did you make her so good-looking?' he asked. 'So you could love her, my son.' 'And why did you make her such a good cook?' 'So you could love her, my son.' The man thought about this and said, 'Well, I don't mean to seem ungrateful or anything, but … why did you make her so stupid?' 'So she could love you, my son.'

* A little boy opened the big family Bible. He was fascinated as he fingered through the old pages. Suddenly, something fell out. He picked up the object and looked at it. What he saw was an old leaf that had been pressed in between the pages. 'Mum, look what I found,' the boy called out. 'What have you got there, dear?' With astonishment in the young boy's voice, he answered, 'I think it's Adam's underwear!'

* A little boy was saying his bedtime prayers with his mother: 'Lord, bless Mummy and Daddy, and God, GIVE ME A NEW BICYCLE!!!' Mother: 'God's not deaf, son.' Boy: 'I know, Mum, but Grandma's in the next room, and she's hard of hearing!'

✳ Late one Saturday night, after a long and difficult day of visiting hospitals, nursing homes and elderly members of the congregation, a vicar was making his weary way home. As he travelled the hilly, curving, country road, he overtook a car. The slow-moving car was weaving from one side of the road to the other in a most disturbing manner. Being familiar with most residents of the area, he recognized the car as belonging to a member of his congregation. 'Oh no,' said the vicar to himself, 'Frank Johnson has fallen off the wagon again. The way that car is weaving, he must be really plastered. I'd better pull up beside him and get him to stop before he hurts himself.' Putting thought to action, the preacher pulled alongside Frank's car just in time for the next swerve to run him off the road. Over the shoulder, down a steep bank, the vicar's car rolled over twice and came to rest against a large pine tree. Not completely senseless to the world, Frank stopped his car and staggered back to a point above the vicar's car. Fortunately, the vicar had been using a seat belt. That and the relatively slow speed had prevented any injury. When Frank saw someone struggling out of the wrecked car, he yelled, 'Who the hell are you?' The vicar yelled back, 'Frank Johnson, don't you talk to me like that.' 'My God, Vicar, that you?' 'Yes, Frank, it is, and I'll thank you not to take the Lord's name in vain. It's already bad enough that you're drunk.' 'You OK, Vicar?' 'Yes, Frank, fortunately the Lord was with me.' 'You better let him ride with me. Way you drive, you gonna kill him.'

✳ When I was a kid I used to pray every night for a new bike. Then I realized that the Lord doesn't work that way, so I stole one and asked him to forgive me.

✳ After the christening of his baby brother in church, a little boy sobbed all the way home in the back seat of the car. His father asked him what was wrong. 'That vicar said he wanted us brought up in a Christian home,' the boy replied, 'but I want to stay with you and Mum!'

✳ A Sunday School teacher was struggling to open a combination lock on the church safe. Finally she went to the vicar's study and asked for help. The vicar came into the room and began to turn the dial. After the first two numbers, he paused and stared blankly for a moment. Finally he looked serenely heavenward and his lips moved silently. Then he looked back at the lock, and quickly turned to the final number and opened the lock.

The amazed teacher said, 'I'm in awe at your faith, Vicar.' 'It's really nothing,' he answered. 'I never can remember the combination, either. That's why I wrote the number on a piece of tape and put it on the ceiling.'

✳ Lord save me from your followers.

✳ Heck is where people go who don't believe in Gosh.

✳ Lead me not into temptation. I can find the way myself.

✳ An atheist is a man who has no invisible means of support.

✳ What kind of lights did Noah use on the ark?
Flood lights!

✳ Forgive and forget, but keep a list of names just in case.

✳ Did you hear about the vicar who tried to convert? A woman in his flock told him she worshipped her body, and he tried to embrace her religion.

✳ If God is watching us, the least we can do is be entertaining.

✳ A confirmed hellraiser began attending church faithfully on Sunday mornings. The vicar was very pleased and told him, 'How wonderful it makes me feel to see you at services with your good wife!' 'Well, Vicar,' said the man. 'Frankly, it's a matter of choice. I'd rather hear your sermon than hers.'

✳ A vicar waited in line at a petrol station to have his car filled just before a long holiday weekend. The attendant worked quickly, but there were many cars ahead of him in the queue. Finally, the attendant motioned him towards a vacant pump. 'Reverend,' said the young man, 'sorry about the delay. It seems as if everyone waits until the last minute to get ready for a long trip.' The vicar nodded. 'I know what you mean. It's the same in my business.'

✳ Atheists can do whatever the hell they want.

✳ What did the Dalai Lama say to the hotdog vendor?
Make me one with everything.

✳ Cult: Not enough people to make a minority.

✳ Did you hear about the rabbi who was drunk on the job?
He got the sack.

✳ Three vicars meet to discuss church matters. 'You know,' says one, 'I
have terrible trouble with bats in the belfry. We've tried poison but
they just won't leave.' 'I know what you mean,' says one of the other
vicars. 'We have the same problem. I tried fumigating them but they
just won't go.' 'You want to do what I did to get rid of them for
good,' says the third vicar. 'I baptized them and made them
members of the church and they haven't been back since.'

✳ How much faith is required to become an atheist?

✳ A father was reading Bible stories to his young son. They came to the
story of Lot's wife: 'The man named Lot was warned to take his wife
and flee out of the city but his wife looked back and was turned to
salt.' His son asked: 'What happened to the flea?'

✳ A man was coming out of church one day, and the vicar was
standing at the door to shake hands with the departing congregation.
He grabbed the man by the hand and pulled him aside. The vicar
said, 'You need to join the Army of the Lord!' The man replied, 'I'm
already in the Army of the Lord, Vicar.' 'How come I don't see you
except at Christmas and Easter?' asked the vicar. He whispered
back, 'I'm in the secret service.'

✳ Who tracks down lost vicars?
The Bureau of Missing Parsons.

✳ A religious war is like children fighting over who has the strongest imaginary friend.

✳ A woman knelt in the confessional and said, 'Bless me, Father, for I have sinned.' 'What is it, child?' 'Father, I have committed the sin of vanity. Twice a day I gaze at myself in the mirror and tell myself how beautiful I am.' The priest turned, took a good look at her, and said, 'My daughter, I have good news. That isn't a sin – it's only a mistake.'

✳ Photons have mass? I didn't even know they were Catholic.

✳ The preacher was having a heart-to-heart talk with a backslider of his flock, whose drinking of moonshine invariably led to quarrelling with his neighbours, and occasional shotgun blasts at some of them. 'Can't you see, Ben,' intoned the parson, 'that not one good thing comes out of this drinking?' 'Well, I sort of disagree there,' replied the backslider. 'It makes me miss the folks I shoot at.'

Nuns

✳ A man is in the hospital recovering from an operation when a nun walks into his room. She is there to cheer up the sick and lame. They start talking, and she asks about his life. He talks about his wife and their thirteen children. 'My, my,' says the nun, 'thirteen children. A good and proper Catholic family. God is very proud of you.' 'I'm sorry, Sister,' he says. 'I am not Catholic, I'm Baptist.' 'Baptist?' she replies. 'You sex maniac!'

* What do you call 100 nuns in a shop?
  Virgin Megastore.

* Are you allowed to kiss a nun?
  Yes. But don't get into the habit.

* There once was a 94-year-old nun back in the 1890s whose worn-out body began to surrender. Her doctor prescribed for her a shot of whisky three times a day, to relax her. However, not to be lured into worldly pleasures, she huffily declined. But her mother superior knew the elderly sister loved milk. So she instructed the kitchen to spike the milk three times a day. Eventually, the elderly pious one approached her final hour. As several sisters gathered around at her bedside, the mother superior asked if she wanted to leave them any words of wisdom. 'Oh, yes,' she replied. 'Never sell that cow!'

RESOLUTiONS

Easy-to-keep resolutions:

1. I must gain weight. Put on at least two stone.

2. Stop exercising. Waste of time.

3. Read less.

4. Watch more TV. I've been missing some good stuff.

5. Procrastinate more.

6. Drink. Drink some more.

7. Develop new interests: smoking.

8. Stop bringing lunch from home: eat out more.

9. Stop giving money and time to charity.

10. Start being superstitious.

11. Have my car lowered and invest in a really loud stereo system. Get the windows tinted. Buy some fur for the dash.

12. Speak in a monotone voice and only use monosyllabic words.

13. Only wear jeans that are two sizes too small and use a chain or rope for a belt.

14. Only wear white T-shirts with those fashionable yellow stains under the arms.

rhinos and hippos

What do you get when you cross an elephant with a rhino?
Elifino!

Why did cavemen draw pictures of hippopotamuses and rhinoceroses on their walls?
Because they couldn't spell their names!

Why does a rhinoceros have so many wrinkles?
Because it's so hard to iron.

🐹 RODENTS

✳ Where do hamsters come from?
Hamsterdam!

✳ A Scotsman was visiting relatives in Canada and one of them took
him on a fishing trip in the wilderness. 'Wow, what's that over
yonder?' the Scotsman asked his cousin. 'That's a moose,' said the
Canadian. 'Aye!' exclaimed the Scotsman, raising an eyebrow. 'If that
be a moose, I'd sure hate to see your rats!'

✳ What squeaks as it solves crimes?
Miami mice!

✳ What's grey, squeaky and hangs around in caves?
Stalagmice!

✳ What's the hardest part of milking a mouse?
Getting it to fit over a bucket!

✳ What have twelve legs, six eyes, three tails and can't see?
Three blind mice!

✳ A mangy-looking guy goes into a restaurant and orders a steak.
The waiter shakes his head and says, 'No way. I don't think you can
pay for it.' The tramp says, 'You're right. I don't have any money,
but if I show you something you have never seen before, will you
give me the food?' 'Deal!' The guy reaches into his coat pocket and

pulls out a hamster and puts it on the counter. The hamster runs to the end of the counter, across the room, and up the piano. He jumps on the keyboard and starts playing Gershwin tunes. The waiter says, 'Wow, you're right. I've never seen anything like that before. That hamster is a really good piano player.' He brings the man a steak, which he promptly eats and asks for another. 'Money or another miracle,' says the waiter. The guy reaches into his coat again and pulls out a frog. He puts the frog on the counter, and the frog starts to sing. He has a marvellous voice and great pitch. A stranger from the other end of the counter runs over to the guy and offers him £300 for the frog. The guy says, 'It's a deal.' He takes the money. The stranger takes the frog and runs out of the restaurant. The waiter says, 'Are you crazy? You sold a singing frog for £300? It must have been worth millions.' 'Nah,' says the guy. 'The hamster is also a ventriloquist.'

ROYALTY

★ The Queen and the Pope are on stage together at a huge charity event. Obviously, they've both done this sort of thing many times before, so to make it a little more interesting the Queen says to the Pope, 'How about a wager? I bet I can make every British person in this crowd go wild with just one little wave of my hand.' The Pope agrees and the Queen waves her hand. Sure enough, the royal wave elicits rapturous applause and cheering from all the Brits in the crowd. The Pope, not wishing to be outdone by someone wearing a worse frock and hat than him, says to the Queen, 'That was impressive. How about another wager? I bet I can make every Irish person in this crowd go crazy with joy merely with a nod of my head. But it won't just last for a minute. This joy will last for months and be talked about for years.' The Queen is sceptical. 'One nod of your head? Show me.' So the Pope head-butts her.

✳ What was the last thing Charles I did?
Took his pet spaniel for a walk round the block.

✳ What happens when the Queen burps?
She issues a royal pardon.

rubbish

What do you get if you cross a goose with a rubbish tip?
Down in the dumps.

scarecrows

What is a scarecrow's favourite food?
Strawberries.

Why don't scarecrows have any fun?
Because they're stuffed shirts.

 **SCiENCE**

* I'm reading an incredibly interesting book about antigravity. I just can't put it down.

* Did you hear about the mad scientist who invented a gas that could burn through anything? Now he's trying to invent something to hold it in!

✳ Who was the most famous ant scientist?
Albert Antstein!

✳ People will accept your ideas much more readily if you tell them
Einstein said it first.

✳ 'A lady with a clipboard stopped me in the street the other day. She
said, "Can you spare a few minutes for cancer research?" I said, "All
right, but we won't get much done."' *Jimmy Carr*

✳ Quantum mechanics: The dreams stuff is made of.

✳ Friction can be a drag sometimes.

✳ Did you hear about the mad scientist who put dynamite in his fridge?
They say it blew his cool!

✳ What is the study of soda carbonation?
Fizzics!

✳ Always turn the radio on BEFORE you listen to it.

✳ Why was there thunder and lightning in the lab?
The scientists were brainstorming!

✳ Why did the scientist install a knocker on his door?
To win the Nobell Prize.

✳ I think animal testing is a terrible idea; they get all nervous and give
the wrong answers.

✳ Biology grows on you.

silence

What breaks when you say it?
Silence!

🐸 SEA-SAILING

✳ What did the water say to the boat?
Nothing, it just waved.

✳ You chatter more than a dolphin by a fish bucket.

✳ Save the whales: collect the whole set.

✳ Which one of these is the non-smoking lifeboat?

✳ Why was the sand wet?
Because the sea weed.

✳ Who is the biggest gangster in the sea?
Al Caprawn!

✳ Sea captains don't like crew cuts.

✳ Why is the sea always so cross?
You'd be cross too if you had crabs all over your bottom.

seals

Two seals walk into a club.

What animals are on legal documents?
Seals!

⓰ SEMi-TRADiTiONAL SAYiNGS

✳ The meek shall inherit the earth … after we're through with it.

✳ If a thing is worth doing, it would have been done already.

✳ Blessed are the flexible, for they can tie themselves into knots.

✳ A closed mouth gathers no foot.

✳ Two rights do not make a wrong, they make an aeroplane.

✳ The things that come to those who wait may be the things left over from those who got there first.

✳ In case of emergency, speak in clichés.

✳ Defeat isn't bitter if you sprinkle dirty revenge on it.

✳ Those who live by the sword get shot by those who don't.

✳ Two wrongs do not make a right, but three lefts do.

✳ Do not walk behind me, for I may not lead. Do not walk ahead of me, for I may not follow. Do not walk beside me, either. Just leave me alone.

✳ If at first you don't succeed, then tightrope walking definitely isn't for you.

✳ A man's home is his castle – in a manor of speaking.

✳ This land is your land. This land is my land. So stay on your land.

✳ Veni, Vidi, Velcro – I came, I saw, I stuck around.

☺ SEX

* **Masochist**: Hurt me!
  Sadist: No.

* Two men were discussing former loves. One confessed that he had once broken up with a girl long ago because she had a seemingly incurable speech impediment. His friend was appalled, 'I'm shocked. I never knew you to be prejudiced against disabilities. What was the girl's problem?' His friend paused and reflected. 'She couldn't say "Yes".'

* Be safety conscious: 80 per cent of people are caused by accidents.

* Jack and his friend Bob went skiing. They loaded up Jack's car and headed north. After a few hours, they got caught in a terrible blizzard and pulled into the driveway of a farm owned by a very rich widow. They went to the door and asked the attractive lady who answered if they could spend the night there. 'Oh, it's such terrible weather out there and I have this huge house all to myself. But I'm recently widowed,' she said, 'and I'm afraid of what the neighbours will say if I let two attractive young men stay in my house.' 'Don't worry,' Jack said. 'We'll be happy if you just let us sleep in your barn. And if the weather breaks, we'll be gone at first light.' The lady agreed, and the two men found their way to the barn and settled in for the night. Come morning, the weather had cleared, and they left and had a great skiing weekend. But nine months later Jack got a letter from an

attorney. It took him a few minutes to figure it out, but he finally determined that it was from the attorney of the attractive widow in whose barn he and Bob had stayed. So he drove to see his friend Bob and asked, 'Bob, remember nine months ago that good-looking widow from the farm we stayed at on our ski holiday up north?' 'Yes, I do.' 'Did you get up in the middle of the night and go up to the house and pay her a visit?' 'Yes,' Bob said, a little embarrassed about being found out. 'I have to admit that I did.' 'And did you stay the night with her?' 'Yes.' 'And did you happen to use my name instead of your own?' Bob's face turned red and he said, 'Yeah, sorry, mate. I'm afraid I did. Why do you ask?' 'She just died and left me everything.'

✸ Now that food has replaced sex in my life, I can't even get into my own pants.

✸ The problem with sex in the movies is the popcorn usually spills.

✸ Except for 75 per cent of the women, everyone in the whole world wants to have sex.

✸ Pretend to spank me – I'm a pseudo-masochist!

✸ A woman takes her sixteen-year-old daughter to the doctor. The doctor says, 'OK, Mrs Jones, what's the problem?' The mother says, 'It's my daughter Frances. She keeps getting these cravings, she's putting on weight, and is sick most mornings.' The doctor gives Frances a good examination, then turns to the mother and says, 'Well, I don't know how to tell you this, but your Frances is pregnant

– about four months would be my guess.' The mother says, 'Pregnant?! She can't be. She has never ever been left alone with a man! Have you, Frances?' Frances says, 'No, Mother! I've never even kissed a man!' The doctor walked over to the window and just stares out it. About five minutes pass and finally the mother says, 'Is there something wrong out there, Doctor?' The doctor replies, 'No, not really, it's just that the last time anything like this happened, a star appeared in the east and three wise men came over the hill. I'll be damned if I'm going to miss it this time!'

✳ I come from a small town whose population never changed. Each time a woman got pregnant, someone left town.

✳ People in cars cause accidents. Accidents in cars cause people.

✳ Chastity is curable, if detected early.

✳ An angry husband returned home one night to find his wife in bed with a naked man. 'What are you doing?' he shouted. To which his wife said to her lover, 'I told you he was stupid.'

✳ I used to be into necrophilia, sado-masochism and bestiality but everyone told me I was just flogging a dead horse.

✳ Are you male or female? To find the answer, see below!

🐑 SHEEP

※ What do you get if you cross a sheep and a waterfall?
A wet blanket.

※ What's a sheep's favourite fruit?
A baa-nana!

※ Who's afraid of Virginia Woolf?
Virginia Sheep.

※ What do you get if you cross a lamb with a spaceship?
The Star-sheep *Enterprise*.

※ What do you get if you cross a cow, a sheep and a goat?
The Milky Baa Kid!

※ A New Zealander is walking along the road with a sheep under each
arm. He meets another New Zealander who says, 'You sheerin'
mate?' and the first guy replies, 'Naw, they're all mine.'

※ What do you get if you cross a lamb and a penguin?
A sheepskin dinner jacket.

※ **First sheep:** Baa!
Second sheep: Moo!
First sheep: What do you mean – moo?
Second sheep: I'm learning a foreign language.

✴ Where do sheep go to get haircuts?
To the baa baa shop!

✴ How do sheep keep warm in winter?
Central bleating!

✴ **Malcolm:** Did you know it takes three sheep to make one jumper?
Sharon: I didn't even know sheep could knit!

✴ You know you should go to sleep when the sheep you're counting start to hit the fence.

✴ Where do sheep like to shop?
Woolworths.

✴ What did the polite sheep say as he waited to let another sheep go through the gate first?
'After ewe.'

✴ Why don't sheep shrink in the rain?

🐺 SHOES AND TRAINERS

✴ A man came across a ticket in an old coat from 'Smith & Sons Shoe Repairs', a local shoe repair shop. The date stamped on the ticket showed it was over eleven years old. He showed his wife and they tried to remember which of them might have forgotten to pick up a pair of shoes over a decade ago. 'Do you think the shoes will still be in the shop?' he asked. 'Not very likely,' his wife said. 'It's worth a try,' he said, and went downstairs, got into the car, and drove to the store. With a straight face, he handed the ticket to the man behind the counter. With a face just as straight, the man said, 'Just a minute I'll have to look for these.' He disappeared into a dark corner at the back of the shop. Two minutes later, the man called out, 'Here they are!' 'Really?' the owner of the shoes called back. 'That's terrific! Who would have thought they'd still be here after all this time.' The man came back to the counter, empty-handed. 'They'll be ready Thursday,' he said calmly.

★ What kind of shoes do all spies wear?
Sneakers.

★ It's time to get new shoes when you stand on a coin and can tell if it's heads or tails.

★ What happens if you eat yeast and shoe polish?
Every morning you'll rise and shine!

★ Did you hear about the little shoe who was upset?
Its father was a loafer and its mother was a sneaker.

★ Wee Billy from Dublin always wanted to look cool. His friend told him that he needed a good designer pair of trainers to go with his shell suit. Billy saved up all his giros and all the money he got back from returning his empty bottles of beer and finally managed to get himself a pair of brilliant white trainers to go with his shell suit.

Proudly, he strutted down the street calling out to all the passers-by: 'See my new trainers? Cool, eh?' One fine upstanding gentleman pointed out that they were indeed a fine pair of trainers but was young Billy aware that he had a lace undone? Billy scornfully retorted that it was part of being cool to have a trailing lace and that on the sole of the trainer there were instructions for the wearer to do such a thing. When asked for proof of this instruction, Billy took off his trainer and held it upside down for the disbeliever to read. 'There y'are! It clearly says ... Taiwan!'

shops

Opening his new store, a man received a bouquet of flowers. He became dismayed when he read the enclosed card which expressed 'Deepest Sympathy'. While puzzling over the message, his telephone rang. It was the florist, apologizing for having sent the wrong card. 'Oh, it's all right,' said the storekeeper. 'I'm a businessman and I understand how these things can happen.' 'It gets worse,' said the florist. 'I accidentally sent your card with a funeral arrangement.' 'Oh? What did it say?' asked the storekeeper. 'Congratulations on your new location.'

What happened to the man who bought a paper shop?
It blew away.

'Hey, you want to feel really handsome? Go shopping at Asda.
Brendon Burns

🐶 SHOPPING

❋ A woman walked up to a cash register in a sporting goods store. She was carrying a package of white athletic socks. 'Will you open this up so I can see how the socks feel?' she asked. Reluctantly the assistant tore open the package, and the customer scrutinized the merchandise. She handed the package back, saying, 'I like them.' Relieved, the clerk started to ring them up on the till, until the customer interrupted. 'Can I have another pack? This one's been opened.'

❋ I went to a general store. They wouldn't let me buy anything specific.

❋ What's the most expensive vehicle, per mile, to operate?
A shopping trolley.

❋ My wife has been missing for four days. I'm not sure if she's left me or gone shopping.

❋ Veni, Vidi, Visa – I came, I saw, I shopped.

❋ Early to rise, and early to bed, makes a man healthy but socially dead.

❋ Whenever my wife looks at my head she puts melon on the shopping list.

✳ I went to buy a watch, and the man in the shop said, 'Analogue.' I said, 'No, just a watch.'

✳ 'Is this a second-hand shop?' 'Yes, sir.' 'Good. Can you fit one to my watch, then, please.'

✳ I went into a shop and I said, 'Can someone sell me a kettle?' The bloke said, 'Kenwood.' I said, 'Where is he?'

✳ A man went into a pet shop. He said, 'Can I buy a goldfish?' The guy said, 'Do you want an aquarium?' He said, 'I don't care what star sign it is.'

🐶 SiGNS

✳ A sign over a gynaecologist's office: 'Dr Jones, at your cervix.'

✳ On the door of a plastic surgeon's office: 'We can help you pick your nose!'

✳ At an optometrist's office: 'If you don't see what you're looking for, you've come to the right place.'

✳ A sign in the non-smoking area of a restaurant: 'If we see smoke, we will assume you are on fire and take appropriate action.'

* Outside an exhaust repair garage: 'No appointment necessary. We hear you coming.'

* Ad on the side of a plumber's truck: 'We repair what your husband fixed.'

* Another slogan on the truck of a plumbing company: 'Don't sleep with a drip. Call your plumber.'

* Pizza shop slogan: 'Seven days without pizza makes one weak.'

* At a tyre repair shop: 'Invite us to your next blow-out.'

* At the psychic's hotline: 'Don't call us, we'll call you.'

* At a breakdown company: 'We don't charge an arm and a leg. We want tows.'

* Billboard on the side of the road: 'Keep your eyes on the road and stop reading these signs.'

* At a car dealership: 'The best way to get back on your feet – miss a car payment.'

* Outside a hotel: 'Help! We need inn-experienced people.'

* On the door of a computer shop: 'Out for a quick byte.'

* Inside a bowling alley: 'Please be quiet, we need to hear a pin drop.'

* In a counsellor's office: 'Growing old is mandatory, growing wise is optional.'

* At a petrol station: 'We will sell gasoline to anyone in a glass container.'

* In a New York restaurant: 'Customers who consider our waitresses uncivil ought to see the manager.'

* On a long-established dry cleaner's: '38 years on the same spot.'

* In a London dance hall: 'Good clean dancing every night but Sunday.'

* In a maternity ward: 'No children allowed.'

* In a chemist's: 'We dispense with accuracy.'

* In the offices of a loan company: 'Ask about our plans for owning your home.'

* In a Yorkshire hospital: 'Mental Health Prevention Centre.'

* On a New York convalescent home: 'For the sick and tired of the Episcopal Church.'

* On a car repair garage: 'Our motto is to give our customers the lowest possible prices and workmanship.'

* At a number of military bases: 'Restricted to unauthorized personnel.'

* On a display of 'I love you only' Valentine cards: 'Now available in multi-packs.'

* In the window of an appliance shop: 'Don't kill your wife. Let our washing machine do the dirty work.'

* In a clothing store: 'Wonderful bargains for men with 16 and 17 necks.'

* Outside a country shop: 'We buy junk and sell antiques.'

* In the window of a Bristol shop: 'Why go elsewhere and be cheated when you can come here?'

* In an Irish restaurant: 'Open 7 days a week and weekends.'

* In the vestry of a church: 'Will the last person to leave please see that the perpetual light is extinguished.'

* In a cemetery: 'Persons are prohibited from picking flowers from any but their own graves.'

* On a rollercoaster: 'Watch your head.'

* On the grounds of a public school: 'No trespassing without permission.'

✻ On a Tennessee highway: 'When this sign is under water, this road is impassable.'

And there's more...

✻ Spotted in the toilet of a London office: 'Toilet out of order. Please use floor below.'

✻ In a launderette: 'Automatic washing machines. Remove all your clothes when the light goes out.'

✻ In a London department store: 'Bargain basement upstairs.'

✻ In an office: 'Would the person who took the stepladder yesterday bring it back, or further steps will be taken.'

✻ In an office: 'After tea break, staff should empty the teapot and stand upside down on the draining board.'

✻ Outside a second-hand shop: 'We exchange everything – bicycles, washing machines, etc. Why not bring your wife along and get a wonderful bargain?'

✻ In health food shop window: 'Closed due to illness.'

✻ Spotted in a safari park: 'Elephants stay in your car.'

✻ Seen during a conference: 'For anyone who has children and doesn't know it, there is a day care centre on the first floor.'

* Notice in a farmer's field: 'The farmer allows walkers to cross the field for free, but the bull charges.'

* On a repair shop door: 'We can repair anything. Please knock on the door – the bell doesn't work.'

skeletons

Why don't skeletons fight each other?
They don't have the guts.

Why didn't the skeleton go to the dance?
Because he had no-body to go with.

What do you get if you cross a skeleton and a detective?
Sherlock Bones.

What is a skeleton?
Bones, with the person off!

Why do skeletons drink a lot of milk?
It's good for the bones.

 SKUNKS

* What's the difference between a skunk and a squirrel?
The skunk uses a cheaper deodorant.

✳ How many skunks does it take to make a terrible smell?
A phew.

✳ How do you stop a skunk from smelling?
Put a peg on its nose.

✳ There once were two skunks. One was named 'In' and one named
'Out'. When Out was in, In was out, and when Out was out, In was
in. One day, Out was in and In was out, and mother skunk said,
'Out, I want you to go out and bring In in.' Out quickly went outside
and almost immediately returned with In. Mother skunk was
amazed and gasped, 'How did you DO that so quickly?' 'Easy,'
said Out. 'In stinked.'

✳ A family of skunks was trapped in a thicket, surrounded by a pack of
hungry wolves that were edging even closer. The mother skunk
calmly instructed her young: 'Quickly, children, let's put our heads
together!' After they obeyed, forming a circle, she continued, 'Now let
us spray!'

🐺 SLEEp

✳ What do you call a sleeping bull?
A bulldozer.

✳ I tried to daydream, but my mind kept wandering.

✳ I can go for more than seven days without sleep – so it's a good thing I sleep nights.

✳ An exhausted-looking man dragged himself into the doctor's office. 'Doctor, there are dogs all over my neighbourhood. They bark all day and all night, and I can't get a wink of sleep.' 'I have good news for you,' the doctor answered, rummaging through a drawer full of sample medications. 'Here are some new sleeping pills that work like a dream. A few of these and your trouble will be over.' 'Great,' the man answered. 'I'll try anything. Let's give it a shot.' A few weeks later the man returned, looking worse than ever. 'Doc, your plan is no good. I'm more tired than before!' 'I don't understand how that could be,' said the doctor, shaking his head. 'Those are the strongest pills on the market!' 'That may be true,' answered the man wearily, 'but I'm still up all night chasing those dogs and when I finally catch one it's hard getting him to swallow the pill!'

✳ A noise woke me up this morning. It was the crack of dawn!

✳ Why didn't the banana snore?
Because it didn't want to wake up the rest of the bunch!

✳ Dawn is nature's way of telling you to go to bed.

✳ What's the definition of a sound sleeper?
Someone who snores.

✳ The best cure for insomnia is a good night's sleep.

✷ What is the best day of the week to sleep?
Snooze-day!

✷ Why is it not safe to sleep on trains?
Because they run over sleepers!

✷ Sleep: A completely inadequate substitute for caffeine.

✷ What kind of fall makes you unconscious but doesn't hurt?
Falling asleep.

✷ It's good to take a bottle of wine for insomnia. It doesn't help you
sleep, but being awake doesn't seem so bad.

smoking

Menthol cigarettes – now you know where the middle of the Polo
mint goes.

Smoking is one of the leading causes of statistics.

Those nicotine patches work really well, but I heard it was hard to
keep them lit.

Smokers are just like everybody else. Just not as long.

SNAILS AND SLUGS

✳ Where do you find monster snails?
On the end of its fingers.

✳ How do snails keep their shells shiny?
Snail varnish.

✳ What did the snail say while riding on the turtle's back?
Weeeeeeeeeee!!!!!!!

✳ What did the slug say to the other slug who had hit him and run off?
I'll get you next slime!

✳ What was the snail doing on the motorway?
About one mile a day!

✳ What did the slug say as he slipped down the wall?
How slime flies!

✳ How do you know your kitchen floor is dirty?
The slugs leave a trail on the floor that reads 'clean me'!

✳ What do you do when two snails have a fight?
Leave them to slug it out!

✳ What is the difference between school dinners and a pile of slugs?
School dinners come on a plate!

✳ Why do the French like snails?
Because they don't like fast food.

✳ What sort of animal is a slug?
A snail with a housing problem!

✳ A snail comes across a leprechaun in the forest. The leprechaun takes pity on the snail, slithering on its belly, and decides to grant it a wish. The snail can't believe its luck. 'I'd like a sports car,' it says, 'with a giant golden "S" painted on the doors and bonnet.' The leprechaun waves his hand, and the car magically appears. The snail is beside itself with excitement and climbs in. It revs the engine up, puts the car into gear and speeds off through the forest. All the other animals gather to watch him career through the trees. 'Look at that crazy "S" car go.'

🐍 SNAKES

✳ What do snakes do after they fight?
They hiss and make up.

✳ What do you get if you cross a canary and a 50-foot-long snake?
A sing-a-long!

✳ An old snake goes to see his doctor. 'Doc, I need something for my eyes... I can't see well these days.' The doc fixes him up with a pair of glasses and tells him to return in two weeks. The snake goes back in two weeks and tells the doctor he's very depressed. Doc says, 'What's the problem? Didn't the glasses help you?' 'The glasses are fine, Doc, I just discovered I've been living with a hose the past two years!'

✳ Two snakes were slithering along through the grass. One snake asked his friend: 'Exthcuth me, are we poisonous?'
  His friend answered: 'Yes, very. Why do you ask?'
  And the first snake explained: 'I jutht bit my tongue.'

✳ What happened when the snake caught a cold?
She had to viper nose.

🐻 SNOWMEN

✳ Where do snowmen keep their money?
In snow banks.

✳ What happened when the snowgirl fell out with the snowboy?
She gave him the cold shoulder!

✳ What do snowmen eat for lunch?
Icebergers!

✳ How do snowmen travel around?
By icicle!

✳ What sort of ball doesn't bounce?
A snowball!

✳ How do you know when there is a snowman in your bed?
You wake up wet!

✳ Why did the snowman call his dog Frost?
Because frost bites!

Life lessons I learned from a snowman ...

✳ It's OK if you're a little bottom heavy.

✳ Hold your ground, even when the heat is on.

✳ Wearing white is always appropriate.

✳ Winter is the best of the four seasons.

✳ It takes a few extra rolls to make a good midsection.

✳ There's nothing better than a foul weather friend.

✳ The key to life is to be a jolly, happy soul.

✳ It's not the size of the carrot, but the placement that counts.

✳ We're all made up of mostly water.

* You know you've made it when they write a song about you.

* Accessorize! Accessorize! Accessorize!

* Avoid yellow snow.

* Don't get too much sun.

* It's embarrassing when you can look down and see your feet.

* It's fun to hang out in your front yard.

* Always put your best foot forward.

* There's no stopping you once you're on a roll.

society

We live in a society where pizza gets to your house before the police.

Laws are like sausages... It's better not to see them being made.

SPiDERS

* Why do female black widow spiders kill the males after mating?
  To stop the snoring before it starts.

✴ What did the policeman say when a spider ran down his back?
'You're under a vest!'

✴ Why did the fly fly?
Because the spider spied 'er!

✴ What would happen if tarantulas were as big as horses?
If one bit you, you could ride it to hospital!

✴ Why are spiders good swimmers?
They have webbed feet!

✴ What do you call an Irish spider?
Paddy long legs!

spies

Who was the first underwater spy?
James Pond!

A man applied for a job as an industrial spy. Together with several other applicants, he was given a sealed envelope and told to take it to the fourth floor. As soon as the man was alone, he stepped into an empty hallway and opened the envelope. Inside, a message read: 'You're our kind of person. Report to the fifth-floor Personnel Office.'

🐻 SpORT

✳ Three men wanted to attend the Olympic Games but they had no tickets to the events. As they stood around watching, they noticed that the participants in the games all went in at a certain gate and that many were carrying sports gear for their event. The three began to get creative and as they looked around, the first spotted some electrical conduit left over from construction work. He picked up a length of this pipe, walked up to the gate, said 'Pole vault' and they waved him in. The second guy discovered a manhole cover, picked it up, walked up to the gate, said 'Discus' and they waved him in. The third guy looked for some time before he spotted a roll of barbed wire. He picked this up, threw it on his shoulder, walked up to the gate and announced, 'Fencing.'

✳ I get enough exercise just pushing my luck.

✳ My grandmother started walking five miles a day when she was 60. She's 97 now and we don't know where the heck she is.

✳ I have to exercise in the morning before my brain figures out what I'm doing.

✳ What season is it when you are on a trampoline?
Spring time.

✳ I like long walks, especially when they are taken by people who annoy me.

✳ What's the hardest thing about learning to ice skate?
The ice.

✳ I have flabby thighs, but fortunately my stomach covers them.

✳ If you are going to try cross-country skiing, start with a small country.

✳ I don't jog. It makes the ice jump right out of my glass.

✳ What did the trampolinist say?
'Life has its ups and downs, but I always bounce back.'

Tennis

✳ What can you serve that you cannot eat?
A tennis ball.

✳ What do you call an elephant that lies across the middle of a tennis court?
Annette!

✳ Don't marry a tennis player. Love means nothing to them.

Cricket

✳ What's an insect's favourite sport?
Cricket!

✴ Why is a cricket team similar to Yorkshire pudding?
They both depend on the batter.

Jogging

✴ If you jogged backwards, would you gain weight?

✴ Marathon runners with bad shoes suffer the agony of de feet.

Squash

✴ What is the noisiest game?
Squash – because you can't play it without raising a racquet!

✴ What games do ants play with elephants?
Squash!

Gym

✴ What's the difference between an aerobics instructor and a torturer?
The torturer would apologize first.

✴ I phoned the local gym and I asked if they could teach me how to do
the splits. He said, 'How flexible are you?' I said, 'I can't make
Tuesdays or Thursdays.'

Football

✳ What do you get if you cross a football team and an ice cream?
Aston Vanilla.

✳ Why is Cinderella such a bad football player?
Because she has a pumpkin for a coach and she ran away from the ball.

✳ Old footballers never die. They just kick off.

✳ Why did the football coach flood the pitch?
Because he wanted to bring on the sub!

✳ What's the difference between England and a tea bag?
The tea bag stays in the cup longer.

Basketball

✳ Why is basketball such a messy sport?
Because you dribble on the floor!

✳ What do you call two Mexicans playing basketball?
Juan on Juan.

✳ Why are baseball players in trouble with the law so often?
They always hit and run.

Boxing

✳ He was a colourful boxer. Black and blue all over.

✳ Did you know you can download the whole Tyson-Holyfield fight off the internet? It doesn't take much memory – just two Bytes.

✳ Boxing razes the consciousness.

✳ Who was the last person to box Rocky Marciano?
His undertaker.

Golf

✳ Did you hear about the small golf course?
You don't have to shout 'Fore!', only 'two and a half'.

✳ Why do golfers wear two pairs of trousers?
In case they get a hole in one!

✳ Why are old socks good for golf?
Because they have eighteen holes.

✳ In primitive society, when native tribes beat the ground with clubs and yelled, it was called witchcraft. In today's civilized society, it is called golf.

✳ Golf is an expensive way of playing marbles.

✳ Golf is a game in which the slowest people in the world are those in front of you, and the fastest are those behind.

✳ Golf: A five-mile walk punctuated with disappointments.

✳ The secret of good golf is to hit the ball hard, straight and not too often.

✳ There's no game like golf: you go out with three friends, play eighteen holes, and return with three enemies.

✳ Golf was once a rich man's sport, but now it has millions of poor players.

✳ An amateur golfer is one who addresses the ball twice: once before swinging, and once again after swinging.

✳ Many a golfer prefers a golf cart to a caddy because the cart cannot count, criticize or laugh.

✳ What do golfers use in China?
China tees!

✳ One fine day, Jim and Bob are out golfing. Jim slices his ball deep into a wooded ravine. He grabs his seven-iron and proceeds down the embankment into the ravine – in search of his lost ball. The brush is quite thick, but Jim searches diligently and suddenly he spots something shiny. As he gets closer, he realizes that the shiny object is, in fact, a seven-iron in the hands of a skeleton lying near an old golf ball. Jim excitedly calls out to his golfing partner: 'Hey Bob, come here, I got trouble down here.' Bob comes running over to the edge of the ravine and calls out, 'What's the matter?' Jim shouts back, 'Throw me my eight-iron! You can't get out of here with a seven!'

✳ A hack golfer spends a day playing golf and enjoying the luxury of a complimentary caddy. As usual, he plays poorly all day. Round about the eighteenth hole, he spots a lake off to the left of the fairway. He looks at the caddy and says, 'I've played so poorly all day, I think I'm going to go drown myself in that lake.' The caddy looks back at him and says, 'I don't think you could keep your head down that long.'

✳ A man got up early on Saturday morning to play golf. He kissed his wife goodbye, and she reminded him they were going out to eat early that evening with another couple. He promised her he would be home in plenty of time. Mid-afternoon came and went, and he did not return home. His wife became angry at first. But her anger turned to worry as the sun began to set. He had never been this late before. Finally, it was completely dark when she heard the back door open and close. Concerned, she ran to greet her husband. 'What happened?' she said. 'You promised you would be home early!' Her husband sighed. 'It was awful. The four of us were on the very first tee when Bill Smith fell over dead with a heart attack.' 'Oh no!' she exclaimed. 'That's terrible.' 'I know,' he said. 'From then on, it was hit the ball ... drag Bill. Hit the ball ... drag Bill.'

✷ The frustrated golfer drove over the river and threw the woods.

Swimming

✷ Why did the man keep doing the backstroke?
He'd just had lunch and didn't want to swim on a full stomach!

✷ What's a swimmer's favourite sport?
Pool.

✷ One day a scuba diver was enjoying a dive. He noticed a man at the same depth he was, but he had on no scuba gear whatsoever. The diver went 20 feet deeper, but the other man joined him a few minutes later. The diver went down another 25 feet, but minutes later, the same man was there too. Confused, the diver took out a waterproof chalk-and-board set, and wrote, 'How are you able to stay under this deep without equipment?' The guy took the board and chalk, erased what the diver had written, and wrote, 'I'M DROWNING, YOU IDIOT!'

✷ There was a competition to cross the English Channel doing only the breaststroke. The three women who entered the race were a brunette, a redhead and a blonde. After approximately fourteen hours, the brunette staggered up on the shore and was declared the fastest breaststroker. About 40 minutes later, the redhead crawled up onto the shore and was declared the second place finisher. Nearly four hours after that, the blonde finally came ashore and promptly collapsed in front of the worried onlookers. When the reporters asked why it took her so long to complete the race, she replied, 'I don't want to sound like I'm a sore loser, but I think those other two girls were using their arms.'

squirrels

How do you catch a squirrel?
Climb a tree and act like a nut!

statistics

42 per cent of statistics are made up on the spot.

Three out of four Americans make up 75 per cent of the population.

STUPIDITY AND IDIOCY

✳ A man is talking to his thick friend, Bob. 'How many biscuits can you eat on an empty stomach?' Bob scratched his head and said, 'Well, five, I think.' 'Wrong,' said his friend. 'You can only eat one. After that, your stomach isn't empty any more! Gotcha!' Bob was impressed, so he decided to pull the joke on his wife when he got home. 'Hey, honey, how many biscuits can you eat on an empty stomach?' She thought for a minute or two and said, 'Six.' Bob was deflated. 'Darn! If you'd said "five" I had a GREAT joke for you!'

* The two most common things in the universe are hydrogen, and stupidity.

* He's so stupid he put a bucket under a gas leak.

* I'm not dumb. I just have a command of thoroughly useless information.

* The trouble with ignorance is that it picks up confidence as it goes along.

* To generalize is to be an idiot.

* A guy walks into work, and both of his ears are all bandaged up. The boss says, 'What happened to your ears?' He says, 'Yesterday I was ironing a shirt when the phone rang and I accidentally answered the iron.' The boss says, 'Well, that explains one ear, but what happened to your other ear?' He says, 'Well, I had to call the doctor!'

* I wondered why the frisbee was getting bigger, and then it hit me.

* I have a thirst for knowledge. I'm just not sure what to drink first.

* When you argue with an idiot, make sure he isn't doing the same.

✳ Don't argue with a fool. The spectators can't tell the difference.

✳ Most people don't act stupid – it's the real thing.

✳ I am infaliable.

✳ You can lead a fool to wisdom but you can't make him think.

✳ I've discovered that I often visit the state of confusion, and I know my way around pretty well.

✳ When it comes to thought, some people stop at nothing.

✳ Sometimes a majority only means that all the fools are on the same side.

✳ I looked up my family tree and found out I was the sap.

✳ I come from a stupid family. During the American civil war my great uncle fought for the west!

✳ I prefer the wicked rather than the foolish. The wicked sometimes rest.

✳ Make it idiot proof and someone will make a better idiot.

✳ What sort of meat do fools like?
Chump chops.

✳ Your kid may be an honours student, but you're still an idiot.

✳ Why did the stupid racing driver make ten pitstops during the race?
He was asking for directions!

✳ You should always write your name on your underwear. See, I'm Machine Wash Cold.

✳ How do you keep an imbecile happy all his life?
Tell him a joke when he's a baby!

✳ Why do idiots eat biscuits?
Because they're crackers!

✳ Never argue with a fool: they will lower you to their level and then beat you with experience.

✳ Never call a man a fool. Borrow from him.

success

Success is a matter of luck, just ask any failure.

If you don't succeed you will never be spoiled by success.

🦁 SURREAL

✳ Why did the boy fall off his bike?
Because someone threw a fridge at him.

✳ What's grey and can't climb up trees?
A car park.

✳ How do you fix a broken tomato?
With tomato paste.

✳ Someone once told me that love makes the world go round. Well, I just had to laugh in their face because, c'mon, everyone knows that what makes the world go round is a mutant gerbil on a treadmill.

✳ A slice of bread will always land peanut butter side down. If, by chance, you put peanut butter on both sides of the slice, it will float for ever.

✳ Is it bad to write on an empty stomach?
No, but it's better to write on paper.

✳ What has two arms, two wings, two tails, three heads and eight legs?
A man riding a horse carrying a chicken.

✳ Did you hear about the man who got a medal for modesty and then had it taken away when they saw him wearing it?

✳ Rock is dead. Long live paper and scissors.

✳ If evolution is outlawed, only outlaws will evolve.

✳ 'I was walking the streets of Glasgow the other week and I saw this sign: "This door is alarmed." I said to myself: "How do you think I feel?"' *Arnold Brown*

🐻 SWINGS AND SLIDES

✳ A man is in bed with his wife when he hears a rat-a-tat-tat on the door. He rolls over and looks at his clock. It's 3.30 a.m. Hell, he thinks, and rolls over. Then a louder knock follows. 'Aren't you going to answer that?' says his wife so he drags himself out of bed and goes downstairs. He opens the door and this bloke is stood outside. 'Eh, mate,' says the stranger, 'can you give us a push?' 'No, get lost, it's half three. I was in bed,' says the man and shuts the door. He goes back up to bed and tells his wife what happened and she says, 'Dave, you're so unhelpful. Remember that night we broke down in the pouring rain on the way to pick the kids up from the baby sitter and you had to knock on that man's house to get us started again? What would have happened if he'd told us to get lost?' So he gets out of bed again, gets dressed, and goes downstairs. He opens the door, and, not being able to see the stranger anywhere, he shouts: 'Oi, mate, do you still want a push?' He hears a voice cry out, 'Yeah, please.' So, still being unable to see the stranger, he shouts: 'Where are you?' And the stranger replies: 'I'm over here ... on the swings.'

✳ Why did the chicken cross the playground?
To get to the other slide!

taxi drivers

A passenger in a taxi tapped the driver on the shoulder to ask him something. The driver screamed, lost control of the cab, nearly hit a bus, drove up over the kerb, and stopped just inches from a large plate-glass window. For a few moments everything was silent in the cab, then the driver said, 'Please, don't ever do that again. You scared the daylights out of me.' The passenger, who was also frightened, apologized and said he didn't realize that a tap on the shoulder could frighten him so much, to which the driver replied, 'I'm sorry, it's really not your fault at all. Today is my first day driving a cab. I have been driving a hearse for the last 25 years.'

A man and a woman are arguing. 'What do you know about love?' she accuses him. 'Loads,' he replies. 'I used to be a taxi driver.'

🐺 TEACHERS

✳ A teacher asked her Sunday School class to draw pictures of their favourite Bible stories. She was puzzled by a boy's picture which showed four people on an aircraft, so she asked him which story it was meant to represent. 'The flight to Egypt,' he replied. 'I see… And that must be Mary, Joseph, and Baby Jesus,' she said. 'But who's the fourth person?'

'Oh, that's Pontius – the Pilot!'

✳ A boy tells his friend that he has a crush on his teacher. The second boy says, 'Man, that is disgusting.' The first boy says, 'What? Everyone has a crush on their teacher.' The second boy says, 'Yeah, but you're home-schooled.'

✳ An overworked English teacher spent a lot of time correcting grammatical errors in her students' written work. She wasn't sure how much impact she was having until one overly busy day when she sat at her desk rubbing her temples. A student asked, 'What's the matter, miss?' 'Tense,' she replied curtly. After a slight pause the student tried again. 'What was the matter? What is the matter? What will be the matter?'

✳ **Teacher**: You boy, what's your name?
Boy: Mickey Jones.
Teacher: We'll call you Jones here. We don't use first names.
Boy: My dad won't like that – he takes offence if people take the Mickey out of my name.

✳ What is the difference between a school teacher and a train?
The teacher says spit your gum out and the train says 'chew chew chew'.

✳ What kind of food do maths teachers eat?
Square meals!

✳ **Teacher**: Billy, name two pronouns.
Billy: Who, me?
Teacher: Very good!

✳ Why don't some teachers like to break wind in public?
Because they're private tooters.

✳ **Teacher**: To which family does the elephant belong?
Pupil: I don't know, nobody I know owns one!

✳ Why did the teacher write the lesson on the windows?
He wanted to be very clear!

✳ What did the music teacher need a ladder for?
To reach the top notes.

✳ **Teacher**: Where is your homework?
Pupil: I lost it fighting this kid who said you weren't the best teacher in the school.

✳ Why did the teacher jump into the lake?
Because she wanted to test the waters!

✳ Early one morning, a mother went in to wake up her son. 'Wake up, it's time to go to school!' 'But why, Mum? I don't want to go.' 'Give me two reasons why you don't want to go.' 'Well, the kids hate me for one, and the teachers hate me, too!' 'Oh, that's no reason not to go to school. Come on now and get ready.' 'Give me two reasons why I should go to school.' 'Well, for one, you're 52 years old. And for another, you're the headmaster!'

✳ A schoolteacher was arrested today at Gatwick Airport as he attempted to board a flight while in possession of a ruler, a protractor, a set square, a slide rule and a calculator. At a morning press conference, the Home Secretary said he believes the man is a member of the notorious Al-gebra movement. He did not identify the man, who has been charged by the police with carrying weapons of maths instruction.

✳ When a teacher closes his eyes, why should it remind him of an empty classroom?
Because there are no pupils to see!

✳ Why did the teacher put the lights on?
Because the class was so dim!

✳ **Teacher:** Can you tell me where Napoleon came from?
Pupil: Course I can.
Teacher: Very good.

✳ What would you get if you crossed a vampire and a teacher?
Lots of blood tests!

technology

Xerox and Wurlitzer will merge to market reproductive organs.

Any sufficiently complicated technology is indistinguishable from bad karma.

🐵 TELEPHONES

✹ What is a name for a phone system in Mexico?
Taco Bell.

✹ Is being a telephone operator a business or a profession?
It's more like a calling.

✹ Local Area Network in Australia: The LAN down under.

✹ What do you get if you dial 87656733462367462?
A sore finger.

✹ Ask not for whom the bell tolls. Let the machine get it.

✹ What happens if you dial 666?
An Australian fire engine arrives.

✳ 'I phoned the local ramblers club today, and this bloke just went on and on.' *Tommy Cooper*

✳ Late one Saturday evening, a woman was awakened by the ringing of the phone. In a sleepy, grumpy voice she said, 'Hello.' The person on the other end of the line paused for a moment before rushing breathlessly into a lengthy speech. 'Mum, this is Karen, and I'm sorry I woke you up, but I had to call because I'm going to be a little late getting home. See, Dad's car has a flat but it's not my fault. Honest! I don't know what happened. The tyre just went flat while we were inside the cinema. Please don't be cross, OK?' The woman who had answered the phone didn't have any daughters, so she instantly knew it was a wrong number. 'I'm sorry, dear,' she said into the phone, 'I don't have a daughter named Karen.' 'Mum,' the young woman's voice replied, 'I knew you were going to be cross, but I didn't think you'd be this angry.'

thanksgiving

'I celebrated Thanksgiving in an old-fashioned way. I invited everyone in my neighborhood to my house, we had an enormous feast, and then I killed them and took their land.' *Jon Stewart*

THEATRE

✳ Two actors are talking. 'I remember, clearly, the first words that I delivered in the theatre,' says one. 'What were they?' asks the other. 'Mummy, I need a wee.'

✳ Did you hear about the terrible ventriloquist? His lips moved even when he wasn't saying anything.

✳ 'So I told my mum that I'd opened a theatre. She said, "Are you having me on?" I said, "Well, I'll give you an audition, but I'm not promising you anything."' *Tommy Cooper*

✳ 'I was once in a play called *Breakfast in Bed*.' 'Did you have a big role?' 'No, just toast and marmalade.'

✳ My life has a superb cast but I can't figure out the plot.

✳ There once was an actor who was obsessed with doing trap-door gags. Some critics thought he would keep doing them the rest of his life, while others said he was just going through a stage.

✳ A man lay spread out over three seats in the second row of a movie theatre. As he lay there breathing heavily, an usher came over and said, 'That's very rude of you, sir, taking up three seats. Didn't you learn any manners? Where did you come from?' The man looked up helplessly and said, 'The balcony!'

🐻 TIME

✴ What do you get if you cross a coward and a clock?
A nervous tick.

✴ I live one day at a time – but I'm three weeks behind!

✴ Why does Father Time wear bandages?
Because day breaks and night falls.

✴ The only reason for time is so that everything doesn't happen all at once.

✴ It's like déjà vu all over again.

✴ He who hesitates is last.

✴ What do you call a grandfather clock?
An old timer.

✴ What is always behind the times?
The back of the clock.

✴ **1st Roman Soldier:** What's the time?
2nd Roman Soldier: XX past VII!

✴ Why did the idiot have his sundial floodlit?
So he could tell the time at night!

✳ I wish I had the time to be patient.

✳ Today is the first day of the rest of this mess.

✳ Today is the tomorrow you worried about yesterday.

✳ A man is giving a best man's speech at his friend's wedding. He gets a bit carried away and talks for two hours. Finally, he realizes what he has done and apologizes. 'I'm sorry I talked so long. I left my watch at home.' A voice from the back of the room says, 'That's no excuse. There's a calendar behind you.'

✳ The speed of time is one second per second.

✳ A clock is a small device to wake up people with no children.

✳ Never throw away a clock. It's a waste of time.

✳ Wear a watch and you'll always know what time it is. Wear two watches and you'll never be sure.

✳ How long a minute is depends on what side of the toilet door you're on.

✳ Time is the best teacher; unfortunately it kills all of its students.

✳ Have you heard about the wonder watch?
It only costs fifty pence. It's called a wonder watch because every time you look at it you wonder if it's still working!

✳ Why did Tommy throw the clock out of the window?
Because he wanted to see time fly!

✳ What do you call it when someone puts a clock on his belt?
A waist of time!

✳ Plan to be spontaneous tomorrow.

✳ Why shouldn't you tell secrets in front of a clock?
Because time will tell.

✳ When is a clock nervous?
When it is all wound up.

✳ What time is it when the clock strikes 13?
Time to get a new clock!

✳ Why is the time in the USA behind that of England?
Because England was discovered before the USA!

🐾 TOILET HUMOUR

✳ A man is driving down the motorway and has to go to the toilet. He
pulls into a services, goes to the gents and sits in a cubicle. The man
in the next stall says, 'How's it going?' He replies 'OK.' Next stall
says, 'What are you going to do now?' Man says, 'I guess I'll drive on
through to London tonight.' The man in the next stall says, 'I'll call

you back later. Some idiot keeps answering whenever I ask you a question.'

✳ Did you hear about the man who fell into the cesspool and drowned? He couldn't swim but he went through the motions.

✳ A farmer walks up to an outhouse and finds a man fishing around in the hole with a long stick. The farmer asks what he is doing and the man replies, 'I dropped my jacket down there and I'm trying to get it back.' The farmer says, 'Are you crazy? Are you really gonna wear the jacket after it's been down there?' The man says, 'Oh, no way! But there's a sandwich in one of the pockets.'

✳ A builder goes to the doctor and says, 'Doc, I'm constipated.' The doctor examines him for a minute and then says, 'Lean over the table.' The construction worker leans over the table, the doctor whacks him on the behind with a cricket bat, and then sends him into the toilet. He comes out a few minutes later and says, 'Doc, I feel great. What should I do?' The doctor says, 'Stop wiping with cement bags.'

🐵 TOOLS

✳ What tools do you need in maths class?
Multi-Pliers.

✳ How can you cut the sea in two?
With a seasaw.

✳ Did you hear about the two cement mixers that fell in love?
Now they have a little path running around the house.

✳ When your only tool is a hammer, all problems start looking like nails.

✳ What do you get when you cut up tofu with a buzzsaw?
Soydust.

☝ TOp TiPS

✳ Before attempting to remove stubborn stains from a garment, always
circle the stain in permanent pen so that when you remove the
garment from the washing machine you can easily locate the area of
the stain and check that it has gone.

✳ Save on booze by drinking cold tea instead of whisky. The following
morning you can create the effects of a hangover by drinking a
thimble full of washing-up liquid and banging your head repeatedly on
the wall.

✳ *X Files* fans. Create the effect of being abducted by aliens by drinking
two bottles of vodka. You'll invariably wake up in a strange place the
following morning, having had your memory mysteriously 'erased'.

✳ Putting just the right amount of gin in your goldfish bowl makes
fishes' eyes bulge and causes them to swim in an amusing manner.

✳ Keep a small chalkboard near the phone. That way, when a salesman calls, you can hold the receiver up to it and run your fingernails across it until he hangs up.

✳ Cheer loudly at 8.00 p.m. each Saturday to fool the neighbours into thinking you have won the Lottery.

toys

What's the last thing they give Tickle-Me-Elmo when he leaves the factory?
A test tickle!

🐶 TRACTORS

✳ As a young boy, Joe was obsessed with tractors. He had pictures all over his bedroom walls, tractor toys, tractor T-shirts, tractor carpet, duvet cover, the whole works. He ate, drank and slept tractors. On his seventeenth birthday he was thrilled to get an invitation to go to a tractor factory and test-drive a brand new tractor. The great day came and he went to the factory. Unfortunately something went wrong with the tractor and it flipped over, breaking his leg. He tried to sue the company for negligence but the company would have none of it and told him there was no liability and he could get lost. He became disillusioned with tractors and shed them from his life completely. All the posters came down, the toys were given away – tractors were GONE. Years later, Joe went into a bar. The smoke was terrible and through it he could see a beautiful girl seated at the bar. Tears were streaming down her face from all the smoke getting in her eyes. Joe looked around and then took a huge breath, sucking in all the smoke. He then walked outside and blew it all out again. He goes back into the bar where the air is now clear and sweet and sits down next to the girl. 'That was amazing!' she said. 'How did you do that?' 'No problem,' said Joe. 'I'm an ex-tractor fan...'

✴ My girlfriend broke up with me last week. She did it cruelly. She sent me a letter saying she ran away with a tractor salesman. I was devastated. It was the first time in my life I've got a John Deere letter.

🐺 TRAFFIC

✴ Why did the traffic light turn red?
You would too if you had to change in the middle of the street!

✴ How do they get the deer to cross at that red road sign?

✴ Save time when crossing a one-way street by only looking in the direction of oncoming traffic.

✴ If all the cars on the earth were lined up bumper to bumper, some idiot would try to overtake them.

✳ The woman was driving her eight-year-old daughter. It was late, there was very little traffic, and they were enjoying a peaceful ride. It was a far cry from the usual chaos surrounding them when they drove to various activities during rush hour. The daughter seemed deep in thought and suddenly said, 'Mom, I have a question.' 'What do you want to know?' 'When you're driving,' she asked, 'are YOU ever the idiot?'

✳ What do you eat when stuck in traffic?
Traffic jam!

✳ A lorry has overturned on the M6 loaded with Vicks vapour rub. Police have said there will be no congestion for eight hours.

🐵 TRAMPS

✳ What's the name for a short-legged tramp?
A low down bum!

✳ After a hard day a tramp needed to go to sleep. He went to a nearby park and covered himself in newspapers. Only a few minutes had passed when a man walked up to him and tapped him on the shoulder. 'Excuse me, mate, have you got the time?' The tramp looked up at him, annoyed at being disturbed. But not wanting an argument, he looked at his watch and told the man that it was 11.30. The man said, 'Thank you' and walked off. The tramp tried to get to sleep again. A few minutes later, a man walked up to him and tapped him on the shoulder. 'Excuse me, mate, have you got the time?' said the man. The tramp looked up at him, annoyed at being disturbed again. But not wanting an argument, he looked at his watch and told the man that it was 11.35. The man said, 'Thanks' and walked off. The tramp tried to get to sleep again. A few minutes later, another man walked up to him and tapped him on the shoulder. 'Have you got the time?' asked the man. The tramp looked up at him. This time he was really annoyed, but he didn't want an argument, so he looked at his watch and told the man that it was 11.40. The man said, 'Thank you' and walked away. The tramp decided that he didn't want to be disturbed again, so he got out a marker pen and a piece of card, and wrote on it: 'I CANNOT TELL THE TIME.' Knowing that he would not be disturbed now, he tried to get to sleep once more. A few minutes later the tramp felt a tap on his shoulder. 'WHAT DO YOU WANT?' screamed the tramp. A man looked down at him and said, 'It's a quarter to twelve!'

🐺 TRANSPORT

✳ PROBLEM: You are on a horse, galloping at a constant speed. On your right side is a sharp drop-off, and on your left side is an elephant travelling at the same speed as you. Directly in front of you is a galloping zebra and your horse is unable to overtake it. Behind you is a lion running at the same speed as you and the zebra. What must you do to safely get out of this highly dangerous situation?

ANSWER: Get off the merry-go-round!

* What do you call a laughing motorcycle?
  A Yamahahaha.

* Drive defensively – buy a tank.

* A bicycle can't stand on its own because it's two-tired.

* Who designed Noah's ark?
  An ark-itect!

* There are two kinds of pedestrians: the quick and the dead.

* What do you call a fast tricycle?
  A tot rod.

Buses

* I wouldn't say the bus was crowded, but even the driver was standing.

* A legless man is waiting at a bus stop. The driver pulls up and shouts, 'How you getting on, Fred?'

* You know you should be insulted when the driver asks you to move to the rear of the bus and it's empty.

* He took the bus home after work, but his mother made him take it back.

✳ What did the bus driver say to the one-legged man?
'Hop on.'

✳ How do you put Pikachu into a bus?
Pokémon.

✳ A married couple trying to live up to a snobbish lifestyle went to a party. The conversation turned to Mozart. 'Absolutely brilliant, magnificent, a genius!' The woman, wanting to join in the conversation, remarked casually, 'Ah, Mozart. You're so right. I love him. Only this morning I saw him getting on the No. 5 bus going to Oxford Street.'

There was a sudden hush, and everyone looked at her. Her husband was mortified. He pulled her away and whispered, 'We're leaving right now. Get your coat and let's get out of here.' As they drove home, he kept muttering to himself. Finally his wife turned to him. 'You're angry about something.' 'Oh, really? You noticed?' he sneered. 'I've never been so embarrassed in my life! You saw Mozart take the No. 5 bus to Oxford Street? You idiot! Don't you know the No. 5 bus doesn't go to Oxford Street?'

Cars

✳ A woman drove her people carrier filled with a dozen screaming kids through the car park, looking for a space. Obviously frazzled, she coasted through a stop sign. 'Hey, lady, have you forgotten how to stop?' yelled an irate man. She rolled down her window and said, 'What makes you think these are all mine?'

✳ The tyre is only flat on the bottom.

✳ When is a car not a car?
When it turns into a driveway.

✳ What occupies the last six pages of the Lada User's Manual?
The bus and train timetables.

✳ How do you top a car?
You tep on the brakes, tupid!

✳ A man having a midlife crisis bought a new BMW and was out on the roads for a nice evening drive. The top was down, the breeze was blowing through what was left of his hair, and he decided to open her up. As the needle jumped up to 80 mph, he suddenly saw flashing red and blue lights behind him. There's no way they can catch a BMW, he thought to himself and opened her up further. The needle hit 90, 100 ... then the reality of the situation hit him. What am I doing? he thought and pulled over. The cop came up to him, took his licence without a word, and examined it and the car. 'It's been a long day, this is the end of my shift, and it's Friday 13th. I don't feel like more paperwork, so if you can give me an excuse for your driving that I haven't heard before, you can go.' The guy thought for a second and said, 'Last week my wife ran off with a cop. I was afraid you were trying to give her back.' 'Have a nice weekend,' said the officer.

✳ My wife wanted a foreign convertible so I bought her a rickshaw.

* Never lend your car to anyone to whom you have given birth.

* Two men are talking. 'My wife drives like lightning!'
  'You mean fast?'
  'No, she always hits trees!'

* Used cars are OK as far as they go.

* People who eat ice-cream cones in cars are sundae drivers.

* Never buy a car you can't push.

* Joy rides: From here to maternity

* I wanted to get a new car for my wife, but the garage wouldn't swap.

* The most dangerous part of a car is the nut that holds the steering wheel.

* There were three bees, a squirrel and a man in a car. They were driving along a country lane and the car broke down. The first bee said, 'Don't worry, I'll give us a few extra miles by peeing in the tank.' It worked – for a couple of miles, that is, until they broke down again. And so the second bee decided to do the same as the first bee, but this lasted another couple of miles until they broke down again, so the third bee did exactly the same. Then the car broke down again. The squirrel said, 'I'll pee in the tank.' The man replied, 'Sorry, mate, this car only runs on BP.'

✳ A tourist is visiting Liverpool when his car breaks down. He jumps out and starts fiddling under the bonnet. About five minutes later, he hears some thumping sounds and looks around to see someone taking stuff out of his boot. He runs around and yells, 'Hey, this is my car!' 'OK,' the man says, 'you take the front and I'll take the back.'

✳ A man was speeding down the highway, feeling secure in a group of cars all travelling at the same speed. However, as they passed a speed trap, he got nailed with an infrared speed detector and was pulled over. The officer handed him the ticket, received his signature and was about to walk away when the man asked, 'Officer, I know I was speeding, but I don't think it's fair – there were plenty of other cars around me who were going just as fast, so why did I get the ticket?' 'Ever go fishing?' the policeman suddenly asked the man. 'Um, yeah...' the startled man replied. The officer grinned and added, 'Did you ever catch all the fish?'

✳ David has just received his brand new driving licence. The family goes out to the driveway and climbs in the car – he is going to take them for a ride for the first time. Dad immediately heads for the back seat, directly behind the new driver. 'I'll bet you're back there to get a change of scenery after all those months of sitting in the front passenger seat teaching me how to drive,' says the beaming boy to his dad. 'Nope,' comes Dad's reply, 'I'm gonna sit here and kick the back of your seat as you drive, just like you've been doing to me all these years.'

✳ Every time my car is in the carwash, the phone on the dashboard starts ringing.

✳ To avoid feeling run down, don't play in the street.

✳ The first thing that struck me when I moved to Paris was a car.

✳ I used to be a safe driver, but I gave it up. Who wants to drive a safe?

✳ Just remember... You gotta break some eggs to make a real mess on the neighbour's car!

✳ What do you call a country where all the cars in it are pink?
A pink carnation.

✳ A State Trooper pulls over a pick-up in the deep south. He says to the driver, 'Got any ID?' The driver says, ''Bout what?'

✳ The DVLA recently divulged they had, covertly, funded a car makers' project for the past five years. The car makers were installing black box voice recorders in cars in an effort to determine the circumstances of fatal accidents in the last fifteen seconds before the crash. They were surprised to find in most areas the recorded last words of drivers in 61.2 per cent of fatal crashes were, 'Oh no!' Only Devon and Cornwall were different, where 89.3 per cent of the final words were: 'Hold my cider. I'm going to try something.'

✳ One day a husband was chiding his beautiful blonde wife about leaving her keys in the ignition of her car. 'If I take them out of the car I lose them,' she reasoned. 'Yes, dear, but what if someone steals your car?' the husband countered. 'Oh, that's OK,' the wife chirped happily, 'I keep a spare key in the glove box!'

✳ A man is driving down the road and a cop pulls him over. The cop asks to see his licence and registration. The man hands the cop the registration of the vehicle and says, 'You guys already have my licence, you haven't given it back yet.'

✳ A blonde tried to sell her old car. She was having a lot of problems selling it because the car had 250,000 miles on it. One day, she told her problem to a brunette she worked with at the salon. The brunette told her, 'There is a possibility to make the car easier to sell, but it's not legal.' 'That doesn't matter,' replied the blonde, 'if I only can sell the car.' 'OK,' said the brunette. 'Here is the address of a friend of mine. He owns a garage. Tell him I sent you and he'll turn the counter in your car back to 50,000 miles. Then it shouldn't be a problem to sell your car.' The following weekend, the blonde made the trip to the mechanic. About one month after that, the brunette asked the blonde, 'Did you sell your car?' 'No,' replied the blonde. 'Why should I? It only has 50,000 miles on it.'

✳ A couple of nuns had gone out to the country for picnic. On the way back they were a few miles from home when their car ran out of petrol. They were standing beside their car on the shoulder when a truck approached. Seeing ladies of the cloth in distress, the driver stopped to offer his help. The nuns explained they needed some petrol. The driver of the truck said he would gladly drain some from his tank, but he didn't have a bucket or can.

One of the nuns dug out a clean bedpan and asked the driver if he could use that. He said yes, and proceeded to drain a couple of gallons into the pan. He waved goodbye to the nuns and left. The nuns were carefully pouring the precious fluid into their petrol tank when the police came by. The policeman stopped and watched for a minute, then he said: 'Sisters, I don't think it will work, but I surely do admire your faith!'

＊ A priest and a rabbi operated a church and a synagogue across the street from each other. Since their schedules intertwined, they decided to go in together to buy a car.

After the purchase, they drove it home and parked it on the street between them. A few minutes later, the rabbi looked out and saw the priest sprinkling water on their new car. It didn't need a wash, so he hurried out and asked the priest what he was doing.

'I'm blessing it,' the priest replied. The rabbi considered this a moment, then went back inside the synagogue. He reappeared a moment later with a hacksaw, walked over to the back of the car and cut off two inches of the exhaust pipe.

＊ A policeman pulled a car over and told the man driving that he was going 50 mph in a 30 mph zone. 'I was only going 30!' the driver protested. 'Not according to my radar,' the policeman said. 'Yes, I was!' the man shouted back. 'No you weren't!' the policeman said.

With that, the man's wife leaned towards the window and said, 'Officer, I should warn you not to argue with my husband when he's been drinking.'

＊ A judge had just fined a man £25 for speeding. When the judge gave the man the receipt, the man yelled sarcastically, 'What am I supposed to do with this? Frame it?!' The judge replied, 'No, keep it. When you get three, you get a bicycle.'

﹡ A truck driver is driving along on the motorway. A sign comes up that reads 'Low bridge ahead'. Before he knows it the bridge is right ahead of him and he gets stuck under the bridge. Cars are backed up for miles. Finally, a police car comes up. The cop gets out of his car and walks around to the truck driver, puts his hands on his hips and says, 'Got stuck, huh?' The truck driver says, 'No, I was delivering this bridge and ran out of petrol.'

﹡ A hesitant driver, waiting for a traffic jam to clear, came to a complete stop on the freeway ramp. The traffic thinned, but the driver still waited. Finally a furious voice from the vehicle behind him cried, 'The sign says Give Way, not Give Up!'

﹡ 'My wife ran off with another man in my new car.'
'That's terrible. Your new car, you say?'

﹡ Why did the truck driver drive his truck off the cliff?
He wanted to try out the air brakes.

Ferries

﹡ A man loved living in Staten Island, but he wasn't crazy about the ferry. If you missed a ferry late at night, you had to spend the next hour or so wandering the deserted streets of lower Manhattan. So, when Bob spotted a ferry no more than fifteen feet from the dock, he decided he wouldn't subject himself to an hour's wait. He made a running leap and landed on his hands and knees, a little bruised maybe, but safe on deck. Bob got up, brushed himself off, and announced proudly to a bystander, 'Well, I made that one, didn't I?' 'Sure did,' the bystander said. 'But you should have waited a minute or two. The ferry is just about to dock.'

Helicopters

✳ What did the impatient helicopter say to its clumsy mechanic? 'Chop chop.'

✳ What's red and flies and wobbles at the same time? A jelly copter!

Taxis

✳ Hailing taxis is even worse than raining cats and dogs.

✳ A young man has just graduated from Harvard and is so excited just thinking about his future. He gets into a taxi and the driver says, 'How are you on this lovely day?' The young man replies, 'I'm the Class of 2002. I just graduated from Harvard, and I just can't wait to go out there and see what the world has in store for me.' The driver turns around to shake the young man's hand and says, 'Congratulations! I'm Mitch, Class of '60.'

Tubes

✳ The tube was so crowded even some of the men couldn't get seats.

Ships

✳ What happens when a houseboat grows up?
It becomes a township!

✳ I like to run my home like a ship, with me as captain. Too bad I married an admiral.

✳ My ship finally came in, only to find my ex-wife waiting at the docks.

✳ I've found a cure for seasickness. A very tight collar.

✳ What do you get when you cross the Atlantic Ocean with the *Titanic*?
About halfway.

✳ Where do broken ships go?
To the doc.

Trains

✳ This is a passenger announcement. The train on platform one, two, three, four, five, six, seven, eight, nine, ten, eleven and twelve has come in sideways.

☀ The best time to miss a train is at a crossing.

☀ What sort of transport gives people colds?
A choo choo train.

Planes

☀ What did Geronimo say when he jumped out of the airplane?
ME!!!

☀ What are the Great Plains?
747, Concorde and Spitfire!

☀ Did you hear about the Irishman whose plane had engine trouble?
He tried to get out and push.

☀ Flying blind: When the instrument panel in the pilot's cabin is in Braille.

☀ The jet age can be defined as breakfast in New York, lunch in Paris, dinner in London and baggage in Buenos Aires.

☀ Who were the first people to invent a plane that didn't work?
The Wrong brothers.

☀ 'Do you have any experience of flying?'
'I fell out of a window once.'

✳ Which airline do teddies use?
British Bearways.

🐺 TRAVEL

✳ I went travelling and I met this bloke with a didgeridoo. He was playing 'Dancing Queen' on it. I thought, that's Aboriginal.

✳ What sort of view do you get from the top of a pyramid?
As Pharaoh as the eye can see.

✳ I've never seen the Catskill mountains, but I did see one of them get a mouse once.

✳ What do you call an ant from overseas?
Important!

✳ I live in London, and my watch is three hours fast. I can't fix it so I'm moving to Moscow.

✳ The horn of plenty is usually the one behind you in traffic.

✳ What's the cheapest way to get to Australia?
Be born there.

✳ What's green, has two legs and a trunk?
A seasick tourist.

✳ Los Angeles is beautiful on a clear day when the fog lifts. Then you can see the smog.

✳ I once drove across Europe in ten days – six days of driving and four to refold the maps.

✳ 'Tell me,' said the tourist to the local yokel. 'Will this path take me to the main road?' 'No, sir!' replied the man. 'You'll have to go by yourself.'

✳ Welcome to Ipswich: set your watch back twenty years.

✳ If you spread out all the sand in North Africa, it would cover the Sahara Desert.

✳ There's no future in time travel.

✳ My bank turned me down for a travel loan. I only wanted enough for a one-way flight to South America.

✳ The shortest distance between two points is under construction.

🦁 TREES

✳ What's part pig and part tree?
A porky pine.

✹ What do you do with a tree after you chop it down?
Chop it up.

✹ What is an icon?
Something that grows on oak trees.

✹ A little old man goes to a large logging company for a job as a tree feller. The logging company owner looks at him in disbelief for the old man looks frail and incapable of wielding an axe. He is invited to go out into the woods and take a few trees down. The old man is directed to an eight-foot-diameter pine tree and promptly takes his double-bladed axe out of its custom case and fells the tree with one blow. Astounded, the owner then points to a stand of six oak trees each about a foot in diameter. The old man takes three swings at each and they fall in quick succession. In disbelief, the owner points to a grove of a dozen giant Douglas fir trees, each well more that three feet across at the base. With six blows on each trunk the mighty conifers fall to the ground. In utter disbelief, the owner gasps, 'Where on earth did you ever learn to cut trees like that?' The old man humbly replies, 'In the Sahara Forest.' The owner attempts to correct him, saying, 'You mean the Sahara Desert?' The old man leans both hands on his axe handle and says, 'Well, yeah … it's called that now.'

turkeys

When is a turkey like a troll?
When it's a-gobblin'.

turtles

Why did the turtle cross the road?
To get to the Shell station!

Deep within a forest, a little turtle began to climb a tree. After hours of effort, he reached the top, jumped into the air, waving his front legs, and crashed to the ground. After recovering, he slowly climbed the tree again, jumped, and fell to the ground. The turtle tried again and again, while a couple of birds sitting on a branch watched his sad efforts. Finally, the female bird turned to her mate. 'Dear,' she chirped, 'I think it's time to tell him he's adopted.'

Did you hear about the lorry full of tortoises that collided with a van full of terrapins?
It was a turtle disaster.

TV

✳ Before TV no one knew what a headache looked like.

✳ A man and his wife are sitting in the living room and he says to her: 'Just so you know, I never want to live in a vegetative state dependent on some machine. If that ever happens, just pull the plug.' His wife gets up and unplugs the TV.

✳ TV teaches us the big ultimate destroying robot always has an easily found and usable self-destruct button.

Iraq TV Guide

MONDAY

8:00 *Husseinfeld*

8:30 *Mad About Everything*

9:00 *Suddenly Sanctions*

9:30 *Allah McBeal*

TUESDAY

8:00 *Wheel of Fortune and Terror*

8:30 *The Price is Right if Saddam Says It's Right*

9:00 *Children are Forbidden to Say the Darndest Things*

9:30 *Iraq's Funniest Public Execution Bloopers*

WEDNESDAY

8:00 *Buffy the Yankee Imperialist Dog Slayer*

8:30 *Diagnosis: Heresy*

9:00 *Just Shoot Me*

9:30 *Veilwatch*

THURSDAY

8:00 *Mahatma Loves Chachi*

8:30 *M*U*S*T*A*S*H*

9:00 *Veronica's Closet Full of Long, Black, Shapeless Dresses*

9:30 *My Two Baghdads*

FRIDAY

8:00 *Judge Saddam*

8:30 *Captured Iranian Soldiers Say the Darndest Things*

9:00 *Achmed's Creek*

9:30 *No-witness News*

UGLY

* A bus carrying only ugly people crashes into an oncoming truck,
  and everyone inside dies. They then get to meet their maker, and
  because of the grief they have experienced, He decides to grant
  them one wish each, before they enter paradise. They're all lined
  up, and God asks the first one what the wish is. 'I want to be
  gorgeous,' and so God snaps His fingers, and it is done. The
  second one in line hears this and says, 'I want to be gorgeous too.'
  Another snap of His fingers and the wish is granted. This goes on
  for a while but when God is halfway down the line, the last guy in
  line starts laughing. When there are only ten people left, this guy is
  rolling on the floor, laughing. Finally, God reaches this guy and asks
  him what his wish will be. The guy calms down and says: 'Make
  'em all ugly again.'

* Why do ginger people burn easily?
  It's nature's way of telling us they should be kept indoors!

✳ A man popped into the supermarket on his way home from work to pick up a few things. He bought a couple of frozen pizzas, a pint of milk and one small tin of beans. As he was at the checkout, the assistant said to him, 'Oh, you must be single.' 'Can you tell that by what I've just bought?' asked the man. 'No, it's because you're ugly,' she replied.

✳ A man's wife asks, 'Do these jeans make my bottom look like the side of the house?'
He replies, 'No, our house isn't blue.'

✳ Everyone is beautiful if you squint a bit.

✳ A little bit of powder, a little bit of paint, makes a girl's complexion seem what it ain't.

✳ Beauty lasts for a moment, but ugly goes on and on and on.

✳ Never get into fights with ugly people; they have nothing to lose.

✳ Two sisters came home from school crying their hearts out. 'What's wrong?' asked their mother. The first sister stopped wailing long enough to say, 'The kids at school make fun of my big feet.' 'There, there,' soothed the mother. 'Your feet aren't that big.' She turned to the second sister. 'Now why are you crying?' 'Because I've been invited to a ski party and I can't find my skis.' 'That's OK,' said her mother, 'you can borrow your sister's shoes.'

✳ A little boy watched with fascination as his mother rubbed cream on her face. 'Why are you rubbing cream on your face, Mommy?' he asked. 'To make myself beautiful,' said his mother. A few minutes later, she began removing the cream with a tissue. 'What's the matter?' he asked. 'Giving up?'

✳ I worked in a pet store and people kept asking how big I'd get.

✳ A woman gets on a bus with her baby. The bus driver says, 'That's the ugliest baby that I've ever seen.' The woman goes to the rear of the bus and sits down, fuming. She says to a man next to her, 'That driver just insulted me!' The man says, 'You go right up there and tell him off – go ahead, I'll hold your monkey for you.'

✳ A healthy male adult bore consumes each year one and a half times his weight in other people's patience.

✳ Her tongue was so long she could lick an envelope after she'd posted it.

✳ I'm not saying he had bad teeth, but he could eat an apple through a letterbox.

✳ She was so ugly that when she looked out of the window people thought it was Halloween.

✳ She must be 25. I counted the rings under her eyes.

✳ She looks like she just stepped out of a beauty parlour, and fell flat on her face.

✳ Please close your mouth so I can see the rest of your face.

umbrellas

A man was in the habit of carrying an umbrella wherever he went. Unfortunately he broke his last good one. Looking at the six useless umbrellas in his umbrella stand, he decided to take them all in and have them repaired. On the bus on the way home he picked up the umbrella of the woman sitting next to him, purely out of habit. She immediately cried, 'Stop, thief!' He surrendered the umbrella and got off the bus, much embarrassed. The next week he went to pick up his merchandise and when he got on the bus with the six umbrellas under his arm he just so happened to sit next to the very same woman. She gave him an icy stare and said, 'Had a good day, huh?'

These two guys were walking down the road when it started to rain. So one guy pulls out his umbrella, but it was full of holes. The other guy said, 'Why'd you bring an umbrella full of holes?' and he said, 'I didn't know it was going to rain.'

🐺 VAMPiRES

※ What do you get when you cross a snowman with a vampire?
Frostbite.

※ Why couldn't Dracula's wife get to sleep?
Because of his coffin.

※ A woman was stealing things in the supermarket today while
balanced on the shoulders of vampires. She was charged with
shoplifting on three counts.

※ Who plays centre forward for the vampire football team?
The ghoulscorer!

※ What's a vampire's favourite dance?
The fangdango!

＊ Why do vampires use mouthwash?
To stop bat breath.

＊ If vampires have no reflection, how come they have such neat hair?

＊ What kind of ship do vampires have?
Blood vessels.

＊ What does Dracula do before he goes on holiday?
Cancels his daily pint of blood.

＊ Did you hear about the two blood cells?
Their love was in vein.

＊ What did the vampire say to his dentist?
Fangs very much.

＊ What's red, oozes and stupid?
A blood clot.

＊ What happened when Dracula broke up with his girlfriend?
They remained just good fiends.

＊ Why did Dracula keep his coffin in a vault?
He liked to have vaulty winks.

＊ Why did the vampire read *The Times*?
He heard it had good circulation!

vegetarianism

Can vegetarians eat Animal Crackers?

Vegetarians coming to dinner? Simply serve them a nice bit of steak or veal. Since they're always going on about how tofu, Quorn, meat substitute, etc. 'taste exactly like the real thing', they won't know any difference.

Invited by vegetarians for dinner? Since you'd no doubt be made aware of their special dietary requirements, tell them about yours, and ask for a nice steak.

I am not a vegetarian because I love animals. I am a vegetarian because I hate plants.

CHICKENS CROSSING

VISITING

* Two friends had not seen each other in many years. They had a long talk trying to fill in the gap of those years by telling about their lives. Finally, one invited the other to visit him in his new flat. 'I've got a wife and three kids and I'd love you to visit us.' 'Great. Where do you live?' 'Here's the address. And there's plenty of parking. Park and come around to the front door, kick it open with your foot, go to the elevator and press the button with your left elbow, then enter. When

you reach the sixth floor, go down the hall until you see my name on the door. Then press the doorbell with your right elbow and I'll let you in.' 'Good. But tell me ... what is all this business of kicking the front door open, then pressing elevator buttons with my right, then my left elbow?' 'You're coming empty-handed?'

🐺 WAR

✳ What lunch meat was responsible for 9/11?
Osalami bin Laden!

✳ General Custer and his aide are in the fort. The aide says, 'General, I don't like the sound of those drums.' From over the hill, a voice yells, 'He's not our regular drummer.'

✳ During the war, people used to say that you needn't worry about the bombs. They would only hit you if they had your name written on them. Which was bad news for my neighbours, Mr and Mrs Doodlebug.

✳ Some people are born to be heroes. Others are born to wave at them in parades.

✳ One day little Billy's teacher has the class go home and think of a story and then conclude the moral of that story. The next day Billy tells his story. 'My dad fought in the Vietnam war, his plane was shot down over enemy territory. He jumped out before it crashed with only a case of beer, a machine gun and a machete. On the way down he drank the case of beer. Unfortunately he landed right in the middle of 100 Vietnamese soldiers. He shot 70 with his machine gun, but ran out of bullets, so he pulled out his machete and killed twenty more, but the blade on his machete broke, so he killed the last ten with his bare hands.' Teacher looks in shock at Billy and asks if there is possibly any moral to his story. Billy replies, 'Yeah ... don't mess with my dad when he's been drinking.'

✳ Osama bin Laden was sitting in his cave wondering who to invade next when his telephone rang. 'Halloo, Mr Laden,' a heavily accented voice said. 'This is Paddy down in County Mayo, Ireland. I am ringing to inform you that we are officially declaring war on you!' 'Well, Paddy,' Osama replied, 'this is important news! How big is your army?' 'Right now,' said Paddy, after a moment's calculation, 'there is meself, me cousin Sean, me next-door neighbour Seamus, and the entire darts team from the pub. That makes eight!'

Osama paused. 'I must tell you, Paddy, that I have one million men in my army waiting to move on my command.' 'Begorra!' said Paddy. 'I'll have to ring you back!' Sure enough, the next day, Paddy called again. 'Mr Laden, the war is still on! We have managed to acquire some infantry equipment!' 'And what equipment would that be, Paddy?' Osama asked. 'Well, we have two combines, a bulldozer, and Murphy's farm tractor.' Osama sighed. 'I must tell you, Paddy, that I have 20,000 tanks and 20,000 armoured personnel carriers. Also, I've increased my army to one and a half million since we last spoke.' 'Saints preserve us!' said Paddy. 'I'll have to get back to you.' Sure enough, Paddy rang again the next day. 'Mr Laden, the war is still on! We have managed to get ourselves airborne! We've modified Harrigan's ultra-light with a couple of shotguns in the cockpit, and four boys from the Auld Shamrock Pub have joined us as well!' Osama was silent for a minute and then cleared his throat. 'I must tell you, Paddy, that I have 10,000 bombers and 20,000 fighter planes. My military complex is surrounded by laser-guided, surface-to-air missile sites. And since we last spoke, I've increased my army to TWO MILLION!' 'Jesus, Mary and Joseph,' said Paddy, 'I'll have to ring you back.' Sure enough, Paddy called again the next day. 'Top o' the mornin', Mr Laden! I am sorry to tell you that we have had to call off the war.' 'I'm sorry to hear that,' said Osama. 'Why the sudden change of heart?' 'Well,' said Paddy, 'we've all had a long chat over a bunch of pints, and decided there's no way we can feed two million prisoners.'

✳ A young, freshly minted lieutenant was sent to a war zone as part of the peace-keeping mission. During a briefing on land mines, the captain asked for questions. Our intrepid solder raised his hand and asked, 'If we do happen to step on a mine, sir, what do we do?'

'Normal procedure, Lieutenant, is to jump 200 feet in the air and scatter oneself over a wide area.'

✳ During WWII an American soldier had been on the front lines in Europe for three months, when he was finally given a week of R&R. He caught a supply boat to a supply base in the south of England, then caught a train to London. The train was extremely crowded and he could not find a seat. He was dead on his feet and walked the length of the train looking for any place to sit down. Finally he found a compartment with seats facing each other; there was room for two people on each seat. On one side sat a proper-looking, older British lady, with a small dog sitting in the empty seat beside her. 'Could I please sit in that seat?' he asked. The lady was insulted. 'You Americans are so rude,' she said.'Can't you see my dog is sitting there?' He walked through the train once more and still could not find a seat. He found himself back at the same place. 'Lady, I love dogs – I have a couple at home – so I would be glad to hold your dog if I can sit down,' he said. The lady replied, 'You Americans are not only rude you are arrogant.' He leaned against the wall for a time, but was so tired he finally said, 'Lady, I've been on the front lines in Europe for three months with no decent rest in all that time. Could I please sit there and hold your dog?' The lady replied, 'You Americans are not only rude and arrogant, you are also obnoxious.' With that comment, the soldier calmly stepped in, picked up the dog, threw it out the window, and sat down. The lady was speechless. An older, neatly dressed Englishman sitting across on the other seat spoke up. 'Young man, I do not know if all you Americans fit the lady's description of you or not. But I do know that you Americans do a lot of things wrong. You drive on the wrong side of the road, you hold your fork with the wrong hand, and now you have just thrown the wrong bitch out of the window.'

✳ Two men were boasting to each other about their old army days. 'Why, my outfit was so well drilled,' declared one, 'that when they presented arms all you could hear was slap, slap, click.' 'Very good,' conceded the other, 'but when my company presented arms you'd just hear slap, slap, jingle.' 'What was the jingle?' asked the first. 'Oh,' replied the other, offhand, 'just our medals.'

✳ During WWII, a lieutenant asked a soldier why he was falling back during a really fierce battle. 'Didn't you hear me say that we're outnumbered four to one?' The soldier replied, 'I got my four, sir.'

✳ What day do wars traditionally start on?
March forth.

water

What is full of holes but can still hold water?
A sponge!

🐺 WEATHER

✳ Did you hear about the man who couldn't tell what the weather was like because it was too foggy?

✳ Why was the weathercock conceited?
Because he was a vane creature.

✳ 'Did you enjoy summer this year? It was on a Thursday.' *Jeff Green*

Rain

✳ Why does Snoop Dogg carry an umbrella?
Fo' Drizzle.

✳ What goes up when the rain comes down?
An umbrella.

✳ A blonde goes over to visit one of her friends. While she is at her friend's house it starts to rain, so her friend suggests she spend the night at her house and go home the next day. The blonde agrees that makes sense and goes into the den to watch TV while her friend goes upstairs to put the kids to bed. When her host comes downstairs, she finds the blonde coming in the front door, soaking wet. She asks, 'Where have you been?'
'I went home to get my pyjamas!'

✳ What doesn't get any wetter, no matter how much rain falls on it?
Water.

✳ Timing has an awful lot to do with the outcome of a rain dance.

✳ Into every life some rain must fall. Usually when your car windows are down.

✳ I believe for every drop of rain that falls, a flower grows. And a roof leaks and a cricket game gets rained off, and a car rusts and...

✳ I can tell if it's raining by my corns. If they get wet, it's raining.

✳ I'd cross the hottest desert,
  I'd swim the deepest sea,
  I'd climb the highest mountain,
  But I can't come over tonight because it's raining.

✳ Why is it that rain drops but snow falls?

✳ Why did the sword swallower swallow an umbrella?
  He wanted to put something away for a rainy day!

✳ What is hail?
  Hard-boiled rain!

Rainbows

✳ Where can you weigh a pie?
  Somewhere over the rainbow: 'Somewhere over the rainbow, weigh a
  pie.'

Sun

✳ A day without sunshine is like night.

✳ I love sunshine. I could sit in the sun day or night.

✳ What holds the sun up in the sky?
  Sunbeams!

WEIGHTS AND MEASURES

* 2,000 lb of Chinese soup: won ton.

* Time between slipping on a peel and smacking the pavement: one bananosecond.

* Weight an evangelist carries with God: one billigram.

* 1,000 aches: one kilohertz.

* Basic unit of laryngitis: one hoarsepower.

* One million microphones: one megaphone.

* 2,000 mockingbirds: two kilomockingbirds.

* 52 cards: 1 decacards.

* Two youngsters were closely examining bathroom scales at the department store.

    'What's it for?' one asked. The other replied, 'You stand on it and it makes you cross.'

* A blonde carrying a baby walks into a chemist store and asks if she can use the shop's baby scale. 'Sorry,' says the pharmacist. 'Our baby scale is broken. But we can work out the baby's weight if we weigh mother and baby together on the adult scale, and then weigh

the mother alone. We just subtract the second number from the first.'
'Oh, that won't work,' says the blonde. 'Why not?' asks the
pharmacist. 'Because,' she answers, 'I'm not his mother. I'm his aunt.'

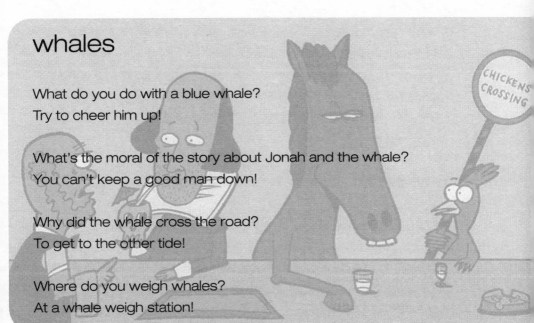

whales

What do you do with a blue whale?
Try to cheer him up!

What's the moral of the story about Jonah and the whale?
You can't keep a good man down!

Why did the whale cross the road?
To get to the other tide!

Where do you weigh whales?
At a whale weigh station!

WISHES

✳ This guy buys an old bottle at a car boot sale. Upon polishing the
bottle, a magical genie suddenly appears. The grateful genie
exclaims, 'Thanks for letting me out of the bottle. I've been in there
for a millennium. I'm pretty old and tired, but I think I've got one wish
left.' The owner of the bottle says, 'I've always wanted to go to

Hawaii, but I'm afraid to fly and I get sea-sick, so build me a road.' 'I'm too old and sick to grant that wish. Got any other ideas?' replied the genie. 'OK,' replied the guy, 'I've always wanted to understand how a woman thinks, to understand her innermost thoughts.' The genie replies, 'Two lanes or four?'

✳ Three guys, stranded on a desert island, find a magic lantern containing a genie, who grants them each one wish. The first guy wishes he was off the island and back home. The second guy wishes the same. The third guy says, 'I'm lonely. I wish my friends were back here.'

✳ **Mr Smith:** I hate to tell you, but your wife just fell down the wishing well.
Mr Brown: It works!

✳ Bill Gates is at the beach when he discovers a bottle in the surf. Gates pulls out the cork and a genie appears. The genie says, 'I have been trapped for 100 years. As a reward you can make a wish.' Gates thinks about it as he carries the bottle back to his beach cottage. Once there, he goes to a bookshelf, pulls out an atlas and turns to a map of the Middle East. 'This area has seen conflict and suffering for hundreds of years. What I wish for is peace in the Middle East.' The genie replies, 'I don't know … I can do a lot, but this? Don't you have another wish?' Bill Gates thinks and finally says, 'OK. The whole world hates Microsoft because we have conquered the software market and because Windows still crashes. I wish you would make everybody love us.' The genie says, 'Let me see that map again.'

🐺 WITCHES

✸ What is a witch's favourite subject at school?
Spelling.

✸ What kinds of tests do they give witches?
Hex-aminations!

✸ How does a witch tell the time?
She looks at her witch watch.

✸ What name did the witch give to her cooking pot?
It was called-Ron!

✸ What would you find on a haunted beach?
A sand witch.

✸ Why do witches ride on broomsticks?
Because vacuum cleaners are too heavy.

✸ What kind of piano music do witches like?
Hagtime.

✸ What happens if you see twin witches?
You won't be able to see which witch is witch!

✸ What did the doctor say to the witch in hospital?
'With any luck you'll soon be well enough to get up for a spell!'

✳ Have you heard about the good weather witch? She's forecasting sunny spells!

wombats

What do you do with a wombat?
Play wom.

woodpeckers

What do you get if you cross a woodpecker with a carrier pigeon?
A bird that knocks before it delivers a message.

wolves

What animal has four wooden legs?
A timber wolf.

What do you call a hairy beast with clothes on?
A wear-wolf!

🐺 WORDS

✳ **Pupil**: My sister and I know the meaning of every word in the world.
Teacher: What does egotistical mean?
Pupil: That would be one of the ones my sister knows.

✳ Some people have a way with words, others not have way.

✳ Don't use a big word where a diminutive one will suffice.

✳ Do not put statements in the negative form.

✳ My secretary spells atrociously, but others can't spell at all.

✳ Which is the longest word in the dictionary?
'Smiles', because there is a mile between each 'S'!

New words

Accidue (AX ih dew) Small pile of broken glass, metal and other debris that remains at the scene several months after a road accident.

Adhokum (ad HOE kum) In television commercials, the belief that because the actor is wearing a white lab coat he must be an expert.

Alfred Hitchcook To stab continuously at a block of frozen vegetables to make them cook faster.

Aquadextrous Possessing the ability to turn the bathtub tap on and off with your toes.

Carperpetuation The act, when vacuuming, of running over a string or a piece of lint at least a dozen times, reaching over and picking it up, examining it, then putting it back down to give the vacuum one more chance.

Circumvaculate (sur kum VAK yew late) To remain in a stationary position while vacuuming in a circle around yourself.

Coinophony (koy NO foh nee) Those annoying concerts conducted by people who jingle change and keys in their pockets, often accompanied by a rocking motion.

Comeondowns (kum ON downz) Depression resulting from knowing all the answers to a game show while confined in your living room.

Coughokum (koff HO kum) In movies, the belief that if someone coughs, he or she has a terminal illness.

Déjà redo (day ZHA ree doo) To do something a second time even though you did it correctly the first time.

Dentocram (DEN to kram) To attempt a year's worth of brushing and flossing in the hour before your dental appointment.

Disconfect To sterilize the piece of confection (lollipop) you dropped on the floor by blowing on it, assuming this will somehow 'remove' all the germs.

Elbonics The actions of two people manoeuvring for one armrest in a cinema.

Enamelisms (ih NAM ul iz umz) Overly embellished names given to interior paints and chocolates, such as Mediterranean Sunset and Haversian Mocha Delight.

Firssue (FUR shoo) The first tissue in a box that gets all the others on the go.

Frust The small line of debris that refuses to be swept onto the dust pan and keeps backing a person across the room until he finally decides to give up and sweep it under the rug.

Gymbols (JIM buls) Those lines and markings on a gym floor that have no purpose whatsoever.

Hatewatch Watching a television programme even though you tell everyone that it's stupid and you hate it.

Hufflechuckle To laugh at someone's joke even though it wasn't funny, just to make them happy.

Idiolocation The spot on a map marked 'You are here'.

Indigestures (in dih JES churz) The half-hearted protestations you feel required to make when someone else offers to pay for the bill.

Intunition (in TEW nih shun) Mentally hearing a song begin seconds before it plays on the album.

Jetschpiel (JET shpeel) The animated safety speech given by flight attendants that regular passengers ignore, but you listen to intently.

Krashtonite (Krash TO nite) The indestructible material that the aircraft's 'black box' is made out of – and how come the rest of the plane isn't made out of it?

Lactomangulation Manhandling the 'open here' spout on a milk container so badly that one has to resort to the 'illegal' side.

Lexplexed (leks PLEKST) Unable to find the correct spelling of a word in the dictionary because one does not know how to spell it.

Peppier The waiter at a fancy restaurant whose sole purpose seems to be walking around asking diners if they want fresh ground pepper.

Phonesia (fo nee' zhuh) The affliction of dialling a phone number and forgetting whom you were calling just as they answer.

Pupkus (pup'kus) The moist residue left on a window after a dog presses its nose to it.

Shoecide (shoo side) One abandoned shoe in the road.

Shoedrive (shoo drive) One shoe hanging from somewhere on an automobile.

Telecrastination (tel e kras tin ay' shun) The act of always letting the phone ring at least twice before you pick it up, even when you're only six inches away.

Todlitter Food debris under the baby's chair.

Tubloids Any newspaper or magazine reserved for reading in the bath.

Wimbledown The fuzz on a tennis ball.

Yaffle To speak loudly to foreigners as if this somehow makes you easier to understand.

Zippyjig (ZIP ee jigg) That dance people perform when a rubber band is pointed at them.

WORDS OF WISDOM

✳ Why choose between two evils when you can choose between five or six?

✷ Just because I look stupid doesn't mean I'm not.

✷ A truly wise man never plays leapfrog with a unicorn.

✷ Fungus is actually alive. Be afraid.

✷ Good judgement comes from bad experience, and a lot of that comes from bad judgement.

✷ When in doubt, poke it with a stick.

✷ A smart man covers his ass; a wise man leaves his pants on.

✷ Those that forget the pasta are doomed to reheat it.

✷ Mother said there would be days like this, but she never said there would be so many.

✷ Do not follow for I may not lead. Do not lead for I may not follow. Just go over there somewhere, please?

✷ If you can't convince them, confuse them.

✷ A clean tie attracts the soup of the day.

✷ What goes around usually gets dizzy and falls over.

✷ Sometimes the best helping hand you can give is a good, firm push.

* Never accept a drink from a urologist.

* **MURPHY'S LAW**: If anything can go wrong, it will.
  J MURPHY'S LAW ADDITION: If anything that could go wrong doesn't go wrong, it would have been ultimately better for it to have gone wrong.

* The road to success is dotted with a heap of parking spaces.

* If you can't love your enemies, compromise. Forget them.

* Things are more like they are now than they ever were before.

* Jumping to conclusions can be dangerous to your health.

* If you get to it and you can't do it, well, there you jolly well are, aren't you?

* Creativity is great, but plagiarism is faster.

* All power corrupts. Absolute power is pretty neat, though.

* Never go to bed angry; stay awake and plot your revenge.

* Originality is the art of concealing your sources.

* Everything is always OK in the end. If it's not OK, then it's probably not the end.

✳ Imitation is not the sincerest form of flattery. Stalking is.

✳ Remember: first you pillage then you burn.

✳ To err is human. To forgive is against company policy.

✳ When everything's going your way, you're in the wrong lane and going in the wrong direction.

✳ A torch is a case for holding dead batteries.

✳ Whatever happens to you, it will have previously happened to everyone else, only more so.

✳ What can you put in a glass but never take out of it?
A crack.

✳ Never do card tricks for the group you play poker with.

✳ No one is listening until you make a mistake.

✳ The hardness of butter is directly proportional to the softness of the bread.

✳ It's not who you know, it's whom you know.

✳ There is no 'I' in 'Team', but there are four in 'Platitude-Quoting Idiot'.

✳ Treat each day as your last; one day you will be right.

✸ Better late than really late.

✸ Follow your dreams, except for that one where you're naked at work.

✸ Birthdays are good for you – the more you have, the longer you live.

✸ By doing just a little each day, I can gradually let the task overwhelm me.

✸ If you're ahead of the pack, take a look back every now and then to make sure it's still there.

✸ Look out for number 1, and don't step in number 2, either.

✸ All true wisdom is found on T-shirts.

✸ 'If the shoe fits, buy it'. *Imelda Marcos*

✸ Those who throw dirt are sure to lose ground.

✸ One dog barks at something, the rest bark at him.

✸ Take my advice; I don't use it anyway.

✸ Man who streaks is unsuited for his work.

✸ I'm proud of my modesty.

✸ Man who places head in sand will get kicked in the end.

✳ Man who gets too big for his britches may get exposed in the end.

✳ All men eat, but Fu Man Chu.

✳ Age is a question of mind over matter. If you don't mind, it doesn't matter.

✳ Quando omni flunkus moritati – when all else fails, play dead.

Confucius say...

✳ Man who want pretty nurse, must be patient.

✳ Man cannot exchange woman of forty for two twenties.

✳ If you don't succeed, redefine success.

✳ Man who keep feet on ground have trouble putting on pants.

✳ Woman who go camping must beware of evil intent.

✳ Man who shoot off mouth, must expect to lose face.

✳ Man who leap off cliff jump to conclusion.

✳ House without bathroom is uncanny.

✳ Those who quote me are fools.

✳ Man who throws dirt is losing ground.

✳ Man who snort coke, get bubbles up nose.

✳ Cow with no legs, ground beef.

✳ Two wrongs not make right, but two rights make U-turn.

✳ Man who smoke pot, choke on handle.

✳ Man who sneeze without tissue take matter into own hands.

✳ Man who sit on tack, get point.

✳ Man who have last laugh, not get joke.

🐵 wORk

✳ You can go anywhere you want if you look serious and carry a clipboard.

✳ Never ask two questions in a business letter. The reply will discuss the one you are least interested in, and say nothing about the other.

✳ I don't mind coming to work, but that eight-hour wait to go home is a bitch!

* Hear about the guy who got fired at the canning factory? He got caught taking a pea.

* Did you hear about the poor man who worked at a sausage factory to make ends meet?

* 'Employee of the month is a good example of how somebody can be both a winner and a loser at the same time.' *Demetri Martin*

* Jones goes to see his manager in the office. 'Boss,' he says, 'we're doing some heavy house-cleaning at home tomorrow, and my wife needs me to help with the attic and the garage, moving and hauling stuff.' 'We're short-handed, Jones,' the boss replies. 'I can't give you the day off.' 'Thanks, boss,' says Jones, 'I knew I could count on you.'

* Start every day with a smile. Then you have the rest of the day to do other stuff.

* What did Chewbacca's boss say to him when he screwed up on his first day of work?
It's a wookie mistake.

* When you're in it up to your ears, keep your mouth shut.

* When you don't know what you are doing, do it neatly.

* When the bosses talk about improving productivity, they are never talking about themselves.

✳ There will always be beer cans rolling on the floor of your car when the boss asks for a ride home from the office.

✳ If it wasn't for the last minute, nothing would get done.

✳ When you don't know what to do, walk fast and look worried.

✳ No one gets sick on Wednesdays.

✳ Why was the employee fired from the orange juice factory? He couldn't concentrate.

✳ I used to be a lifeguard, but some blue kid got me fired.

✳ Confession is good for the soul but bad for your career.

✳ An unemployed court jester is no one's fool.

✳ It is much easier to apologize than to ask permission.

✳ It's a thankless job, but I've got a lot of karma to burn off.

✳ This isn't an office. It's Hades with fluorescent lighting.

✳ Hard work never killed anyone, but why chance it?

✳ Voluntary work? I wouldn't do it if you paid me.

✳ I told my girlfriend I had a job in a bowling alley. She said, 'Tenpin?' I said, 'No, it's a permanent job.'

✳ I'd whistle while I work – but all I know are happy songs!

✳ Admit nothing, deny everything and make counter-accusations.

✳ Somebody who knows how will always have a job. Working for someone who knows why.

✳ Employer to employee: I didn't say it was your fault. I said I was going to blame you.

✳ **Boss**: Experts say that humour on the job relieves tension in this time of down-sizing. Knock, knock.
   Employee: Who's there?
   Boss: Not you any more.

✳ All work and no play will make you a manager.

✳ If things get any worse, I'll have to ask you to stop helping me.

✳ Of course there's no reason for it, it's just our policy.

✳ The manager is reviewing a potential employee's application and notes that she has never worked in this area of business before. 'For a woman with no experience you are certainly asking a high wage.' 'Well, sir,' the applicant replies, 'the work is so much harder when you don't know what you're doing...'

✳ Do it tomorrow. You've made enough mistakes for today.

✳ Work is for people who don't have internet access.

✳ For every problem there is one solution which is simple, neat and wrong.

✳ A bad plan is better than no plan.

✳ I'm late for work because the train driver had an out of body experience and didn't come back for a day and a half.

✳ An office manager arrives at his department and sees an employee sitting behind his desk, totally stressed out. He gives him advice: 'I went home every afternoon for two weeks and had myself pampered by my wife. It was fantastic, and it really helped; you should try it too!' Two weeks later, when the manager arrives at his department, he sees the man happy and full of energy at his desk. The faxes are piling up, and the computer is running at full speed. 'I see you followed my advice.' 'I did,' answers the employee. 'It was great! By the way, I didn't know you had such a nice house!'

✳ I'm late for work because I set half the clocks in my house ahead an hour and the other half back an hour Saturday and spent 18 hours in some kind of space-time continuum loop reliving Sunday (right up until the explosion). I was able to exit from the loop only by reversing the polarity of the power source by exactly e*log(pi) clocks while simultaneously rapping my dog on the nose with a rolled-up newspaper. This was strange as I don't own a dog. Accordingly I will be late for work, or early.

✴ Chaos, panic, pandemonium – my work here is done.

✴ Beat the five o'clock rush: leave work at noon.

✴ Department of Redundancy Department.

✴ Drilling for oil is boring.

The advantages of going to work naked

✴ Your boss is always yelling, 'I wanna see your ass in here by 8.00!'

✴ Can take advantage of computer monitor radiation to work on your tan.

✴ Inventive way to finally meet that hunk in Human Resources.

✴ 'I'd love to chip in, but I left my wallet in my trousers.'

✴ To stop those creepy guys in Marketing from looking down your blouse.

✴ You want to see if it's like the dream.

✴ So that – with a little help from muzak – you can add 'Exotic Dancer' to your exaggerated CV.

✴ People stop stealing your pens after they've seen where you keep them.

✳ Diverts attention from the fact that you also came to work drunk.

✳ Gives 'bad hair day' a whole new meaning.

✳ No one steals your chair.

🐛 WORMS

✳ What do worms leave round their baths?
The scum of the earth!

✳ What reads and lives in an apple?
A bookworm!

✳ What's the difference between a worm and an apple?
Have you ever tried worm pie?

✳ If the early bird catches the worm, what about the worm?

✳ What did the woodworm say to the chair?
It's been nice gnawing you!

✳ What's a glow worm's favourite song?
'Wake Me Up Before You Glow Glow!'

✳ What do you get if you cross a worm and a young goat?
A dirty kid!

✳ What did the maggot say to another?
What's a nice maggot like you doing in a joint like this?

✳ What is the best advice to give to a worm?
Sleep late!

✳ Did you hear about the rival maggots?
They were fighting in dead Ernest.

✳ What do you get if you cross a glow worm with some beer?
Light ale!

✳ Why do worms taste like chewing gum?
Because they're wrigleys!

✳ What happened to the glow worm who was squashed?
He was de-lighted!

✳ What is life like for a woodworm?
Boring!

✳ A chemistry teacher wanted to teach his class a lesson about the evils of liquor, so he produced an experiment that involved a glass of water, a glass of whisky and two worms.

'Now, class. Observe the worms closely,' said the teacher, putting a worm first into the water. The worm in the water writhed about, happy as a worm in water could be.

The second worm he put into the whisky. It writhed painfully, and quickly sank to the bottom, dead as a doornail. 'Now, what lesson can we divine from this experiment?' the teacher asked. A hand went up at the back, 'Drink whisky and you won't get worms?'

✳ One winter, Billy Bob and Jethro decided to go ice fishing. They got to the lake early in the morning, cut two holes and dropped their lines into the frigid water. A few hours later, Billy Bob had a dozen nice fish, while Jethro hadn't even had a nibble. 'Billy Bob, what's your secret?' he finally asked. 'Mmu motta meep yer mmrms mmmrm.' 'What?' Jethro said. 'Mmu motta meep yer mmrms mmmrn!' 'If you think I can understand...' Before Jethro could finish, Billy Bob spat into his hand and said, 'You gotta keep your worms warm!'

✳ Did you hear about the lucky fisherman?
He married a girl with worms.

🔊 WORRIES

You know you should worry when...

✳ You let your twelve-year-old daughter smoke at the table in front of her kids.

✳ You've been married three times and still have the same in-laws.

✳ You think a woman who is 'out of your league' bowls on a different night.

✳ Jack Daniel's makes your list of 'Most Admired People'.

✳ You think Genitalia is an Italian airline.

✳ You wonder how football grounds keep their toilets so clean.

✳ Someone in your family died right after saying, 'Hey, watch this!'

✳ Your school disco had childcare.

✳ You lit a match in the bathroom and your house exploded right off its wheels.

✳ You can't get married to your sweetheart cos there's a law against it.

✳ You think loading the dishwasher means getting your wife drunk.

✳ Your toilet paper has page numbers on it.

✳ Did you hear about the man who paid a friend £10,000 a week to do all his worrying for him?
When asked how he could afford that he said that was his friend's problem.

🐵 WRITERS AND WRITING

✳ What's the difference between joist and girder?
One wrote Ulysses, while the other wrote Faust.

✳ Tolkien enjoyed writing fairy tales so much it became a Hobbit.

✳ What is posthumous work?
Something written by someone after they are dead!

✳ Don't read everything you believe.

✳ Why doesn't Jack Kerouac pay his bills?
Because he's a dead beat.

✳ Spelling is becomming a lossed art.

✳ Proofread carefully to see if you any words out.

✳ What was Carl Sagan's druid name?
Carl Pagan!

✳ What did Anton Chekov?
Everything on Franz Lizst.

✳ Three boys are in the school playground bragging about their fathers. The first boy says, 'My dad scribbles a few words on a piece of paper, he calls it a poem, they give him £500.' The second boy says, 'That's nothing. My dad scribbles a few words on a piece of paper, he calls it a song, they give him £1,000.' The third boy says, 'I got you both beat. My dad scribbles a few words on a piece of paper, he calls it a sermon, and it takes eight people to collect all the money!'

✳ A backward poet writes inverse.

✳ Why did the ink spots cry?
Because their mother was in the pen doing a long sentence.

✳ Graffiti written on a wall: 'Make Bread Not Bombs.' Scratched out
and written underneath: 'Tried Bread, Didn't Explode.'

ZEBRAS

* What is a zebra?
  A horse behind bars.

* What is a zebra?
  26 sizes larger than an 'A' bra.

* Why are there no zebras in Czech zoos?
  Czechs and stripes don't mix.

* What's black and white and makes a lot of noise?
  A zebra with a drum kit.